For Susan and Eric
    With love and thanks
for decades of friendship —

Steven

Washington
1989.

# BY HOOK OR
# BY CROOK

MULLER

The Swami, the Sultan, the Princess and the Author.

# BY HOOK OR BY CROOK

## Steven Martindale

FREDERICK MULLER
London Sydney Auckland Johannesburg

First published in 1989 by
Frederick Muller an imprint of
Century Hutchinson Ltd, Brookmount House,
62–65 Chandos Place,
London WC2N 4NW

Century Hutchinson Australia (Pty) Ltd
89–91 Albion Street, Surry Hills, NSW 2010

Century Hutchinson New Zealand Ltd
PO Box 40–086, 32–34 View Road, Glenfield, Auckland 10

Century Hutchinson Group (SA) Pty Ltd
PO Box 337, Bergvlei 2012, South Africa

A CIP catalogue record for this book is available from the British Library

Printed and bound in Great Britain by
Butler & Tanner Ltd, Frome, Somerset

For my mother, Clarissa Parkinson Martindale,
and my father, Addington A Martindale

# Acknowledgments

This is my first book. Many friends took the time to read sections, ask questions, and suggest ways to clarify and simplify a complicated yarn. Special thanks to: Cellina and Henry Barth, Lucy and Chris Buckley, Robert Charles, John Chesterman, Mehri Esfandiari, Deecy Stephens Gray, Sir Eldon Griffiths, Marc Jaffe, Gloria and Michael Lewis, Charlotte Mayerson, Valorie McGhee, Kay Meehan, George O'Sullivan, Brian Petty, David Ridd, Leona and Jerry Schecter, Lily Tomlin, Nancy Brown Wellen, Sir Oliver and Lady Wright and Jane Wagner.

My agent, Desmond Elliott, was resolute and professional. He has been a close friend for years and this experience served to enhance our relationship.

Paul Sidey, my editor, weathered many legal storms with grace and made me realize most of my jokes were not particularly funny.

I am blessed with certain friends who have enhanced by life beyond measure. Not all of them had to endure the ups and downs of my first book, but I shall never forget those who cheered me, loved me and supported this endeavor. A rose to: Buffy Cafritz, Oatsie Charles, Mehri Esfandiari, Joan Gardner, Sir Eldon and Lady Griffiths, Mimi Harris, Keith Henderson, Tina Lyle-Harrower, Carrie Lee and Gaylord Nelson, Nancy Howar O'Sullivan, Brian Petty, Robert Simon, Sharad Tak and my beloved Helen Verstandig (Madame Wellington).

Acknowledgment

# Contents

# CONTENTS

# Introduction

This book profiles three men: Adnan Khashoggi, Mohamed Fayed and Chandra Swamiji (an Indian guru known either as Swamiji or the Swami). Each were men of humble birth who became larger than life in the public arena and enjoyed lives of private luxury and advantage most men never attain. All cut a swath through the worlds of finance, international political affairs and public relations. At the peak of their success, Khashoggi, Fayed and the Swami were the world's most successful con artists. Virtually all public and private assessments supported their claims of wealth and good intentions.

Khashoggi and Fayed became known throughout the world as billionaires. Khashoggi appeared on the cover of *Time* magazine 19 January 1987 in an article telling of his 'high life and flashy deals'. Mohamed Fayed has stacks of press cuttings which describe him as a billionaire and a descendant of a wealthy Egyptian business family.

The Swami was depicted by his operatives as a saint. They addressed him reverentially as 'Your Holiness'. He traveled the world for years visiting with heads of state. To confirm his status, his disciples always carried a photo album featuring intimate pictures of the Swami with everyone from Richard Nixon and Elizabeth Taylor to the King of Jordan and the President of Zaire.

A major reason the men I profile ranked first in a world plagued by swindlers was their ability to gain access and become advisors to His Majesty The Sultan of Brunei. The monarch is officially designated: The Sultan and Yang Di-Pertuan Negara Brunei Darussalam. He is the richest man in the world (net worth $40 billion), a status which he tried unconvincingly to dispute in a rare press interview with the editor of the *Sunday Telegraph* on 29 May 1988.

Whether or not the Sultan deserves to be at the top of *Fortune* magazine's top ten richest list, he was certainly the richest man in the world willing to open his doors and his bank accounts with impunity to adventuresome businessmen. One by one they came, playing upon his innocence and isolation. They used the Sultan to fill their pockets and to entrap others in their webs of deception.

More important than their individual fates, however, are the consequences of their greed:

1. On 21 October 1988, the United States of America indicted Adnan Khashoggi for racketeering and obstruction of justice. His co-defendants are the former President and First Lady of the Philippines, Ferdinand and Imelda Marcos. If convicted, Khashoggi could be sentenced to decades in prison. His flagship company in America, Triad Salt Lake City, was forced into bankruptcy in 1987. The yacht, the planes, the homes, and his reputation are gone.

2. On 9 April 1987, the UK Secretary for Trade and Industry, Mr Paul Channon, appointed Inspectors, under a provision of the UK Company Law applicable when the circumstances suggest fraud or similar misconduct, to investigate the acquisition of shares of House of Fraser (HOF) by Mohamed Fayed, whereby this little known Egyptian had gained ownership of the world's most famous department store, Harrods.

The Inspectors were asked to consider whether the assurances provided to the Government by the Fayeds, on which the Secretary of State based his decision to allow the takeover without a referral to the Monopolies and Mergers Commission, were known to be false by the Fayeds who thereby intentionally violated the law in purchasing HOF.

On 23 July 1988, the Inspectors submitted their report to the Secretary of State.

In late September 1988, the British Government disclosed that it had referred the report on the House of Fraser (HOF) matter to the Serious Frauds Office which must determine whether or not to bring criminal charges against Fayed.

The HOF matter was elevated to unprecedented confusion on 25 November 1988. The Secretary of State, Lord Young, announced that he would not refer it to the Monopolies and Mergers Commission, having previously announced that he would not publish the Inspectors' report on advise from the Serious Frauds Office that publication might be prejudicial to their investigation.

The *Telegraph* applauded Lord Young's ruling in an editorial which explained that the DTI report 'indicated the existence of previously undisclosed material facts' in the three-year-old acquisition of Harrods by the Fayeds. 'Since the report has been referred to the Serious Frauds Office, it is reasonable to conclude that the inspectors unearthed *prima facie* evidence that offenses may have been committed. If so, that is a matter not for the Monopolies Commission but for the courts,' it concluded.

The *Sunday Times*' Ivan Fallon took Lord Young's ruling to mean the following: 'By ruling as he did, Young was in effect saying the Fayeds can keep Harrods – and Tiny Rowland, the scourge of so many secretaries of state, can never own it.'

After an exhaustive judicial review, the HOF matter was sent on appeal to the Law Lords who will decide whether to overturn Young's decision and refer the matter to MMC or let it stand.

3. In October 1987, Chandra Swami was arrested in India on charges of fraud, income tax evasion and foreign exchange offenses. He has yet to come to trial, but the evidence against him is substantial. Of greater concern to the Swami, the hundred-odd million dollars once controlled by his 'financial advisor', Ernie Miller, is spent. The bulk of it was lost in what the Swami understood to be business ventures with Khashoggi, the most publicized of which was funding the sale of US arms to Iran.

How can reason explain the thinking of Khashoggi, Fayed and the Swami? At the same moment as they were being lionized by the world media and had everything to lose with essentially nothing to gain, they engaged in major international fraud and deception.

Unwittingly, I became a personal witness to the rise and fall of Khashoggi, Fayed and the Swami. It was a point in my life when I had determined to make a fortune. The capitalist ethic which Americans of the sixties generation were taught promoted the notion that a wealthy man was never drunk or crazy, merely eccentric in a humorous way. It was a lexicon, moreover, that a rich man never lied or cheated in business matters. I sought out these men described in the press and elsewhere as billionaires. Initially, I too believed their lies.

By virtue of ambition, luck and the kindness of both family and strangers, I was educated at the best schools, lived in Europe and Asia, and was exposed to the work of many of the influential intellectuals of our time. Foremost among them were James Baldwin, Martha Graham, David Hockney, Karen Horney, Claire Booth Luce, Margaret Meade,

Rheinhold Niebur, Nelson Rockefeller, Adlai Stevenson and Paul Tillich. My life so far has been one of privilege and unique experience.

The maturation process never ends, I hope. On the other hand, it will please me greatly if this book concludes the period in my life which began when I learned there was no Santa Claus.

There is every reason for the reader to pause, from chapter to chapter, to ponder how I could have been so simple-minded. Please know, I ask myself the same question. My hope is that the leaders of the world who took these men at their word will do the same.

My editor wanted to cut many of the personal asides in the book, but I needed to explain how I became involved with these men. The anecdotes are intended to convey a sense of the magic and the luck of the moment. The settings do not fully explain how the events came about, but do illustrate the power of personal contact and interaction. They matter because the unlikely circumstance often leads to a decision of consequence.

In spite of the disillusionment these experiences brought, I remain an optimist. A positive approach to life, however, is no excuse for agreeing to buy the Brooklyn Bridge from a stranger. One must know the danger of believing, or wanting to believe, that all men are good.

# – 1 –
## A View from the Air

28 October 1986

For the first time in over two years, I knew exactly why I was boarding an airplane. The next day Shri Chandra Swamiji Maharaj, the young Hindu holy man from India, and I were to meet in Los Angeles. Many times before I had flown to London, Tokyo or Singapore on the vague promise by the Swami that I would return either with a contract designating me the government affairs representative for the Sultan of Brunei in the US, or be retained as a lawyer by a Saudi prince to negotiate a huge international business deal. Alas, none of those potentially lucrative work assignments were ever consummated. I had spent two of the most fascinating and frustrating years of my life accomplishing little or nothing. Worse, I felt betrayed by the Swami, Adnan Khashoggi, the Sultan and others. This trip to see the Swami would allow me to observe the scene one last time and perhaps make the appropriate, final exit.

In the past few months the Swami had received a great deal of press coverage. The *Onlooker* magazine of India quoted him as saying: 'Look at this photograph album. It carries pictures of all the most famous people in the world. And in each one you will find me beside them. Kings, prime ministers, princes, sheiks. I have control over all of them.' He specifically mentioned several individuals that had received him at my request. Not only did this cause great embarrassment, but I was

1

furious with the Swami for attempting to exploit my friends. In the past he had kept his word and declined all press interviews. Now he and Khashoggi seemed to seek them out. And what the Swami was saying was exaggerated. These royals and heads of state had received him only once at my request. They were merely being gracious to the Swami who said he was representing, first, Indira Gandhi, then later, the Sultan of Brunei. He was pulling the age-old trick of name dropping to project himself as the world's most important guru. When I expressed my anger, he laughed and said: 'You should be happy I am becoming such a famous Swami.' His parting words were: 'Adnan and I know what is best.'

The Swami knew I was disillusioned and that I no longer considered him a trusted friend. He also realized I had been exposed to a great deal of information about him and his close associates. In recent weeks he had been telephoning constantly to reaffirm our friendship and to try to bring me back into his orbit. Over and over he spoke of a television interview he had just given to the Indian Cable Television network in which he had described me as his 'brother' and acknowledged with extra emphasis that it was I who had introduced him to the Saudi billionaire, Adnan M Khashoggi.

At this point, the Swami's words no longer mattered. In the past few months I had caught him in a series of lies which had begun to confirm my worst thoughts about many of his dealings with his disciples and friends. I knew the Swami wanted to lure me back. I also knew that would never happen.

When I had first met the Swami in February 1983 he seemed a good and original man. I had never met a Swami before or been exposed to the Hindu religion. Both fascinated me. Of course, I had read of other gurus and the US press at the time was filled with stories about the Bhagwan Shree Rajnesh, the guru who started a town in Oregon and owned scores of Rolls-Royce motor cars. Swamiji, however, distinguished himself at once. He carefully explained that his brand of religion was critical of the Bhagwan. His stated goal was to be an advocate for a world religion that respected and included all religions. He appeared to live simply and spoke convincingly of his desire to help the poorest of the poor around the world.

At our first encounter, the Swami was dressed in an unpretentious white robe and wore sandals. Jet black hair framed his deep brown eyes which sparkled when he laughed. He spoke almost no English, but conveyed the feeling he might indeed have a 'third eye' which could enable him to perceive my values and motivations at once. A red dot was placed slightly above his eyes and centered on his forehead. Above the dot was an impressive scar which, he explained, had been caused by a fall from a tree. As a teenager he had studied with the great Hindu saints and monks for seven years in the Himalayas. During this period they all lived in trees, he revealed, and once while deep in meditation, he had fallen. The scar had become a symbol of his spiritual awakening.

With the Swami was his general secretary, K N Agerwal, known to all as Mamaji (Hindi for uncle). Mamaji was older, shorter and thinner than the Swami. He looked after every detail of the Swami's life including preparing his vegetarian meals which, he made a point of professing, could contain no garlic or onions. Food seasoned with garlic and onions activates the male hormones. The Swami, being celibate, avoided such stimulation. When someone else prepared the food, Mamaji acted as the Swami's taster.

Mamaji was the Swami's translator as well. After a long, emotive statement from the Swami in Hindi, Mamaji would tell the listener what 'His Holiness' had said. Later, I learned Mamaji would tell the listener what he wanted the Swami to have said! It was all done with great flair. I can still hear Mamaji's words to me at our first meeting: 'His Holiness wishes you to know that he values your friendship a great deal. He recognizes you are a man of consequence in the United States and he wants to work with you and help you translate your desire for public service into something solid. He senses your deep spiritual dedication, and he understands your vocational and financial problems. Together we will work through both of these dilemmas. We will achieve a success not out of greed or exploitation, but by means of our mutual understanding of the ideals needed to make the world a better place for all mankind.'

Mamaji and Khashoggi always referred to Swamiji as 'His Holiness'. For reasons probably best known to the Pope, people invariably seemed to take the Swami more seriously and attend to him with greater respect upon hearing Mamaji say: 'His Holiness will receive you now'.

It had been an extraordinary two years. As the airplane lifted off the runway at Dulles Airport for Los Angeles, I could only shake my head in disbelief.

The next day, 29 October 1986, was the Swami's thirty-eighth birthday, and Adnan Khashoggi was hosting a party for him at the house currently occupied by his daughter, Nabila, in Bel Air. Initially, I had been told the party would be hosted by Elizabeth Taylor at her Bel Air mansion, but for some reason the location of mansions had been changed. In telephone conversations, the Swami had begged me to attend. He could have saved his energy. I wanted to be present to check who would turn up, and to take one last look at this iconoclast Khashoggi called a 'selfless Indian spiritual saint'.

During the flight, I tried to focus on the positive things that had happened because of my friendship with the Swami. Certainly he had introduced me to India. In the past two years I had traveled from the north to the south many times and had come to love the country and its people. In addition, I had met many Americans of Indian origin while traveling in the US. Several remain close friends.

At the initial meetings, the Swami and I had agreed our goals required the assistance of a network of important and powerful friends. Accordingly, I had made most of the Swami's early introductions to heads of state such as Philippine President Marcos, the President of Panama, the Prime Minister of Jamaica, the Prince of Monaco, the Prince of Liechtenstein and others. He had in turn introduced me to the King of Jordan, the President of Zaire and the President of Egypt, to name a few. These meetings were arranged to further our plan.

The Swami's most intriguing introduction on my behalf was to the Sultan of Brunei. The young ruler was new to the world stage and controlled a fortune. Our association should have made it possible to change history.

Filipino businessman, Enrique Zobel met Swamiji at the palace in Manila on a trip I had orchestrated in July 1984. President Marcos had been very ill before the Swami's visit. After their meeting and the Swami's prayers, the President's health made a dramatic turnaround. Much later in conversation with the exiled President in Hawaii, Marcos confirmed his belief that the Swami had saved his life. True or not, Zobel encountered the Swami at that lucky moment and was won over by the guru's spiritual powers. He determined the Swami could save his relationship with the Sultan. Although the Swami had met the Sultan before, it was Zobel that took him to Brunei and promoted his unique activities.

Overnight, the Sultan became the focus of the Swami's life. I will never really know how close the two were, but the Swami made the most of their friendship. Mamaji, at one point, even bragged to Tiny Rowland that the Sultan had given the Swami $100 million. I do know they spent a great deal of time together and that I was introduced to the Sultan by the Swami on at least three occasions, and spoke with him on the telephone many more times.

4

The reality of their friendship may remain a mystery, but the perception of the Swami as the Sultan's close friend and advisor was nurtured and made tangible by the Swami and Adnan to those in pursuit of the Sultan's wealth. It was both comical and sad to see men attempt to gain the Swami's favor in order to obtain an entree to the Sultan.

Because of the Swami's alliance with the Sultan, I became involved with another major player on the world scene: Mohamed Fayed. Even though we never met, I was compelled to learn a great deal about him. In the end it became clear that these three disparate characters – the young Indian guru, the Egyptian born in the slums of Alexandria, who resided in London, and the Saudi arms dealer known around the world for his flamboyant lifestyle and enormous wealth – were cut from the same cloth. My adventure with them during the last three years was both painful and instructive. I had been allowed to visit a world few people have ever known.

As the lights of Los Angeles appeared below, I continued to ponder what I had yet to fully piece together.

Mohamed Fayed was known as a friend of the Sultan of Brunei. He had negotiated the Sultan's purchase of the Dorchester Hotel and been involved in other business dealings with him over the years. In March 1985, Fayed and his brothers succeeded in purchasing the prestigious London company, House of Fraser, holding company of the world's most famous department store, Harrods. From foreign banks, Fayed proffered £615 million to close the deal. Fayed and his newly retained investment bankers, Kleinwort Benson, claimed the money was cash in hand.

Fayed's bold move caused a furor in the UK which is yet to be resolved. The chief executive of Lonrho plc, a publicly held British conglomerate, Roland 'Tiny' Rowland, had been attempting to buy House of Fraser for seven years, but Lonrho's offers had been repeatedly blocked by the British Government. Suddenly a private, little known family from Egypt was given the blessing of Her Majesty's Government to accomplish what a well-known, public corporation had been inexplicably stopped from acquiring. The City of London went wild with rumors!

Rowland argued that Fayed deceived the UK Secretary for Trade and Industry, Norman Tebbit, in statements made on his behalf by Kleinwort Benson. Tiny was convinced the funds used in the takeover were not the Fayeds, because his company had been privy to more solid financial information on the Fayeds than almost anyone. Kleinwort Benson were, after all, newly retained bankers. Mohamed had ditched his previous investment bankers and retained Kleinwort Benson specifically for the Fraser deal. They knew little about these Egyptians.

Since the Fayed takeover, Rowland has done everything in his power to convince the British Government and the citizenry that the money Fayed used to purchase House of Fraser was not his own but the Sultan of Brunei's. It has been the business feud of the century.

Adnan Mohamed Khashoggi was born the son of a highly regarded doctor in Saudi Arabia. His father became the physician to the King, and as a result, Adnan was given many opportunities at a young age to act as the agent for the royal family in transactions with Western corporations. There seems to be little doubt that he made a great deal of money in less time than any other commoner. He also spent that money at a record pace.

I had known Khashoggi at a distance from infrequent encounters at social functions in New York and the south of France. The billionaire myth, the bodyguards and his odd social style put off any real personal contact.

Khashoggi telephoned me in Washington on 2 September 1985, to ask for an introduction to the Swami. It was a point in his life when he desperately needed to restore his relationship with the Sultan of Brunei. Adnan had been told that his only hope was to convince the Swami to recommend and support him.

I arranged for them to meet the next day in Toronto, believing AK's promise that if the Swami restored his relationship with the Sultan, I would be paid a commission. Fourteen months later as the plane pulled up to the gate at Los Angeles International Airport, I marveled that they had become inseparable.

The Swami's birthday celebration was scheduled for 6.30 pm the next evening. The better to observe the occasion, I arrived a bit early to the apparent relief of Adnan's daughter, Nabila. She appeared to have little knowledge of what was about to transpire. Nabila was in residence at 1088 Summit Drive in Bel Air, a grand 'showbiz' style mansion over-looking Beverly Hills. The house had always been rumored to have been a gift to actor George Hamilton from the First Lady of the Philippines, Imelda Marcos. Shortly after the Marcoses had been driven out of their country, the press reported that Nabila had purchased it for $7 million. Since I knew her father was struggling with what we delicately called a cash-flow problem, the transaction fascinated me.

Being the first to arrive, I stationed myself in the foyer to observe the proceedings. Typically, the Swami and Khashoggi were late. Always prompt, his disciples from throughout the US turned up at 6.30. Most were Americans of Indian origin who had become successful doctors or businessmen. They were consistently shy, gentle people who had done nothing but work for the past twenty years, and now wanted to be recognized for their achievements. The Swami portrayed himself to them as the guru with the power to help them and their children enter the higher echelons of American society. It riveted them that the Swami was able to bring together people from important sectors of the power structure.

Next came the usual entourage the Swami had collected over the years: Ernie Miller of Toronto, his follower and financial manager; Congressman Mervyn Dymally, the former Lt Governor of California who courted the Asian/Indian community by proclaiming he was 25 per cent Asian/Indian and 75 per cent black; Dr Pretab Reddy, a brilliant heart surgeon from Madras who founded the first chain of private hospitals in India; and – of course – Mamaji.

They were followed by the entire Khashoggi family guiding the Swami to his seat of honor in the center of the vast living room. Trailing this group was Adnan's wife, Lamia, still trying to secure the clasp on one of the many jeweled bracelets that adorned her. Lamia seemed the perfect wife for Adnan.

AK had met Laura Biancolini in Paris when she was a young girl of 17. Quite simply, she was the most gorgeous woman he had ever seen. In 1979, he divorced his first wife, Soraya, to marry this Italian beauty. At Adnan's insistence, Laura changed her name and converted to the Moslem religion.

Lamia always gave the impression she knew nothing significant about her husband's life. She appeared at public functions on command draped in jewels and wearing striking designer clothes. I was aware they were seldom together and rumors circulated that he forced her to spend time with other men when he needed their money. One story that surfaced again and again, hinted that President Mobutu of Zaire had invested $6 million in one of Adnan's hopeless business schemes on his agreement that Mobutu would have Lamia's company for a weekend.

Lamia was captivating beyond her incredible beauty. She seemed a tragic figure in Adnan's world of male domination. When together we spoke in her native Italian. It was our common bond. At large parties I made a point of ascertaining she was not alone in a corner while the men talked business.

Surveying the room, she seemed pleased to see a familiar face and

7

suggested a walk in the garden. Glancing across the clear blue swimming pool at the lights of Beverly Hills, the evening seemed perfect if somewhat surreal. A melting pot of religion, race, and status swirled around the Swami. It was not just a celebration of his birthday, but of the common goals of world peace, and the shared concern for the wellbeing of mankind that attracted this impressive crowd.

Barbara and Cary Grant arrived fashionably late to the absolute thrill of everyone except the Swami. He had no idea Cary Grant was one of the world's most cherished film stars. Once informed, he requested they be brought to him. As the Swami sat in his chair like an Indian Buddha, the Grants dutifully greeted him as they would the Pope.

Later, Cary Grant asked, as only Cary Grant possibly could: 'Who the hell is that guy?'

Suddenly there was a hush over the sprawling mansion. Elizabeth Taylor and George Hamilton had arrived. Totally losing his composure, the Swami leapt to his feet to greet them. Elizabeth was the most famous personality the Swami had ever met. He treated her like a goddess and bragged to everyone that she had become his disciple.

Adnan had arranged their introduction a few months earlier at the Cannes Film Festival in France. The moment did not permit questions to Elizabeth about the Swami. I can only surmise she had been enchanted by his psychic powers in much the same way as he had wooed the Sultan and others. Obviously, she thought enough of him to attend his birthday celebration.

This was a moment in Elizabeth's life when she was 'at her fighting weight' (her words). Dressed in white and exuding the radiance of a twenty-year-old prom queen, she was devastatingly beautiful.

As the excitement grew, Adnan assembled everyone around the Swami for a tribute. To my surprise, he asked me to speak. Without hesitation, I thanked the Swami for my introduction to his country and the deeper understanding I had gained of India's culture and dedication to the principles of democracy. I meant it. He taught me a great deal about a vast nation most Americans do not know or fully appreciate.

Elizabeth also spoke and impressed everyone with her praise of the Swami. She talked movingly about his love of man and his inspiration to her. She is a great actress, after all.

Within two weeks, the *National Inquirer* ran a cover story on the relationship between Elizabeth and the Swami, obviously promoted by Mamaji. Several months later, Burt Bacharach, the famous composer and a neighbor of Elizabeth's in Bel Air, told me the Swami had given her an emerald necklace valued at over $300,000. The next year, friends in France reported that she had asked him to accompany her to Paris to be present when President Mitterand decorated her with the Legion d'Honeur.

Since I had been the first to arrive at the party, it seemed proper to be the first to leave as well. My mind had absorbed enough for one night.

As the large iron gate to the entrance of 1088 Summit Drive closed, I dissolved with laughter. Into this mansion, allegedly owned by Nabila Khashoggi, had come the Swami's current list of 'photo album' friends to honor him. The charade would no doubt continue, but I knew it would be impossible to break bread with the Swami or Khashoggi again.

# – 2 –
## The Chief

---

The telephone call from Khashoggi fourteen months before the LA trip had caught me off guard. It was 2 September 1985. Actually, the call was placed by Adnan's chief of staff, Robert Shaheen. In time I learned that Shaheen was to Khashoggi what Mamaji was to the Swami.

Shaheen was a fast talking, wise-cracking American of Arab origin. He had worked for the 'Chief', as he always called Khashoggi, for over twenty years. A slender man, about six feet tall, he knew the importance of projecting an image. He appeared in public dressed always in a dark suit and wearing conservative wire rimmed glasses. It was he who enabled AK to bridge the gap between the Arab and Western worlds. He spoke Arabic, French and, of course, English; gave information on a 'need to know' basis; and, above all, took care of the 'Chief'.

Shaheen placed the call from AK's Paris office to request a meeting between Khashoggi and the Swami. 'Come on,' I remember saying, 'Why on earth would Adnan want to meet Swamiji?' 'Steven, dear boy,' he replied. 'We need to better our relationship with the Sultan of Brunei. Those in the know tell us your Swami is the man for the job. If this can be accomplished, you will be handsomely rewarded.'

The minute the conversation with Shaheen ended, I telephoned the Swami in Canada at the home of Ernie Miller. 'Khashoggi?' he shouted into the telephone, 'Khashoggi! Tell him he must meet me here tomor-

10

row. Otherwise, I cannot see him.' He could, of course, have seen Khashoggi any time in the next few weeks. The command for a meeting the next day was intended to signal to AK that the Swami was accustomed to giving orders to the high and mighty.

When I telephoned Shaheen with the Swami's message, the suddenness of the meeting caught him and Adnan off guard. Adnan came on the telephone to explain that his plane was on loan to President Mobutu of Zaire the next day. It meant he would have to fly to Canada on a commercial airline and cancel several appointments. Diplomatically, I explained the Swami was adamant. AK sighed and agreed.

For the first time in years, AK was awakened at the scheduled morning hour and driven to the Paris airport, where he had to endure the indignities of security and customs like any ordinary traveler. On his private plane, the authorities always came on board and cleared the passengers with no delay. AK reported it was the first time he had queued up for anything and that it was most unpleasant.

It was 3 September 1985. Adnan took the Concorde from Paris to New York, chartered a small jet, and flew to Toronto. In order to facilitate the meeting, I had flown to Toronto earlier that day, hired a limousine and instructed the driver to request permission to enter the restricted section inside the gates of the terminal. This positioning would allow me to receive Adnan and Shaheen as they stepped off the plane. I decided against a red carpet.

The Chief's jet arrived at exactly 11.00 am. AK, Shaheen, and a manservant emerged looking refreshed and full of anticipation. As we were being driven to Ernie Miller's house in Gormley, Ontario, a house which the Swami always referred to as his own, I attempted to brief Adnan and Shaheen on the Swami. AK seemed totally uninterested, but did let me know I was in the company of a man who understood the big leagues. When the driver inquired how the Concorde flight had been, Adnan enthused: 'It was great. I haven't been on a public aircraft in over fifteen years. Wonderful speed.'

By this time, I had met Ernie on many occasions. Adnan, of course, had never heard of him. When asked, I merely explained he was a Canadian businessman and a devoted follower of the Swami's.

In truth, Ernie was my nemesis. To say the man was arrogant, overweight, crude, ill-tempered and mean-spirited, fails to take cognizance of his many other shortcomings. I have rarely met a man I disliked more.

Over a year before, in a private meeting with the Swami and Mamaji,

11

I had asked about Ernie. Mamaji, sensing my negative attitude, leapt to Ernie's defense. He explained that the man had been an alcoholic in the early seventies. At that time, Ernie was part owner of the Black Hawk Motor Inn in Richmond Hill, just north of Toronto. The Black Hawk was a flea-bag motel frequented by the leather and motor-cycle crowd. An Indian pianist performing at the motel was worried about Ernie and convinced him to attend a meeting with the Swami in New York.

Ernie and the Swami became comrades. The Swami persuaded Ernie to stop drinking and prayed for his financial success. As Ernie tells the story, his life was transformed. Soon after his conversion to the Hindu faith, he achieved financial success, went off the booze, and married, for the second time, a lovely young woman, Kim. When we first met, he was the father of two little girls, ostensibly wealthy, and the Swami's most loyal supporter. Whenever money was needed for one of His Holiness' causes, Ernie provided it. I took this to be the highest form of devotion and did my best to get along.

After a thirty-minute drive, we arrived to be greeted by the Swami, Ernie, his wife and children, and Mamaji. Ernie was wearing a tie, the little girls looked like they were prepped for their Sears family photo session, and the Swami was sporting a new multi-jeweled bracelet which, he said, was a gift from the Sultan.

I began to worry that I might be guiding Adnan into a trap.

Obviously, the Swami and Ernie were primed for this meeting.

After the standard vegetarian lunch and inconsequential conversation, the Swami took Adnan into the sitting room where, I was told later, he demonstrated his psychic powers and added a routine where another swami – Swamiji always liked to have one or two lesser swamis around for effect – produced dirt in his hand by the power of concentration and prayer. Swamiji explained that this guru could produce anything in his hand by intense concentration. AK was evidently wowed by the Swami's astrological insights, but not impressed by the other guru's sleight of hand. 'If that swami can actually produce a diamond, like the Swami says, why didn't he? Who needs the dirt!' he complained.

In spite of this disappointment, the visit was a success. After four hours of dialogue, the customary photo session, and the unending proclamations of brotherhood, AK, Shaheen and I returned to New York on the private plane. While AK slept, Shaheen explained that they had invited the Swami to spend time in New York, where he was to reside in the Chief's guest apartment in the Olympic Towers. Swamiji had agreed to move into the apartment in less than a week and big things were contemplated. 'Sure,' opined Shaheen, 'the Sultan is important, but he is not the only show in town. The Swami tells us he knows Prince Rainier, Prince Hans Adam of Liechtenstein, the President of the Philippines . . . the list is endless. We can definitely work together.'

At this point it was impossible to tell who was telling the truth. One thing is certain: none of us knew that when AK excused himself from our meeting to make urgent telephone calls, he was speaking to the key players involved in the sale of US arms to Iran.

If someone had then suggested that AK and the Swami would spend the next two years virtually living together, I would have thought them mad. But that is what happened.

Unknown to his disciples and friends, the Swami had amassed a fortune of over $100 million. The money was controlled by Ernie Miller, but he took orders from the Swami and Mamaji. Unlikely as it may seem, what had been kept from virtually everyone, Adnan and Shaheen discovered in one day: the guru was loaded.

The Swami had always been told Adnan was a multi-billionaire and, therefore, trusted him completely. Swamiji was elated to have won the friendship of this important statesman/billionaire, and instantly agreed to AK's invitation to spend time with him in New York. Looking back, the Swami probably told AK he controlled over $100 million when he apologized for not being a billionaire.

It was all in a day's work for Khashoggi and Shaheen. In the months ahead, they would promote the Swami, who would order Miller to transfer over $63 million to the Chief's bank accounts.

Once the introduction to AK had been made, Swamiji relied on me less and less, and began a process of distancing himself. He no longer needed my help. Also, he began to sense my growing recognition of his real ambitions as opposed to his pontifications. At AK's insistence, however, I continued to be included on many trips with them and, as always, they encouraged me to believe future business would result. Instantly, we entered a heady world of private planes, yachts, appointments with heads of state, and constant deal-making. AK befriended me, put me at ease, and included me whenever nothing confidential was being discussed. Alas, closing the deal inevitably required one more journey or my bringing another major investor into the deal. Nothing was ever finalized.

Shaheen seemed even more sympathetic. In fact, it was Shaheen who cautiously disclosed some of the financial transactions between AK and the Swami. When he revealed, three months after the fact, that Miller had loaned AK over $30 million shortly after their first meeting and that

13

the Swami had insisted the money be transferred in twenty-four hours without being secured by anything but AK's promise to repay it, I fell off my chair.

Virtually everyone in the media, and even most of those who had a business involvement with Khashoggi, failed to recognize that he had fallen into deep financial trouble. Practically all of the circumstances AK had exploited to make large profits no longer existed, or had changed dramatically. Not only had oil prices gone down, but the oil sheiks had learned they no longer needed him. Their own sons had returned from American universities (usually MIT or Harvard) trained to evaluate the terms of contracts with foreign corporations and were eager to earn commissions on the deals. The number of Third World leaders able to hand Khashoggi large portions of their country's resources to broker in return for enormous kick-backs (secretly transferred to their private Swiss bank accounts) was steadily declining. AK's last major effort at a mega-deal collapsed in 1985, when President Numeiry of the Sudan was deposed in a coup. Numeiry had entrusted the economic future of the Sudan to AK, thus hastening his downfall.

Triad America, the Khashoggi flagship entity in Salt Lake City, Utah, was forced to declare bankruptcy for two reasons: AK tried to do too much too fast, but more important, he covertly drained the company of over $130 million in cash to pay for his lavish life-style. Prior commissions allegedly due him from his 1970s deals with Lockheed and Northrop were tied up in court battles. He had pledged these commissions to Triad, but the creditors considered his word meaningless.

Everything AK owned of value had been encumbered long ago to obtain cash. Frequently, the amount of the loan was greater than the value of the asset used to secure it. Many of these transactions were, in effect, secured by his reputation as the richest man in the world.

It is amazing that while Adnan was in the process of virtually losing everything, he was able to use the media to conceal the truth. In 1986, Ronald Kessler wrote a fairy-tale book about AK, *The Richest Man In The World*. On the book jacket, Kessler is described as: 'an award-winning investigative journalist who had worked for *The Washington Post* for fifteen years'. Yet, he chronicled and gave credence to the Khashoggi fictions.

It was soon after the Irangate scandal became news, that AK appeared on the 19 January 1987 cover of *Time* magazine. The article, which also featured a photo of AK with the Swami, was another puff piece that

14

might as well have been written by Shaheen.

At about the same time, Barbara Walters persuaded Adnan to be interviewed on a special television segment of ABC's '20/20'. In the grand Khashoggi style, he flew Barbara to the south of France on his DC–8 while the program was being filmed. Her interest, of course, was the role Adnan had played in the arms sale. But, even though Barbara asked the right questions, AK masterfully used this television opportunity to conceal the real story, and, in so doing, encouraged the viewers to continue to believe he was one of the world's richest men. Virtually no one fathomed the dimensions of his financial crunch. Once again, AK successfully manipulated the media to keep the billionaire myth alive.

In contrast, Khashoggi's money problems were discussed quite openly among his staff. Even Shaheen talked 'poor' all of the time. At first, I thought he was trying to discourage me from asking for expenses. J Paul Getty made his guests use a pay telephone installed in his home, I recalled. Perhaps this was just a quirk of the billionaire's club.

The staff, however, was schooled by the master himself. They liked the life they were leading and, naturally, hoped AK would again be on top. Thus, in all of their dealings with the outside world, they protected his reputation with skill and determination.

My first clue to AK's money problems came on the day the Swami was to move into the Khashoggi apartment at the Olympic Towers – 6 September 1985. The Swami had asked me to help organize his arrival. When I explained the purpose of the visit to the elevator operator, he advised me not to encourage AK's new guest to become too well settled. 'Mr Khashoggi has not paid his condo fees in months,' he said. 'My guess is that he will be out of here in two weeks.'

During this period, Adnan skillfully transcended these troublesome money matters with humor and convincing logic. The financial ups and downs, he mused, were merely a matter of bad management. 'Maintaining and staffing twelve homes around the world, not to mention three airplanes, is complicated,' he would sigh. In time, I observed it was not only complicated, but unspeakably expensive. The irony of this particular period was that the money he continued to pour into short-term interest payments and public displays of wealth, estimated to be over $200,000 per day, was provided by the Swami.

In the spirit of my father's old adage, 'When you are really broke, buy a new Cadillac', Adnan kept pouring borrowed millions into sustaining his image and lifestyle. He even pledged $5 million to The American University in Washington, DC, to endow the Adnan

Khashoggi Sports Center. Lamia and Adnan presided over the ground-breaking ceremony on the university campus, and at the Swami's request, I hosted an impressive luncheon in their honor.

Driven by this grim financial crisis, Adnan flew frantically from nation to nation in search of a quick 'hit'. In December 1985, he traveled to India, Jordan, Egypt and Zaire in six days exploring potential business deals. Nothing gelled.

In the spirit of the California forty-niners, AK was the first to call on 'Baby Doc' Duvalier in the French Alps and former president Marcos in Hawaii, two of the world's most corrupt and wealthy leaders in exile.

From September 1985 until October 1986 I accompanied Adnan on countless trips. When he wanted to relax, he would ask me to join him in his section of the plane or offer dinner with a group of friends. After two or three cocktails, his conversation became open and expansive. In the pattern of most men with great self-esteem, he spoke in inflated terms about his movements and business projects. Most of what he said is no longer credible, but certain comments, especially with the assistance of more reliable points of reference, were instructive.

While my day-to-day involvement with AK began long after the plan to sell arms to Iran had been put in motion, I realize now that he was unwittingly dropping clues all of the time. Money was the only thing that really mattered to him, but he did fancy himself to be a statesman of sorts as well. When he actually possessed a fortune, the lure of international diplomacy was a fascination. Now he used the fiction of statesmanship to justify his actions and encourage the real statesmen of the world to trust him and invest in his business projects.

In one late night conversation, Adnan told me he had been considering business opportunities in Iran for some time. After many discussions with knowledgeable observers of that country, AK said he had asked his staff to take a closer look. The fall of the Shah and the terrorist antics of the Ayatollah had isolated Iran from most normal business relations with the free world. 'Without getting too involved, and without any desire to be associated with the current Iranian government,' Khashoggi observed, 'there may be housing, medical or other areas in which I can do business.'

On 25 November 1986, the US Attorney General announced that the government had taken part in a covert action in which the Israelis were given permission to buy arms from the US and sell them to Iran. My shock turned to horror when it was revealed that a key figure in this debacle was Adnan Khashoggi. Adnan reportedly had loaned money to intermediaries at the request of the US Government to enable the Israelis to buy the arms and sell them to Iran. The bridge loans were necessary, according to statements approved by various government officials, because neither side trusted the other. In short, only Adnan M Khashoggi had the confidence of the US Government, the Government of Israel and the Revolutionary Government of Iran, as well as the money required to carry out the foreign policy of the US.

Had Khashoggi and the Swami floated the most disastrous foreign policy initiative of the Reagan Administration? The scheme sounded like something Khashoggi might have masterminded. It seemed more than a little odd that the US Government needed Khashoggi to loan money to Israeli intermediaries so the government of Israel would cooperate in a major US foreign policy initiative. Ship arms to the moderates in Iran? What moderates?

I was prepared to come to terms with the fact I had been made a fool of, but now it appeared the leaders of the free world had been taken in as well.

Few of those around AK had a clue what he was really selling to Iran until the sale of arms was disclosed by the media. Adnan was able to do what seemed impossible to other arms dealers, in part, because he understood the needs and the vulnerabilities of the key nations involved. Others had this intelligence, but did not have the advantage of being regarded as billionaire statesmen.

Iran needed arms in the war against Iraq and AK recognized the business potential at once.

Years before, he had made himself the Saudi royal family's go-between with Israel and had developed high level contacts in the Israeli government. These officials had informed Adnan many times that they considered Iraq a constant threat, and that they were increasingly nervous about the possibility that Iraq might defeat Iran and direct its forces against Israel.

It was no secret that the Americans were preoccupied with the hostage issue. President Reagan raised the matter daily to his national security staff. Adnan saw Iran's isolation, his carefully cultivated relationships in Israel, and the US preoccupation with the hostages as a perfect opportunity to make some desperately needed money.

While I know it should not have taken so long to comprehend the Swami/Miller financial arrangement – what Khashoggi learned in a day took me three years to figure out – my failure to recognize that AK could manage to involve the governments of the United States and Israel in the sale of arms to Iran might be forgiven. No matter how immoral and money hungry AK and his agents might have been, the policy of the United States government was unequivocally against the sale of arms to Iran. Not only would the US reject any such proposal, the President had instructed the Secretary of State to strongly urge other governments to adopt the US position. Sell arms to the Ayatollah Khomeini? Never.

# – 3 –

# How AK Masterminded the Sale of US Arms to the Ayatollah

News of the sale of arms to Iran shocked the world. I felt like the doorman at a whore house who never understood what happened inside. My anger on learning of AK's and the Swami's involvement motivated me to learn what actually transpired in greater detail, and to factor in bits of information I had acquired while associated with them.

In order to examine the Iran-Contra matter, I put aside other projects and client matters for months, read the report of the Tower Commission and, subsequently, followed the hearings in Congress diligently. Both of these official inquiries were wide-ranging and instructive from the point of view of the US Government. My particular fascination, however, was that the old Watergate admonition, 'follow the money', was not more thoroughly pursued in the inquiries, even though it was given lip service.

This is not to say the investigations were poorly organized or lacking in leadership. In a short time period, a great deal of information was considered and conclusions of essential importance were formulated. For some obscure reason, however, both the Tower Commission and the Congressional Committee accepted the sequence of events put forward by Khashoggi and the other middlemen as fact.

19

Once I began to integrate the information garnered from AK with the official documents, another dimension to the story suddenly coalesced. If the committees had 'followed the money' in their examinations of the bridge loans and the roles played by Khashoggi and Ghorbanifar, instead of accepting their testimony as fact, I suggest they would have reached another painful conclusion. Khashoggi succeeded in corrupting the foreign policy of the US by a clever series of phoney initiatives undertaken solely for his financial benefit.

Adnan was the world's most experienced and most publicized arms merchant. Others may have considered it an impossible task, but AK was convinced his contacts and his reputation would enable him to succeed in buying arms from the United States and selling them to Iran.

AK's first move, as directed by a master plan formulated in late 1984, was to approach an old friend, Manucher Ghorbanifar. They had met years before when Ghorbanifar was a shipping executive in Tehran and had seen each other from time to time in Paris. The two had discussed many potential projects immediately after the revolution, a few of which Khashoggi said, actually materialised.

It amused AK that while Ghorbanifar had once been loyal to the Shah, he determined there was no money to be made from political sentimentality and, in a matter of days after the Shah fell, did an 'about face'. Even though Khomeini confiscated his businesses, Ghorbanifar soon became a trusted advisor to Mir Hossein Mousavi, the Ayatollah's Prime Minister. Shortly thereafter, Mousavi had made Ghorbanifar the head of Iranian intelligence in Western Europe.

By sheer happenstance, AK introduced me to Ghorbanifar, already his partner in the sale of arms to Iran for several months, in December 1985. We were meeting in his Paris apartment at 11 Avenue Montaigne, when Shaheen announced that a delegation of Iranians had arrived. AK said he did not want them to enter a room in which he was meeting with an American and, apologetically, asked me to leave by the rear entrance and return in two hours. Jokingly he said, 'They will assume you are an agent for the Great Satan.'

Taken aback and a bit angry, I walked to the hotel George V, sat at the bar for two hours, and returned just as he was ushering out Ghorbanifar and two mullahs. To my surprise, AK made a point of introducing us. 'My Iranian friends must know I am involved with many important Americans,' he said, 'but it would have offended them if they thought I had received you before them.' Their names and purported political influence in Iran meant nothing at the time.

Sensing my dismay, AK explained that Ghorbanifar had been close to the Shah and, therefore, could be trusted. He said he had known Ghorbanifar for years and understood the significant, complicated role he played in relations between Iran and the West. He was a pragmatist, according to AK, and in no way an agent of the Ayatollah. Shaheen also confirmed that Ghorbanifar was a major player between Iran and Western Europe and that AK had known him a long time. Also, Shaheen reminded me that Adnan was a citizen of Saudi Arabia and able to engage in commercial dealings with Iran. The arms sales and AK's involvement with the US government were never mentioned in these conversations, but Khashoggi had been hard at work for some time.

In a series of meetings initiated by Adnan in January 1985, he and Ghorbanifar devised the scheme to buy arms for Iran and, more importantly, sold the plan over the next five months to the governments of Iran, Israel, and the United States.

Needless to say, before the first 96 TOW missiles (the press reported 100 TOWs had been shipped, but the missiles were packed in pallets of twelve missiles each, and no unpacked missiles were shipped for safety reasons) were shipped to Iran in August 1985, AK needed to do a great deal of political groundwork in Washington, Jerusalem and Tehran.

The Chief had to factor certain 'givens' into his scheme: (1) Ghorbanifar was essential because of his contacts in Iran, but would not be 'OK'd' by officials in the CIA. (2) Israel would not ship the missiles without US approval. (3) To convince US officials to accept the plan, the arms sales had to almost appear to be an afterthought. While it was always proposed as a covert operation, the possibility of public disclosure could not be ignored. Above all, if the plan was uncovered, it could not be perceived to be a deal to sell arms to the Revolutionary Guards in Iran as a swap for the hostages. Rather, it had to be seen as an opening to those who would lead Iran after Khomeini, the so-called 'moderates'. (4) Finally, the arms sales had to be orchestrated in a way which kept AK in the money pipeline. The enterprise made no sense unless both AK and Ghorbanifar were clearly in control of the funds and able to benefit from immense profits down the line.

Lies, secrecy and evasion were the tools AK used to skillfully overcome each obstacle. He also had the benefit of Ghorbanifar's knowledge of the day-to-day political situation in Iran.

Ghorbanifar had fallen out with the CIA in 1983. A devastatingly negative profile on him had been filed by George Cave, a CIA officer stationed in Tehran before the overthrow of the Shah. In 1985, he was then on assignment at CIA headquarters in Langley, Virginia. The CIA had evidence that AK and Ghorbanifar had worked together for years.

So rather than describe themselves as long-time friends and trigger background checks with the CIA, Ghorbanifar and AK deduced that it would be more effective if AK said he had just been introduced to Ghorbanifar.

CIA Director William Casey was well aware that the professionals in his agency would kill the Iran initiative if they were appraised of Ghorbanifar's involvement. Casey deliberately deceived CIA officials, and asked a mutual friend of his and Khashoggi's, Roy Furmark, to be his 'beard'. All agreed to the cover story that Furmark had just introduced Ghorbanifar to Khashoggi in January 1985. This pretense enabled AK to appear to check him out with other intelligence sources, apparently ignorant of prior history. By this time Casey, Oliver North, and their cabal were actively creating 'the Enterprise' – a secret, illegal entity conceived to implement their particular foreign policy decisions. The Enterprise bought AK's plan, and agreed to go along with whatever cover was required.

No CIA official has ever denied that solid information existed to prove Khashoggi and Ghorbanifar had known each other before January 1985. The current director of the CIA, Judge Webster, confirmed this in a private conversation. Khashoggi carefully stuck to the Furmark story in interviews with *Time* magazine and in his testimony before the Tower Commission. At all events, Casey successfully used Furmark as his cover to help Khashoggi and Ghorbanifar leap-frog the CIA.

Knowing the best way to avoid the CIA, in obtaining the US government's approval of Ghorbanifar, was through Jerusalem, AK decided to first approach his friend, then Israeli Prime Minister Shimon Peres. He intended to persuade Peres that his plan was in Israel's best interest and convince him that, in order to obtain their desired ends, he needed the necessary clearances on Ghorbanifar from Israel's intelligence agency, the Mossad. Key Israeli officials could then be instructed to speak to President Reagan's national security staff about Ghorbanifar and explain the value of working with him, thus minimizing any negative reports on his past.

AK had other factors working in his favor: (1) He had known for a long time that the Israelis were keen to resume arms sales to Iran. They had sold over a billion dollars in arms to the Ayatollah since the fall of the Shah, but had been forced to stop by the United States. (2) Not only had Iraq long been considered Israel's most dangerous enemy, it also was known that Iraq had come within an eyelash of building a nuclear bomb. Only a lightning air strike by Israel, obliterating the atomic reactor, stopped Iraq from developing a nuclear capability. (3) Finally, the safety of the large Jewish population in Tehran was an issue that gave the Israeli leaders another reason to favor Iran over Iraq.

Obviously, AK realized his plan to buy US arms and sell them to Iran would be considered with greater sympathy and taken more seriously if it was proposed to Washington by Israel. With this in mind, Adnan orchestrated the flow of information to the NSC staff by Israeli officials in a way which seemed informed and uncalculated.

Once he had cleared the plan with Ghorbanifar, Khashoggi quickly arranged a meeting with Peres in New York while the Prime Minister was attending meetings at the United Nations. In a low-key, off-the-record discussion, AK outlined the plan in both practical and positive global political terms. The Prime Minister, as AK reported in a later memo, was 'excited'. Whatever the Mossad thought about Ghorbanifar, Peres liked the plan and was willing to go to bat for him. As planned, AK's meeting with Peres in New York was followed within two weeks by a visit to national security advisor Robert McFarlane from Adolph Schwimmer, a friend of Peres, carrying a letter from the Prime Minister to President Reagan supporting the initiative. There is no evidence the letter ever reached the President's desk. Five days later, David Kimche, former director general of the Israeli foreign ministry, met McFarlane at the White House to advocate the plan go forward. Both Schwimmer and Kimche said Ghorbanifar could be trusted.

Never greatly experienced in the minutiae of foreign affairs, McFarlane accepted the Israeli officials' explanation of the merits of the undertaking. The Israelis persuaded McFarlane to work with Ghorbanifar and the other middlemen in order to gain the confidence of the 'moderates' in Iran and to avoid public knowledge of the sale of arms. They also advised the CIA be left out of the loop in the early stages of the operation.

NSC consultant Michael Ledeen recommended Ghorbanifar as well. Ledeen even met with Peres in Israel without the knowledge of the Secretary of State or the US Ambassador. On his return, he confirmed that Peres' agreed Ghorbanifar was a necessary ingredient.

In his book, *Perilous Statecraft* (Scribners, 1988), Ledeen seems to agree with me on Iran-Contra: 'In many ways, Khashoggi was the originator of the entire enterprise', he writes, 'for, contrary to the widespread theory that the Iran initiative was purely an Israeli plan to advance its own interests by luring the United States in supporting Israeli arms sales, it was Khashoggi who realized that the shortest route for Ghorbanifar to reach Washington lay through Jerusalem.' Ledeen was certainly in a position to know.

In spite of his constant interplay with Khashoggi, however, he missed the point. Ledeen believed Khashoggi to be an international diplomat, 'a man to be taken seriously in Western capitals', not a calculating rogue in desperate need of money.

During the months of April and May 1985, AK initiated confidential discussions with McFarlane, usually by telephone, on a variety of foreign policy issues. He did not disclose his interest in the arms sales, at first, rather he sought to convince McFarlane of his knowledge and statesman-like interest in world affairs, especially the Middle East.

On 1 July 1985 Adnan sent McFarlane a forty-seven-page memorandum classified 'Confidential' by the NSC. The memo was a follow-up document to their many prior telephone conversations. It detailed the political situation in Iran and suggested one group, in particular, that might be able to change the direction of history, thus bringing Iran back into – or near – the Western orbit. AK basically identified and defined 'moderates' for McFarlane. Further, he gave his personal assurances of the validity of Ghorbanifar's assumptions and outlined why only he, with the help of Ghorbanifar, could succeed in bringing about an 'opening' in Iran. The release of the hostages was never referenced in any of the documents, but always promised in secure telephone conversations and in the many meetings held in London, Hamburg and elsewhere among NSC officials and the middlemen.

Still fearing the CIA would kill his plan, AK repeatedly emphasized that recent meetings with world leaders confirmed the intelligence provided by Ghorbanifar. As further proof, he asserted that he would not risk dealing with Ghorbanifar unless he was certain of his veracity (never mind that AK at this point had virtually nothing to risk). The McFarlane memo, in fact, was grounded in the thesis that the covert action not be discussed or coordinated in any way with the CIA. The agency could not be trusted in matters of such a 'top secret' nature, AK emphasized. Only the NSC had the sophistication and intelligence to be relied upon. AK was always a master of inflating the egos of those he needed. In spite of Ghorbanifar's previous attempts to work with the Departments of State and Defense which were rejected out of hand, Ghorbanifar remained the key middleman. That great statesman/billionaire, Adnan Khashoggi, had rehabilitated him.

Selling the fiction of 'moderates' in Iran was not easy, but it was essential for US approval of the plan. Adnan and Ghorbanifar obviously succeeded. To this day, Reagan justifies the sale of arms to Iran in their words.

Finally, through a clever series of misrepresentations about the finan-

24

cing arrangements between Iran and Israel, the two kept control of the flow of money. In public statements made after the arms sales became an issue of concern to the world, Khashoggi consistently said he had been asked to loan the money to buy the arms because of the lack of trust between the Israelis and the Iranians. In short, the Israelis would not ship the missiles until they had been paid and the Iranians would not pay until they had received the arms. This lack of trust, it was universally assumed, made Khashoggi's bridge loans essential.

The need for the NSC staff to keep the plan hidden from the CIA, Congress, and the other branches of government, along with the NSC's lack of experience in covert operations, enabled the middlemen to put forth this invention unchallenged. It was unimportant to the Israelis and the Iranians exactly how the technicalities of paying for the arms were reported to the US government. As long as Israel had Washington's approval and the arms were actually delivered, both sides were happy with the end result.

Contrary to public statements, Adnan never actually loaned the money to buy the arms. Khashoggi's loans were a scam unknown even to Ghorbanifar. He wrote checks which were made good only after 'real' money came into his account from the Iranian payments. AK's relationship with the Swiss banks allowed this kind of 'kiting'.* His first check for $1 million, written on 7 August, did not clear his account until his so-called loan was repaid on 29 August from the funds received from Iran. The loan from AK was said to have been deposited in an Israeli intermediary's account. The intermediary, however, was never identified in testimony before the Tower Commission or Congress.

According to AK, he went along with the second loan of $4 million because the first had been repaid, and on the information and belief that the loan request had come from officials of the US Government at the highest level.

* Personal experience taught that the banks gave AK the kind of consideration not available to most people. After hounding him for weeks, Khashoggi finally handed over a check to reimburse me for out-of-pocket expenses. On advice from Shaheen, I deposited the check the next day with Credit Suisse in Geneva, the correspondent bank to AK's bank in Monte Carlo on which the check was drawn. The bank manager was instructed to wire the money to my Washington account after the check had cleared. He said it normally took three days. Weeks passed before I was able to get any information. Finally the manager explained there was no money in Mr Khashoggi's account, and advised me to be patient. It was, he said, standard operating procedure for Khashoggi. Incredibly, there were always outstanding checks waiting payment. Five weeks passed before the check was honored. In EEC countries, writing a bad check is a criminal offense, but that never troubled Adnan Khashoggi.

Apparently, even the co-conspirators became confused at this point. Their testimonies of what happened differ rather significantly. In the Tower Report, Ghorbanifar, contradicting AK, stated that the second check for $4 million was actually his, which he sent to AK on 12 September. Not until AK received Ghorbanifar's check on 14 September did he forward his own check for $4 million to be deposited in the intermediary's account.

The Iranians transferred $5 million to the Swiss bank account controlled by Ghorbanifar and Khashoggi on 18 September, to pay for the second shipment. Ghorbanifar then notified AK to negotiate his check, thus enabling AK to instruct his bank to honor the 14 September check which he alleged he had given to pay for the second shipment of TOW missiles.

AK did, indeed, give a new definition to the word loan. Basically, he was using his reputation as a billionaire to win credibility for the scam in order to skim off whatever profits he could. Exactly why AK's loans were needed was never critically examined.

The government of Israel was not paid for the TOW missiles until March 1986, when the Ministry of Defense accepted $3 million for 504 TOWs. This is confirmed by both the Tower Commission and the Congressional Committee report, although the reports do not disclose who actually made the payment. On the basis of Ghorbanifar's and AK's statements, the committees note that Iran transferred $6,217,410 to Ghorbanifar's Swiss account to pay for the missiles. This figure cannot be verified, of course, the committees had no way of knowing whether the middlemen were giving accurate figures. For all we know, it could have been $100 million.

Khashoggi used the Iran arms sale to swindle the Swami as well. By April 1986, the Swami and Miller had loaned him over $40 million. Miller, especially, was distraught over Triad's financial tailspin and had begun to complain to the Swami that the collateral AK had pledged was worthless. Mamaji and Ernie made the Swami promise that no more money would go to Adnan.

To convince the Swami to advance more money AK cleverly dazzled him with reports of his involvement in the Iran arms sale. He described it as an international exploit of untold possibilities. In spite of Ernie's objection he persuaded the Swami to risk another $15 million in return for his promise of high profits from arms sales and other ventures in Iran.

In public statements, AK said he borrowed $15 million from the Swami's bag men (Miller and Co.) to finance the third shipment of arms to Iran. AK did not use the Swami's money in the arms deal however. Actually he never intended to do anything other than keep the DC-8 in the air. Footnotes in the Congressional report indicate that the money was slow to appear in the proper accounts, a laughable description of bank accounts totally out of the control of the US Government.

The official reports state that Khashoggi deposited $15 million into the Lake Resources account in Geneva. The account was supposedly controlled by American middlemen, but other insiders aver that Ghorbanifar was also able to activate it. Adnan testified that Ghorbanifar gave him postdated checks at the same time for $18 million, his $15 million investment and 20 per cent interest. It all sounds plausible until the numbers are compared with the Israeli Historical Chronology which was carefully reviewed and highlighted in the Tower Report. At B-179, the Report reveals that Iran advanced $40 million in late 1985 to accounts controlled by Ghorbanifar (and, one suspects Khashoggi) for future arms transactions. To repeat, why was AK's loan needed? A better question perhaps is, what happened to Iran's $40 million?

Whether Khashoggi loaned the money, or merely represented to have loaned it, was obfuscated by the public outrage over the disclosure of the arms sales. When the Iranians discovered the middlemen were grossly inflating the price of the arms, they gave the story to the press. It was the Reagan Administration's darkest hour.

AK, in a clever diversionary move, prevailed upon Roy Furmark to approach CIA Director Casey with the threat that his Canadian business partners would take legal action against the US Government if the money he allegedly loaned (Adnan said they were owed $10 million), was not repaid. As usual, the world media reported every word Adnan said uncritically and unconditionally.

AK also gave several interviews in which he said he had made no profits from the sale of arms, had not been repaid his last loan, and that, moreover, he had lost money in his noble efforts. These public protestations succeeded in misleading everyone, and saved AK from any serious examination of his part in the debacle.

It has yet to be disclosed how most of the profits from the arms sales were diverted and where. The public record suggests the amount unaccounted for was $8 million. This figure recurs because that amount was in the only Swiss account actually acknowledged by the middlemen. Knowing how these men operate, the amounts involved had to have been much, much more. As a rule of thumb, when $8 million is disclosed under pressure, the figure is probably $80 million. Worse, it is impossible to trace the transfers of the money due to the sophistication of the middlemen and the banking regulations of the countries in which they had secret or numbered accounts.

The self-appointed implementors of foreign policy on the NSC staff planned that the profits would be diverted to the Contras. The Contras received almost none of this money according to official reports.

One can imagine AK finally was able to pay the fuel bill on his DC–8 or buy Lamia an emerald necklace as insurance against the future.

The bottom line: AK did not loan the money to purchase the arms sold to Iran. In order to make money, he promoted a scheme he knew to be bogus from the start. He literally invented moderates in Iran in this specific instance to make the deal palatable to the US. The arms were sold to the Revolutionary Guards in Tehran. Only one hostage was released as a ploy to keep the scam going. And, when the Iranians discovered they were being cheated out of millions of dollars by the middlemen, they blew the whistle. The Khashoggi/Ghorbanifar foreign policy initiative was mercifully over.

In his testimony before the Iran–Contra Committee of Congress, former White House Chief of Staff Donald Regan commented: 'We were all snookered by a bunch of rug traders and phonies,' as he closed his briefcase and left the hearing room.

# – 4 –

# Smoke and Mirrors

In Ledeen's book, subtitled: 'An Insider's Account of the Iran-Contra Affair', he makes a statement, most likely fed to him by Adnan, which is laughable: 'There are references to the two Canadians ... In fact, the Canadians did not exist. The story was made up for the occasion by Khashoggi, in a clever attempt to get his money back from the United States government'. Even Adnan could not have invented Ernie Miller and Don Fraser. They existed, and invested money with AK who promised the Canadians enormous profits from the sale of arms to Iran.

Ledeen's preposterous notion was another smokescreen offered to the press and knowledgeable insiders by Adnan on orders from Miller. There was nothing illegal in Miller loaning money to Khashoggi, but the Iran arms sale generated a torrent of press interest and raised a number of questions Miller did not want to answer.

It is a wonderful irony of the association between the Swami and Khashoggi that neither was able to ultimately achieve for the other what was promised. The Swami pledged to persuade the Sultan to once again befriend Khashoggi and invest in his projects, and Khashoggi vowed to make the Swami a billionaire.

It soon became apparent that Ernie and the Swami were not in Adnan's league when it came to operating with smoke and mirrors. They never doubted for a moment Adnan was one of the world's richest men. As mentioned above, Khashoggi persuaded the Swami to instruct Ernie to stake him for several million dollars the day they met in Canada. AK's explanation for his urgent need of $7 million the next day must have been worthy of an Academy Award. Ernie would never have loaned me $1 if my life depended on it.

Thinking back to 3 September 1985, as soon as Adnan, Shaheen and I boarded the chartered Lear jet for the return trip to New York, Khashoggi immediately began to ask questions about the Swami's wealth. In all honesty, I did not know the guru had any money other than what Ernie and other followers provided.

No one seemed to know the extent of Ernie's wealth. He bragged about his success in the stock market and was constantly monitoring the ups and downs of the price of gold, but he was the biggest cheapskate I had ever met. 'Ernie throws money around like sewer lids!' I remember someone saying.

To this day, the revelations about the Swami's wealth are staggering. Khashoggi must have assumed I was either following orders to reveal nothing about the financial resources of the Swami or was just stupid. He never comprehended I had no inkling that Ernie was managing the Swami's fortune. Thereafter, both Adnan and Shaheen confided in me whenever they felt I could encourage the Swami to agree to their proposal over Ernie's objection.

It requires little research to learn Ernie had no obvious source of money until he joined forces with the Swami. The records of the Supreme Court of Ontario, which granted Ernie a divorce from his first wife in 1979, disclose that his net worth at the time was $450,000. His 1977 tax return, filed with the court, listed a gross income of $32,450. Yet, five years later, Ernie was sporting a new Rolls-Royce Corniche convertible with LUXMI, the Hindu goddess of wealth, in bold print on his vanity license plates. Ernie also acquired a Falcon 50 jet. To cover, the Swami explained that the Sultan had loaned the jet as a gesture of friendship. Later, I learned it was actually registered to one of Ernie's offshore companies. He had bought it from the Bank of Mexico for $7 million.

The Toronto *Globe and Mail*'s Peter Moon recently reported that Miller deposited $56 million in one of his local bank accounts during a four week period in 1985. An educated guess puts the amount of money controlled by Ernie for the Swami at over $100 million in 1985. According to Moon, Miller 'told his banker that he was the director of a foreign bank and owned a $10 million rubber plantation in Malaysia'.

How did the guru manage to accumulate such wealth? He started the old-fashioned way. One con at a time. No amount, apparently, was too small. The story of the 'pickle man' captures the essence of the Swami's scam. In the end, it also enabled the Government of India to capture the Swami.

The pickle man was Mr L G Patak of Wigan, Lancashire, the proprietor of Patak's Spices ('Internationally acclaimed as manufacturers of the world's finest quality Indian Pickles, Pastes and Chutneys'). In December 1983, Patak claims he gave the Swami $100,000. The checks were made payable to the Canadian Imperial Bank of Commerce and endorsed by Ernie Miller, allegedly as a commission to the Foreign Minister of India to secure a contract for Patak with the Government of India to supply pulp and other materials used to make paper. The agreement between the Swami and Patak was that if the contract was not signed by the following April, Patak's money would be refunded with interest.

A transaction of this kind is not only inept, but unenforceable in a court of law. Yet Patak, like others before and after, took the Swami at his word. Deals such as this are said to be common in India, a country where 'black' money (cash paid under the table to avoid taxation) continues to exist in spite of efforts by the Gandhi government to control it.

April passed without a contract to Patak from the Government of India. The 'pickle man' tracked down the Swami and demanded his money be refunded. The Swami told him to get lost. When Patak continued to hound the Swami, the guru began to muddy the waters by asserting Patak was insane, and merely trying to cajole him into using his influence to keep him from being sent to prison in India.

Patak may have been a bit daft, but he was persistent. By August 1984 he was sending letters to the Indian community around the world castigating the Swami, Mamaji and Miller for their actions. He called Swamiji every name in the book: crook, liar, blackmailer, cheat, bloodsucker, etc. People in the Indian community eventually began to ask questions and show some concern over the negative fallout from Patak's campaign.

At no time did I act as the Swami's attorney, nor was I ever retained by him or any of his advisors to act as his attorney. He often described me to friends as his 'American advisor'. I volunteered my best thoughts on various matters as I would for any friend. When he asked what he should do about Patak, I suggested he file a legal action to restrain Patak from spreading these false stories. This advice was based on the categorical statements of Mamaji, Miller and the Swami that nothing Patak proffered was true. I had no first-hand knowledge of the facts in the dispute.

31

As a favor to the Swami, I did suggest solicitors in London skilled in defamation law, as well as a highly regarded barrister. The case of *Chandra Swami v. Lakhubhai Patak* was filed in the High Court of Justice Queen's Bench Division, on 26 November 1984.

Since I had made the initial introductions between the Swami and the lawyers, many mistakenly took for granted that I was the man to contact when a decision had to be made. The solicitors could never locate the Swami, let alone understand what he was saying. Predictably, they refused to work with Ernie because he was so obstreperous. *Ipso facto,* I became the go-between. That meant I was a glorified secretary with no authority in this confusing legal action. The case was the beginning of the Swami's downfall.

What was meant to be a simple legal action in defamation became a quagmire. Patak was not a rich man and the financial burden of such an action almost forced him to give up. But just when it appeared that his family had prevailed upon him to surrender before he lost his health along with what little was left of his family savings, the Swami double-crossed Tiny Rowland. Once the Rowland–Swami dispute became public, Patak approached Tiny, who agreed to help him defend the action brought by the Swami. Shortly afterward, Patak was successful in having the action dismissed on procedural grounds. The matter also was brought to the attention of the Indian Criminal Bureau of Investigation (CBI). Based on this information, the CBI filed a claim against the Swami in the courts of India.

The Swami was arrested in October 1987 on charges that arose from the Patak litigation of fraud, tax evasion, and failure to abide by India's foreign exchange regulations. At the time of writing, a date for the Swami's trial has not been set. The courts in India proceed at a pace similar to those in the UK and the US. Investigators from the CBI have traveled the world since the Swami's arrest gathering as much evidence as possible. Not an easy job.

# – 5 –
## Tricks of the Trade

At a critical point in Tiny Rowland's struggle to prove Fayed had given false information about the source of funds used in his takeover of House of Fraser, Rowland purchased a document from Khashoggi and the Swami that purports to establish that Fayed had taken the son of the British Prime Minister, Mark Thatcher, to Brunei on 24 October 1984.

Brunei is the only country in the world to have a hologram on all passports and official documents. The hologram is a pattern of a mosque produced on a photosensitive medium that has been exposed by holography and then photographically developed. It is impossible to forge.

Moreover, after the Swami's first meeting with the Sultan, at about the same time Fayed and Thatcher were allegedly in Brunei, the Swami discoursed many times that he had been kept waiting because the Sultan was meeting with the British Prime Minister. The Swami knew nothing of Fayed's intent to buy HOF in late 1984. He mentioned 'Mrs Tatcur' as a way of impressing his listeners with the fact that he was next on the monarch's appointment list. Since we know the Prime Minister was not in Brunei, his braggadocio makes the possibility of Mark Thatcher's visit more viable.

A photo of the document was printed in the *Observer* on 12 January 1986, along with a story disclosing the alleged Thatcher-Fayed trip to

Brunei. In a matter of hours, conceivably before the Sultan had even been made aware of the disclosure, it was declared a forgery by the Sultan's representative in London, Major Christopher Hanbury. It is well known that Major Hanbury had been an aide to the Sultan and had lived in Brunei. At that point, he acted as the Sultan's envoy without ambassadorial portfolio in London and lived in Southall, Middlesex, where the Sultan owned a home as well. It was not widely known, however, that Hanbury had become closely allied with Fayed in business matters. Among other connections, he was serving as a director of Hyde Park Investment Holding SA, one of the entities that funded Fayed's takeover of House of Fraser. Given his involvement with Fayed, it seemed a bit clumsy for the first public comment on the validity of the document to come from Hanbury.

Whether or not Mark Thatcher stopped in Brunei was a small piece of the puzzle Tiny was trying to put together in 1986. There was certainly nothing illegal or unethical in such a visit, and the matter has no part in the investigation of the Serious Frauds Office of the Fayed takeover. The possibility of the sojourn, however, suggested other potentially critical movements. In short, while it may never be proven beyond a reasonable doubt, I tend to believe Mohamed Fayed prevailed upon the son of the British Prime Minister to accompany him to Brunei in late October 1984. Fayed's mission was to convince the Sultan, once and for all, that he was the anointed representative of Mrs Thatcher's government, charged with the duty to bring the two countries closer together. Rumors of the visit have never been denied by Whitehall or Mark Thatcher. More to the point, the events that followed promote the notion that Fayed used Mark Thatcher to convince the Sultan that the Prime Minister approved of his bid for Harrods in order to gain his tacit cooperation.

Try as I might, it is impossible to fully explain what happened in this saga strictly on the basis of facts known to me as I would be required to argue before a judge and a jury.

The Swami, Fayed and Khashoggi systematically defied legal boundaries and restrictions. They had the ability to lie with such conviction and consistency that they made their critics seem fraudulent. Each perfected an ability to compartmentalize their deceptions. They were not split personalities, they adopted a different persona for every victim or useful friend.

None of these characters could have remained in the country of their birth and still managed to claw their way to fame and fortune. Like Magellan, they set out to conquer foreign lands. Modern transportation and communication systems made it simple to cross the globe. Centuries of religious education and cultural heritage almost prevented these men from being exposed. The men I profile operated in the same world that proclaimed that the Mafia did not exist, and that there was no Holocaust.

Numbered Swiss bank accounts, Shell corporations based in principalities that refuse to honor the laws of other nations, and the tacit cooperation of Third World leaders struggling to survive in a chaotic world, enabled men like the Swami, Fayed and Khashoggi to succeed.

The spectacle of Imelda Marcos appearing before a New York court in October 1988, to be arraigned on charges of racketeering is an extra illustration to this story. The former First Lady of the Philippines presented herself to the judge in a full-length ball gown as though she were attending a state dinner. After she entered a plea of 'not guilty', the judge instructed her lawyers to post a bond of $5 million. This 'iron butterfly' and her husband, the former President, had looted their country's treasury of billions of dollars. Yet, she honestly explained that circumstances required them to live off money borrowed from friends. If Imelda or Ferdinand dared acknowledge other holdings or bank accounts, they would have been seized or frozen by the Filipino government. Alas, the standards of proof and the procedural rules of the American legal system may prevent the Marcoses from being found guilty, and the money being returned.

Rather than being limited by my legal training which presupposes a grounding in Western civilization and a world order in which international law is defined by our rules, I have sought to employ legal terms and principles in a creative way to factor in other civilizations, customs, and circumstances to illustrate this story.

To better explain, therefore, I introduce a concept meant to help the reader understand the events of the last four years: *the important person set up*.

**The Important Person Set-up:** Fayed, Khashoggi, and the Swami were masters of the important person set-up. Herewith, I offer two explanations of how it works, one an outline of the tactic in general terms, and the other a totally and utterly fictitious account of what might transpire.

**1. The Outline:** The principal target, say a wealthy man like the Sultan, is told by the hit man, say an upwardly mobile businessman like Fayed, that he has a very important person in his orbit who can greatly influence matters critical to the target, say the personable son of a political leader like Mark Thatcher. The hit man greatly exaggerates the power and influence of the important person to the target as well as his control over him. At the same time, the hit man assures the important person that he wants to involve him in an altruistic, mutually beneficial course of action which will also benefit the target, and asks his permission to arrange a meeting.

When the three meet, the atmosphere is euphoric. Thinking the important person is able to move mountains, the target makes an extra effort to pay him respect and to charm him. The important person responds to this flattery with a new sense of his own worth and an instant eagerness to please the target. Once the introductory meeting is over and a sense of warmth and trust has been established, the important person is sent away to rest or to attend to other critical matters reinforcing his VIP status.

Without the knowledge of the important person, the hit man then extracts what he specifically wants from the target under the guise that the important person expects the target to take such action or he would not have attended the meeting. The hit man never allows the target and the important person to talk alone, and often instructs the target that it would be inappropriate for him to openly discuss the matter with the important person. Less direct instructions are given to the important person. In general terms the hit man thanks him for his good work and asks him to do what he can, never mentioning anything specific, and pays him a small fee. Next, the hit man extracts whatever he can from the target with the double justification that he has done him a great service and that, of course, he had to pay the important person, and probably many others involved, an enormous fee.

**2. The Fictional Account:** [Please note I have bracketed a few nonfictional asides. These comments are intended to give the reader a larger canvas on which I paint, in the spirit of Lewis Carroll, the fairy-tale of 'Fayed and Thatcher in Brunei'.]

If Fayed had actually inveigled Mark Thatcher to accompany him to Brunei, the interaction between him and the Sultan most likely would have followed the above pattern.

First, Fayed would have tantalized the Sultan with notions of Mark Thatcher's close relationship with his mother. Then he would describe Mark's great admiration for the Sultan. In a whispered tone, Fayed might suggest that the Prime Minister had delegated her son to approach the Sultan on her behalf. No doubt British intelligence had warned the Prime Minister that His Majesty's father and brother were conspiring against him. Out of concern, she was sending her son to offer her support. Fayed would then, of course, inflate his own prominence by mentioning that he routinely saw the Prime Minister and had brought the Sultan's enlightened rule to her attention on many occasions.

Once Fayed knew the Sultan was intrigued by the idea of meeting with Mark Thatcher, he would then have gone to Thatcher with a somewhat different story.

[Foreign middlemen have always targeted the close relatives of heads of state to give their schemes or policy positions credibility. It happened to Don Nixon and Billy Carter, brothers of US presidents who were neither qualified to serve in top-level government jobs or willing to be kept in a closet. Money, of course, was always a compelling reason for them to become involved in vaguely defined projects initiated in distant lands. President Carter never even considered confining brother Billy to an attic in the White House under constant surveillance as President Lyndon B Johnson did with his brother, Sam. Relatives of US presidents are not given a staff and procedural rules to protect and guide them from self-serving middlemen, as are members of the British royal family.]

Returning to my fairy-tale account of the set-up, Fayed probably figured Mark was never a strong-willed or financially successful person and was, therefore, a prime candidate for his scheme. In this fictional account, one can imagine Fayed portraying himself to young Thatcher as head of a major business empire, a billionaire, and a new and devoted resident of the UK. He would flatter Mark and offer him a discreet, totally confidential way to help England and to make money.

Fayed would quietly explain that the richest man in the world, the Sultan of Brunei, had been put off by many of the bureaucrats and career men at Whitehall, and that much good would be done if they were able to convey that Her Majesty's Government had a high regard for him and that future relations would reflect a more informed appreciation of his position and point of view. As they were both young men with many things in common, Fayed, closing in for the kill, would further explain that he had mentioned Mark to the Sultan. Instantly, enthused Mohamed, His Majesty requested that Fayed bring him to Brunei. The Sultan was most keen to meet him and very much wanted to exchange thoughts on many important matters.

[This technique has varying degrees of success, but definitely works better when there are cultural differences, religious differences and language barriers.]

To continue this fictional explanation of an oft-used ploy, Fayed would have flown Thatcher to Brunei on an impressive Gulfstream III, describing it as a bit outdated, but tolerable. He would apologize that the C-IV he had ordered was not yet ready because he had insisted on numerous alterations and an upgrading of the communications equipment. He would make clear to Mark that His Majesty was a special friend and that he had been charged by the Prime Minister of Singapore and others to give him direction. There was, of course, nothing he, Fayed, needed from the Sultan. He was, after all, a wealthy man. But, with great wealth comes a duty to serve Allah and to do His work here on earth.

Finally, Fayed would conclude by admonishing Mark to say nothing of this to anyone, except of course, the Prime Minister. Fayed's explanation might even be: 'I am a private man. I do not desire any recognition or publicity. Our mission will only be successful if it is kept away from the press and the jealous bureaucrats at Whitehall.'

[It is impossible to travel to Brunei as an honored guest of the Sultan without being overwhelmed. A retinue of guards and officials welcome you at the airport and direct you to a chauffeur-driven brown Mercedes. Each guest has her or his own Mercedes and driver which remains within eyesight throughout the visit. Two guests, two cars and drivers; twenty guests, twenty cars and drivers. Next one arrives and is escorted into a comfortable, almost cozy guest house, staffed by a cook, two maids and a man-servant. I have often wondered if anyone had the temerity to ask why he was relegated to the guest house when the palace had 1788 rooms? That minor perplexity aside, excitement builds as the gates to the palace open and His Majesty's perfectly appointed assistants perform the overture to an audience with the Sultan.

The guards escort the visitor to the escalators which, although they make the palace look like Macy's, transport all honored guests to the official rooms, and ultimately into the presence of the Sultan. A small and unprepossessing man, the Sultan seems totally out of place in the enormous rooms of the palace. Shy and uncomfortable when first introduced, he appears aloof and disinterested.]

In Brunei, Fayed has learned that only a joke or an obsequious remark seems to relax the Sultan and catch his attention. Fayed tells a story, to the delight of all, and continues to do most of the talking, focusing on superficial issues and often speaking for both parties. 'Your Majesty,' he might begin, 'Mark is an enormous supporter of your effort to modernize Brunei. He wanted to meet with you to convey the conviction of his mother, the Prime Minister, that you are greatly admired in Great Britain and especially by her.' Not wishing to do the wrong thing, Mark nods his assent.

Turning to Thatcher, Fayed could say, 'His Majesty and I have had many discussions about the over-emphasized misunderstandings between our two countries. He is pleased you are here in Brunei to join in his effort to set past dissensions aside.' Fayed might conclude with a cheerful and knowing hand gesture of unity. The Sultan conceivably would invite Mark to sit near him in a chair the size of most sitting rooms, offer tea, and chat briefly about the trip over, the time change, his impressions of Brunei on first glance, and whatever small talk entered his mind.

Knowing that the Sultan of Wonderland has an attention span of five minutes for any official meeting regardless of the topic, Fayed might again take control and suggest that their honored guest, doubtless, was fatigued and should be permitted to rest. Relieved, if somewhat confused, Thatcher would then be escorted to the guest house to relax until summoned to dinner.

Alone with the Sultan, Fayed would fill in the specifics, not known or uttered by Thatcher, and re-emphasize the significance of his visit to Brunei.

Bear with me as I invent the dialogue.

Fayed: 'Few know how important and how close Mark Thatcher is to his mother, the Prime Minister. She is devoted to her son and does whatever he asks. It is our luck that Mark has a special interest in Brunei and that because you are nearly the same age he especially wants to help you. He will never speak it, but he knows about the difficulty you are having with your father and brother. If anything should happen, he can persuade the Prime Minister to side with you and do whatever is necessary to put down the coup.

'On another matter – and, again, he will never say this to you directly – the Prime Minister was taken by surprise when you transferred so many billions from the Crown Agents to American and Japanese banks. The pound fell dramatically against the dollar and it was seen as an insult to her.

'Also, you must know that no one in the UK will do business with Zobel. He is not respected. Yet, everyone talks of his influence over you and explains he convinced you to take the money out of England. He has done you great harm.

'We both know Khashoggi is a joke. He is considered a fool by those in power in England. Mark Thatcher especially mentioned that his mother feels you should not be associated with men like Khashoggi and Zobel.

'You have put great trust in me. I have ended many arrangements in which people who call themselves your friends were stealing your money. I want nothing. Thatcher wants nothing. Our only interest is your wellbeing. Do what you want, but please consider my words.

'One final matter, Your Majesty. The Prime Minister and many others in her Government have asked me to seriously consider purchasing Harrods. It is, as you know, the most famous and important department store in the world. They are afraid it will fall into the wrong hands. You have trusted me with many personal and financial matters. May I have your permission to do whatever is necessary to achieve the takeover requested by the Prime Minister? Do not worry, your name will not be associated with the purchase. It may be necessary to proffer funds controlled by our joint account, but whatever the outcome, I will return the money to you within a few weeks or months. Mrs Thatcher will know that you supported me in this effort and be grateful.'

The Sultan: 'Mohamed, I am late for polo. Do whatever you feel is right and in our mutual interest.'

# – 6 –
# Serendipity

*'Young men ... look at the good side rather than the bad, not having yet witnessed many instances of wickedness. They trust others readily, because they have not yet often been cheated.'*

Aristotle, *Rhetoric*, Book II, Chapter 12.

In the Introduction, I alluded to the odd moment that often leads to important decisions. The thought explains my involvement with the Swami which began, for no particular reason, in Paris. In 1982, I was on holiday staying in the guest apartment of Baron Thyssen-Bornemizza's sister, Baroness Bentinck, on Avenue Charles Floquet. Everyone in residence had gone for lunch, but I had declined another rich French meal with the explanation that the time could be better utilized writing post cards and letters. Minutes after I was happily seated by the window, overlooking the Parc du Champs du Mar, to pen a letter to Gloria Vanderbilt. Gloria had spent many of her childhood years in this house and I wanted her to know how it looked now and to know I was thinking of her, the maid summoned me to the telephone. A young actress friend was calling to invite me to join her for dinner at Nella Rubinstein's home on Avenue Foch. Maestro Rubinstein had died recently after a rather unseemly affair with his secretary. The plan was to cheer Nella and, of course, enjoy her fabulous Polish cuisine. Never being one to turn down a fascinating and good-hearted evening, I agreed at once.

For the most part, it did turn out to be a pleasant evening in the company of good friends. Marion Pike, the California artist who painted Nancy Reagan, was my dinner partner. Milton Goldman, the celebrated theatrical agent from New York, was jovial and spirited as always. The man I remember most vividly, however, was a rather flaky fellow called Darius De La Rouchefoucauld. He seemed intensely interested in Washington political affairs, and appeared at my side every moment with a penetrating question. I had to sneak into the kitchen to capture a few moments with Nella before dinner, and departed rather wishing Mr Darius – 'whateverhisname' – had been elsewhere.

Darius emerged again in Washington in February 1983, and called my office telling my secretary we were good friends. Suddenly, he was on the line. While my mind was thinking, 'What does he want!', my voice gave away nothing.

Somehow, Darius had known of my friendship with John Lennon. Lennon and I had become friends in the early Seventies when the US Justice Department had attempted to deport him due to his arrest for possession of marijuana in the UK ten years earlier. My role in preventing punitive action against him was minor, but we did spend many happy days together, and the local press chronicled our every move.

Darius had called to offer lunch with an 'incredible Asian-Indian beauty, Asha Putli'. My interest peaked when he said Asha had made records with Lennon and that she was also a film star, a writer, and someone I simply had to meet. Of course, I accepted with alacrity.

Asha, it turned out, was everything Darius had said and quite a bit more. She was funny, she was worldly, she was exotically beautiful and she was totally captivating. Her ability to bridge both Western and Eastern civilizations with grace and intelligence was extraordinary.

The lunch, which lasted for hours, made time seem unimportant. We agreed to meet again. Asha lived in New York City, but promised to come to Washington often, and I promised to call on my next visit to the Big Apple. As I was about to leave, Asha asked, rather offhandedly, if I would like to meet an Indian guru who happened to be visiting Washington. Her eyes sparkled with laughter at my lack of interest, but when she confided he was a close friend, and that she was certain the experience would be enjoyable, I agreed.

As we entered the elevator, Asha became serious about the moment, and instructed that the guru be addressed as 'Your Holiness', explained he was considered a saint in India, and urged me to relax in his presence.

As the elevator stopped at the third floor, two official-looking men immediately opened the door at the end of the hall, and, suddenly, I was face to face with Shri Chandra Swamiji Maharaj.

The Swami was a large, bulky man dressed in simple white robes and wearing no jewelry. He had glistening black hair, a long black beard, and eyes which both twinkled and burned at the same time. His youth and contagious laugh were unexpected. The room was without pretense and he projected a quiet dignity reminiscent of the Dalai Lama.

At the Swami's side was a small, bald-headed man, known as Mamaji. He was introduced as the Swami's general secretary. Since the Swami spoke little English, Mamaji acted as his translator.

After the usual perfunctory remarks, Asha volunteered to leave us alone for a more intimate conversation and vanished. The Swami proceeded to converse as if we were old friends and began to explain his mission. Having studied at Harvard Divinity School, I found his theology predictable and simplistic. However, his apparent ability to cross national, cultural, religious, and racial boundaries was impressive. He spoke of being the only Hindu to be welcomed in many Muslim states and of his affinity for all the religions of the world.

After the conversation had continued for about thirty minutes, I stood to thank him and depart. Shaking his head and saying 'no, no', he insisted I remain a little longer. Offering a notepad and pen, he asked me to write a name, a seven digit number, and a goal or wish, fold it, and put it in my coat pocket. I did. The Swami closed his eyes and appeared for a moment to be in a trance, then in his own voice sang out: 'Florence Parkinson, 333–5229, and US Ambassador to the Court of St James' – the name of my maternal grandmother, my parent's telephone number in Pocatello, Idaho, and my fantasy of the moment. His English might have been dreadful, but his mind-reading ability was utterly amazing. Even with the benefit of hindsight and the skepticism that inevitably followed, I still marvel at the Swami's psychic skills. He then proceeded to say everything that I wanted to hear. Pondering my birth date, he predicted that in spite of recent set-backs, I would be able to start over, and one day play an important role in public affairs. Articulating what he called our mutual goals, he spoke of his meetings with Third World leaders and his keen desire to form a coalition of individuals that truly were color-blind, valued all religions, and understood the needless waste and suffering caused by war.

Swamiji was born in the small town of Behror in Rajasthan in northeastern India on 29 October 1949, and named Nemi Chandra Jain.

Shortly thereafter, his family migrated to Hyderabad, Andra Pradesh, in southern India. He was a precocious child, and at an early age showed a great interest in politics, involving himself in the Youth Congress when he became a teenager. Frustrated by his lack of success in politics, he rightly observed that religious leaders played a more powerful and unique role in Indian affairs. With this in mind and with his parents approval, he became an apprentice to Mahaupadhyay Shri Amar Muni Maharaj and studied religion in the Nepalese mountains for several years. Chandra Swami tells of months of quiet meditation and a daily recitation of prayers. The young supplicant lived in a tree, or so he said, until he attained his spiritual self realization from the Maa Goddess Bhagwath. Then, with the blessings of Lord Balajee Vyankatesh of Thurupati, he emerged as a swami and tantrik Yogi, at the age of twenty-one, to begin his career as a saint.

Most swamis combine religion, politics and show business. Chandra Swami clearly understood this and managed to beat the competition at an early age. He gave forceful speeches on the necessity of preserving ancient Hindu rituals, befriended many important political figures, and brought it all together by organizing the sacred fire ceremony known as the Yagna throughout India and around the world. He had become a leading spiritual figure in India at an early age.

It was impossible to verify the Swami's credentials. To the best of my knowledge there was no registry of who had resided in the trees in the mountains of Nepal. The man looked like a swami, spoke like a swami, dressed like a swami, ate like a swami, chanted mantras like a swami, and had countless numbers of followers who referred to him respectfully as 'Your Holiness', so I figured he had to be a swami. Add to this his unusual ploy of showing a photo album of himself with various heads of state while explaining that the Indian Prime Minister, Indira Gandhi, had asked him to be her envoy to the world. It would have been bad form to doubt his veracity, or to appear indifferent to his noble goals.

The Swami's pitch was not revolutionary or new, his style was clumsy and I had heard it all before. Yet, strangely, the simplicity of the man and his words made an impact. When I explained that my interest in the Hindu religion did not imply any desire to convert, and that, furthermore, I could never become a disciple, he thanked me for my honesty. Mamaji then graciously escorted me to the door, remarking: 'His Holiness, would never ask you to turn your back on your history and your faith. He desires that you help him demonstrate that Christians, Hindus, Jews, Muslims, and all men of good will can work together to build a better world.'

With that, I said farewell and never thought about the Swami again until he wrote in late March 1983, with the news that he planned to return to Washington the following week, and looked forward to continuing our discussions.

Thinking back, the letter from the Swami was so amateurish and poorly typed that it only served to confirm his image as the real thing. There was nothing slick about his operation. Rather, it was fascinating that this simple, unsophisticated man had emerged on the world scene at such an early age.

Nonetheless, I took the precaution of calling a man known to have close ties to Madame Gandhi for a second opinion.

A distinguished Member of Parliament and a long time personal friend, Sir Eldon Griffiths, had encouraged me to become involved in Indian/American affairs. Sir Eldon is Co-Chairman of the Indo-British Association, with a prominent British businessman of Indian origin, Swraj Paul. When I mentioned the Swami to Eldon, he urged me to contact Swraj. Not only was Swarj a man of intelligence and stature, he also was Madame Gandhi's close personal friend. On the telephone and in person, he vouched for the Swami. Any doubts I might have had were put aside.

The Swami next made contact several months later to ask me to come to Chicago to participate in a Yagna ceremony organized for 9 April 1984.

Organized, I came to learn, was not a word that had any real definition for the Swami. He seemed to float on a cloud of unknowing, with the absolute conviction that sooner or later someone would appear to cope. Indeed, people did appear – later rather than sooner – and I found myself in Glen Ellyn, Illinois, at the Wagner School attending my first Yagna. Considering that I could not understand a word of Hindi and that fire ceremonies tend to be a bit uncomfortable at normal temperatures, it otherwise was an enjoyable adventure. Most impressive were the participants. The festival was my first introduction to the Asian/Indian community in the US. There must be exceptions, but I have never met an American of Indian origin who was not unfailingly polite, understated, well-educated, and hard-working. The Swami clearly brought joy to their lives and they were especially keen to have their children participate in and learn more about the Hindu culture. It was a positive experience.

The printed program for the Yagna stated that the celebration was sponsored by Hindu Satsang, Lombard, Illinois, with the blessings of Maa Goddess Bhagwath. Among the patrons listed were Mr Swraj Paul,

45

London, UK; Mr Thomas Pritzker, Chicago, (the Pritzker family own the Hyatt Corporation and Continental Airlines), and Mr Mohamed Fayed, London, UK.

I had meant to ask the Swami about Mr Mohamed Fayed, a name unknown to me and never mentioned before.

I forgot.

# – 7 –

# Still the Advance Man

*'Young men ... have exalted notions, because they have not yet been humbled by life or learnt its necessary limitations; moreover, their hopeful disposition makes them think themselves equal to great things ... They would always rather do noble deeds than useful ones: their lives are regulated more by moral feeling than by reasoning.'*

Aristotle, *Rhetoric*, Book II, Chapter 12.

The day after I had returned to Washington from attending the Yagna, the Swami telephoned to thank me for my interest in his work. Then he put Mamaji on the line to pass on another message. In summary, Mamaji explained they were going to Canada for three weeks to visit His Holiness's disciples and have a short rest. In early May, they planned to travel to the Caribbean en route to Los Angeles where the Swami had an ashram. While His Holiness had traveled almost everywhere in the world, he had never been to the Caribbean before and was hopeful I could arrange for him to call upon important leaders in the area.

Mamaji also dropped an attention getting aside: 'His Holiness has been speaking with our Prime Minister about you, and she is most anxious to meet you. We are organizing a major Yagna in Delhi in late October. It would be a great honor to have you attend and no doubt at

that time you can have important talks with Madame (Gandhi) as well.'
I was hooked.

The Swami entered my life just four years after I had reluctantly come
to terms with the fact that I would never realize my childhood ambition
and become President of the United States! I devoted over thirty years
of my life preparing to become the president.

For reasons which probably never merited a good psychiatrist, I was
a lonely child. I like to think it was because I was more intelligent and
inquisitive than other kids my age. In Twin Falls, Idaho, where I lived
in my formative prekindergarten years, for example, most children
played 'doctor'. Too small a scope for me. I organized a hospital in our
backyard. It all went on with great success until my mother walked in
one day, nearly fainted at the sight of naked children before her, and
closed the doors forever. Not only did much of the excitement fade
from my young life, but I became something of a loner.

Shortly thereafter, for reasons of my father's employment (during this
period he was a traveling salesman for a paint company and then for
S&H Green Stamps), we moved house and town at least once a year,
sometimes twice. Under such circumstances, it was impossible to make
friends. Finally, the family moved to the place of my birth, Pocatello,
Idaho. Father had always been a star athlete. Many of his happier years
were spent in Blackfoot, Idaho as the head high school coach. Blackfoot
had no hospital in 1944 which is why my mother had to be driven the
25 miles to Pocatello for the occasion of my birth. By 1954 the old man
had finally become frustrated with the life of a salesman and taken a job
as director of athletics for the Pocatello school system. Thus Pocatello
became our real home and my parents promised to stay put. The time
had come to win friends and influence people.

Obviously, I do not wish to suggest similar experiences motivated
other aspirants to seek the presidency, but for the reasons stated above,
I decided to overcome my isolation, throw myself into politics and
prepare to enter public life. Like most candidates for public office, I
made this decision alone and without honestly reflecting on or evaluating
the odds.

It helps a great deal to grow up in the rarefied air of the mountain
West. No one tells you it is impossible to become the president. It was
even more formative to be born and raised in the Mormon Church, The
Church of Jesus Christ of Latter Day Saints. Mormon doctrine proclaims
the church to be the one true religion. The Mormons were the chosen
people. I was taught that 'as God is, man may become'. The formula

for success was simple: no booze, no smoking, no sex out of wedlock, and total commitment to the institution of the church. The word 'ambiguity' was never spoken, let alone contemplated. The church had an answer to every question. Of course, I could become the President!

With my ultimate goal firmly in mind, I began to test the waters by organizing and heading the Idaho Teenage Republicans, helping the local mayor win election to the US Congress, and befriending the state leaders. I attended church diligently, won the romantic lead in the school musical, sang at weddings and funerals on request, earned all As in school, played on the golf team, and not only was voted the guy most likely to succeed by my graduating class, but succeeded in being awarded a full scholarship to Stanford University in Palo Alto, California.

All freshmen at Stanford were required to take a course on the history of Western civilization. Immersing myself in the writings of the Greek philosophers, the history of the Reformation, and the entire panoply of thoughts, debates and values which form the basis of our Judeo-Christian heritage, I began to panic. Had I been on the wrong track until now? Perhaps the Mormon church was not the one true religion.

In this world of academic exploration the word 'ambiguity' was used often. Wise men stated that in order to know the truth, other options had to be studied and considered. It began to seem less and less likely that success resulted from the simple steps outlined by the Mormon church. Even *Time* magazine ran a cover story asking the question: 'Is God Dead?'

In the midst of this confusion, Paul Tillich became the guest-in-residence at my Stanford dormitory. Tillich was one of the truly great intellectuals of this century and a theologian of immense stature. It was as if God had sent him to me to say, 'No, I am not dead!' Time spent with him gave new depth and meaning to the words of theology which had become empty. Tillich enabled me to appreciate the good of the Mormon church and the uncomplicated world from which I came. He challenged me to be affirmative, not bitter, and he enabled me to redefine morality in a personal and contemporary framework still grounded in the Judaeo-Christian tradition.

After endless hours of soul-searching and counsel by Tillich, I accepted a Rockefeller Fellowship to the Harvard Divinity School in 1966. Studying under the guidance of men like Richard Niebur, Christor Stendall and Harvey Cox gave me renewed self-confidence and a greater determination 'to participate in history', Cox's contemporary summation of the lessons in the Old Testament. In the back of my mind, I still yearned to run for public office, but one way or another, I intended to work for change.

Within a year an opportunity presented itself.

Ever since founding the Teenage Republicans in Idaho, and the resulting involvement with other Republican groups around the country, I had been an admirer of New York Governor Nelson A Rockefeller. When he ran for president in 1964 and 1968, I worked on his campaigns. During that period, Rockefeller had introduced me to a bright, young Congressman from Jamestown, NY, Charles E Goodell. On Nelson's recommendation, I had spent a summer in Washington working for Goodell as a Congressional intern. He was one of the finest men I have ever met in or out of political life.

In most ways, my first real chance to become involved in the national political scene resulted from a tragic series of events. 1968 was a period of great turmoil in America. The Vietnam War and issues of civil rights, especially, dominated the public debate. Also, it was the year in which two of America's heroes, Robert Kennedy and Martin Luther King, were assassinated, changing forever the political landscape of America.

It was the sad duty of Governor Rockefeller to appoint a senator to complete the term of Senator Robert Kennedy. Among others, I urged Rockefeller to appoint Congressman Goodell. The day Goodell's appointment was announced, I took a leave of absence from law school and moved to Washington to become his executive assistant.

Charlie was a great senator. He took positions and risks not expected from the conservative record he had established in Congress. In November 1969, he joined Mrs Martin Luther King and Senator George McGovern in leading the Vietnam Moratorium March on Washington. It was Goodell who first introduced legislation to cut off the defense appropriations for the war. He also took other moderate positions which caused Richard Nixon to hate him and Spiro Agnew, the former Vice President, to call him the 'Christine Jorgensen of the Republican Party'. Charlie allowed me to participate in all of these legislative decisions and events, and I began to believe that my hopes and aspirations might be realized.

In the 1970 general election in New York, Goodell was defeated. As the deputy campaign manager, I had worked night and day to raise over $7 million for the campaign. But, Charlie was both betrayed by the Republican party and outspent by his opponents.

Discouraged but thus enlightened, I returned to Washington and in quick sequence finished law school, passed the bar exam, organized more charity benefits than Mrs Astor, formed a law firm and, finally, set out to become rich and famous. Alas, neither endeavor was accomplished.

The Swami entered my life during a mid-life crisis. He and Mamaji seemed to understand both my desire to enter public life and the need to be in a financial position to sustain a public career.

So when Mamaji telephoned the next day from Canada, I asked if the Swami would be interested in meeting with the Prime Minister of Jamaica, Edward Seaga, and the President of Panama, Jorge Illueca. Without hesitation, he answered in the affirmative and requested the necessary arrangements be made.

In the world of politics and public affairs, the moniker 'advance man' is given to the person in charge of the schedule, details of transport and virtually everything else involved in moving the candidate from one place to another. I had been an advance man for both Rockefeller and Goodell. Often on a date or traveling with friends outside Washington, I still catch myself walking ten steps ahead, opening doors and giving orders to strangers. My explanation for this odd behavior is: 'once an advance man, always an advance man'. If anyone could organize an impressive trip for the Swami, I remember thinking, I could!

The extra effort was made because it was important for the Swami to be impressed with my contacts and skills. When he next saw the Prime Minister of India, I wanted to be certain he would be able to speak about me from personal and positive experience.

In short order, the Caribbean mission was arranged and the Swami and his party set off for Kingston, Jamaica and Panama City. Financial restraints prevented me from traveling with them, but a member of my staff was sent to coordinate all of the details and to deal with any problems. I was, of course, in constant communication with the group and pleased to get the glowing reports of their visits.

Prime Minister Seaga received the Swami at Jamaica House as he would a head of state. They spent several hours together and the Prime Minister insisted the Swami join him at breakfast the next day to allow his wife the honor of meeting him. Their official appointment was featured on the front page of the *Gleaner*, Jamaica's respected newspaper. Under a picture of the Swami with the Prime Minister was the caption: 'His Holiness Shri Chandra Swamiji Maharaj, one of India's spiritual leaders of the Hindu faith ... is seen in conversation with the Prime Minister The Rt Hon Edward Seaga, on whom he called yesterday morning at Jamaica House. The Hindu spiritual leader has been traveling to various Western countries to bring "a message of peace through cultural understanding." Here since Friday, he has been meeting with Jamaicans of Indian origin and also paid a courtesy call on the Governor General, Sir Florizel Glasspole, at Kings House. He leaves the island today. At left is his interpreter, Mr K N Agar Wat'. [Mamaji]

When I next heard from the Prime Minister, he thanked me for making the visit possible and expressed the hope that he and the Swami would meet again.

The Panama segment of the trip also worked out exceedingly well. My staffer returned elated at the reception they had received, and the Swami telephoned from Los Angeles to report everything had been extremely beneficial. 'The President of Panama now considers you a better friend,' enthused the Swami. 'Wait one minute, Mamaji will tell you more.'

At that, Mamaji briefed me on the trip at some length, then remarked that His Holiness had become especially fond of the President of Panama in whom he saw great potential as an ally in the cause of world peace. As a way of thanking the President for his many kindnesses, Mamaji continued, the Swami had insisted that he be allowed to persuade his American brother to host a reception in his honor in New York City at the time of the United Nations General Assembly. 'Please make the necessary arrangements for the reception on 26 June. His Holiness and I must return to India, but we will join you in New York,' he remarked, ending the conversation before I could respond.

Not knowing what to make of all this, I rang Asha in New York. 'This is wonderful news,' intoned Asha. 'We can host the reception together. I know good things will come of it!'

Jorge Illueca became President of Panama upon the resignation of former President Ricardo de la Espriella on 14 February 1985. Illueca was a career diplomat who had been serving as president of the United Nations General Assembly while holding the post of Panamanian vice president. He had been a figure in the UN virtually since its founding in 1945, having served as a member of the Panamanian delegation off and on since the second session of the General Assembly. It was Illueca who opened talks with the US twenty years ago on the Panama Canal Treaty. He was a gifted man and I was sorry that his tenure as president would be so short. National elections were scheduled for late May and he vowed to hand over power to his successor in October. Illueca was probably the last decent man to run Panama. It was an honor to host a reception for him.

I had recently become a member of the Harvard Club and booked the reception in the Biddle Room hoping to project a more serious image for the occasion. Press reports at the time were laudatory. The President and the Swami could not have had a better time. Once again, it seemed my new-found friendship had merit and might well be the ticket to success.

Newspaper columnist, Suzy, summed it all up rather well: 'Asha Putli, who thinks nothing of bridging cultures and countries, and Steven Martindale, the Washington lawyer, gave a reception for President Jorge Illueca at the Harvard Club, which seemed like the thing to do. After all, Illueca went to Harvard Law. Mrs Neil Sedaka, one of the guests, said she heard someone say the gathering was the kind of dazzling array one hopes for at New York parties but seldom gets.

'The mix was exotic, or something – everyone from Maureen Stapleton to Jonas Salk and his wife, Francoise Gilot to Christine Biddle (who was admiring the pictures of her family in the Biddle Room where the reception was held) to Sir James and Lady Murray to Swami Chandra Maharaj, the Indian religious leader and friend of the Panamanian President and his wife. Asha, a well-known singer, has become a liaison in the political and international corporate area. "East is East and West is West" doesn't seem to apply to this Indian lady.'

I never saw Jorge Illueca again and I doubt the Swami did.

# – 8 –

# The Swami Meets the World's Richest Man

*'Young men ... overdo everything ... they love too much and hate too much, and the same with everything else. They think they know everything, and are always quite sure about it; this, in fact, is why they overdo everything.'*

Aristotle, *Rhetoric*, Book II, Chapter 12.

Basking in the glow of the press notices and compliments on the reception for the President of Panama, I returned to Washington to attend to legal matters on behalf of my clients. The Swami and Mamaji were scheduled to fly to India via the Far East where they would organize a grand Yagna ceremony for mid-October. It was agreed that I would join other non-Indian friends of the Swami as a special guest. 'You must come,' the Swami said: 'I want to introduce you to my disciples in India. So many important people you must know, ministers, industrialists, journalists, actors ... all are my disciples.'

I barely had walked into my office the next day when Mamaji was on the telephone. The Swami had had word from his disciples in the Far East that President Marcos of the Philippines was a spiritual man – to be called a spiritual person was the Swami's highest praise – and wondered if I could arrange a stopover in Manila as they journeyed back to India. Not wishing to come across as anything less than enthusiastic for the Swami's mission, I promised to do my best.

Imelda and Ferdinand Marcos were not my favorite couple on the world scene and certainly were not close friends. Why the Swami wanted to meet them and how they added to his ambitious plans for a better world eluded me. But, I figured the introduction could do no real harm, and perhaps might even have a positive impact on the Filipino President. Why not?

The last time I had seen Mrs Marcos was a near disaster. For over seven years, I served as a volunteer member of the board of directors of Save The Children, a private, non-profit agency based in Westport, Connecticut, dedicated to helping the poorest of the poor throughout the world and closely allied with Save The Children in the UK. In 1983, Save The Children had organized a dinner to honor the Queen of Thailand for her exemplary work with the boat people fleeing Cambodia. The dinner was at the Waldorf Hotel in New York City. David Rockefeller acted as chairman, and everyone involved had gone to great lengths to make it a night the Queen would enjoy. The occasion was an opportunity to raise funds and, as chairman of the development committee of the board, I spent hours filling the tables with wealthy friends that I wanted to become involved.

The night of the dinner arrived without any major problems and as the reception began, all heaved a sigh of relief. Then, uninvited and with no advance warning, in walked Imelda Marcos with at least ten security guards (the Queen had none). Recognizing me from past, brief social encounters, she offered the explanation that she had found herself in New York unexpectedly and wondered if it might not be appropriate to attend the tribute to her dear friend. Thinking quickly, I said I knew the Queen would want to receive her, but that it was impossible to change the head table at this late hour. Save the Children simply could not allow the First Lady of the Philippines to attend such a dinner as anything other than an honored guest. Imelda looked displeased, but got the point. Dutifully I escorted her around for about ten minutes allowing her to greet the Queen (who looked very surprised to see her) and the honored guests. To the First Lady's added displeasure, I had asked the security guards to wait at the entrance. In the end, however, she seemed grateful for the proper reception and thanked everyone profusely as I returned her to her entourage. It occurred to me at the time that she had expressed her gratitude with a grudging admiration. She had been treated with every courtesy, but had not been able to steal the spotlight from the dignified, unobtrusive Queen.

When I placed a telephone call to the Maiacanang Palace and asked to speak to the First Lady, my guess was the odds were about 50/50 that she would accept it. But, after a long wait and being transferred to several secretaries, Imelda came on the line. 'Are you coming to Manila?' she began.

As best I could, I explained that while I was not traveling to Manila, a Hindu holy man was passing through on his return to India. Then, I launched into my standard introduction of the Swami, his close relationship with Prime Minister Gandhi, his world mission for peace, and his close association with many other heads of state. Imelda seemed nonplussed, which was to be expected, but agreed to receive him as a favor.

'The President has not been well,' she said. 'Perhaps this holy man can pray for him. He needs inspiration at this moment.'

The specific details of the visit were worked out with Imelda's brother, Benjamin Romualdez, who was at that time the Ambassador of the Philippines to the US. Once the details were confirmed, I never gave the matter another thought.

In late September 1984, I received a letter from the Swami in which he asked for another favor. As an aside he wrote: 'In the Philippines the interest was spontaneous and overwhelming. I was indeed touched by their sincere desire to come closer spiritually to God. The President of the Philippines, Mr Marcos, and his gracious lady, Imelda, looked after me extremely well and accorded me the honor of being a state guest'.

That visit was the beginning of an incredible saga, although the full story was unknown to me for almost two years.

As planned, I arrived in New Delhi in mid-October 1984, to take part in the much anticipated Yagna. This was my first visit to India. From the minute the plane landed at Indira Gandhi Airport until my departure six days later, I was spellbound. No other place on earth can match, let alone better, this marvelous picture of color and confusion.

According to the schedule, the guests of honor were to assemble in the lobby of the Maurya Sheraton Hotel at ten the next morning to be driven to the ceremony. The time change and jet-lag had not left me in perfect form, but upon entering the holding room, I livened up at the sight of Imee Marcos. The daughter of the President of the Philippines was a classic beauty. At that moment, she was a Member of Parliament in the Philippines.

Imee could not wait to tell me how grateful the Marcos family was for the prayers of the Swami. As she told it: the President had been terribly ill, none of the doctors were able to pull him out of his decline, and the family was fearful that the end of his life was near. The Swami had spent many hours with him, chanting the mantras and praying. Miraculously, he recovered completely.

Imee was there to represent the President who wanted to be with us, but could not attend. She praised the Swami's spiritual powers, especially his healing powers, to everyone.

The fire ceremony was tedious and hellishly hot. The Yagna goes on for hours and my hunch is that even if you understood what was being said, it would still be boring. Honored guests at the Yagna were in a hopeless position. Since we were the center of attention, it was impossible to leave. Worse, we had to sit adjacent to the fire and toss flowers, fuel and whatever was required on the flames on cue. 'Hell could not be this hot!' I whispered to Imee. 'I wish Cardinal Sin were here,' she replied.

Eleven months before we had gathered in Delhi, Benigno Aquino had been assassinated as he stepped down the ramp of a commercial airplane which had flown him from exile to his homeland. A few days before Imee left Manila, a commission of inquiry appointed by the government published its report concluding that Aquino's murder had been a military conspiracy. Aquino's death proved to be the turning point in Filipino politics. His assassination united the Marcos opposition. One of the leaders of the anti-Marcos movement in the Philippines was the prelate of the Catholic Church, Cardinal Sin. For some reason the Marcos family never understood that even burning the courageous Cardinal would have made no difference.

Once the rituals were completed, the Swami kept his word and set up meetings with several ranking Indian officials. The Prime Minister, I was told, had been called out of Delhi on matters of state. Our meeting would have to be postponed until my next visit. Not being able to see Madame Gandhi was a disappointment.

The meeting was rescheduled for 1 November. I was about to leave for the airport to return to Delhi when news of her brutal assassination flashed around the world.

In her stead, I was to see the Minister of Defense and the Foreign Secretary.

Whenever appointments required transport in Delhi, I was driven in a white air-conditioned Mercedes, guided to my destination by accommodating security men, and made to feel like a maharaja. That day was no different and I arrived at the home of the Foreign Secretary, Romesh Bhandari, on Akbar Road, at the appointed hour. Bhandari was a career civil servant who had risen to the top on merit. At the end of our first meeting, I meant to pay him a compliment by saying I knew only one other man on earth with his diplomatic skill, the foreign minister of Pakistan, Yaqub Khan. Confirming my opinion while ignoring my less than consummate skill, he laughingly accepted the praise.

The Minister of Defense at that time was P V Narasimha Rao, an impressive little man with a long history in government. He remains the senior minister in Rajiv Gandhi's Government to this day. The Swami had befriended Rao years ago in Hyderabad. There was more than mutual respect between them, and they conducted themselves as long time friends. The Minister received me both in his office and later at his residence exactly as he would have welcomed a visiting secretary of state. This was heady stuff. In the course of our conversation which covered the high points and the low points of Indo-US relations, he pointed out the stumbling-blocks that prevented closer ties between our two countries and suggested ways to put them aside. 'Please convey this message to your friends in Washington,' he implored.

My stay in India turned out to be more exciting and rewarding than I could have imagined. Not only was I introduced to a fascinating country and many of its leaders, but it was gratifying to see the Swami treated with regard.

It should have been obvious the Swami was no saint. Chalk it up to cross-cultural differences, my total lack of exposure to the Indian ethos, the excitement of discovering kindred spirits in a totally different world, the intense desire to work with the leaders of India and the US in bettering relations, a naive notion that my account of the visit to India would matter to US opinion leaders, the royal treatment I received, personal ambitions, the Indian propensity to tell a guest what he wants to hear, or whatever. For the first time since Charles Goodell had been defeated, a specific mission of conspicuous importance to the world (I thought) had been proposed.

Once again, I returned to the nation's capital to resume work. The Swami, it turns out, was marching off to a different drummer, the Filipino businessman, Enrique Zobel.

Zobel had met the Swami at the Maiacanang Palace. The Swami routinely would size up the people around his host, determine who had the most influence, and request a private meeting later in the day. It is doubtful the Swami had ever heard of Zobel before, but in the course of their conversation he told Zobel that he could sense he was under great pressure, and asked Zobel what was troubling him. The Swami's deep brown eyes must have widened when he heard the name Mohamed Fayed and the horror of Fayed's power play against him in Brunei. Zobel confided to me later that he was totally taken back when the Swami said he knew Fayed well and knew how to handle him. It seemed almost too good to be true. It was important for Zobel to regain his position in the Sultan's Court. With his usual barrage of influence and names, the Swami apparently tempted Zobel with the notion that he could turn the Sultan around. Zobel had wanted to take the Swami to Brunei at once, but the guru explained that he had to perform the Yagna ceremony first. They agreed to go in late October instead.

Recall that Fayed had given the Swami some money to sponsor the Yagna in Chicago. That was early in the Swami's assent and he tended to promise more than he could deliver. Only Fayed and the Swami know what was discussed, but Fayed, according to Mamaji, had become disenchanted and was telling friends the holy man was a fraud. With the benefit of hindsight, it is more than plausible to suggest that Fayed had asked the Swami if he could help him establish a close business relationship with the Sultan. It would have been typical of the Swami to have promised the recommendation to Fayed in spite of the fact that he had never heard of Brunei. This may explain Fayed's question to Tiny Rowland at about the same time. Rowland recalls Fayed asking about the Swami and handing him the front page of the guru's brochure. Tiny later told Fayed the Swami was not reputable according to international sources, but by that time the Swami had met the Sultan and accepted $500,000 from Fayed in return for his support.

Realizing he could make more money by playing games with the two men, the Swami had later shifted his support away from Fayed. Hearing of the Swami's duplicity no doubt made Fayed angry that he had wasted his money.

Whenever the Swami was told of negative remarks about him, he reacted with anger. It was another form of bluff. His outrage actually made his critics seem vengeful. Hearing again of the Sultan, this time from an insider who told of his vast wealth, as well as Fayed's involvement made the Swami eager to enter the fray.

The Swami was never adequately prepared or sufficiently sophisticated to enter the big league. What he had was an uncommon determination, an unexpected pitch and the nerve and drive of a rhinoceros. After a casual meeting with a head of state or film star, he would brag to everyone that the individual had become his loyal disciple and would do whatever he asked. It was clear he had no shame.

Minutes after Zobel had effected introductions, the Swami dismissed him so he could have time alone with Princess Mariam, the Sultan's second wife, and his Majesty. Zobel had no choice but to let the Swami work his magic. The Swami, meanwhile, expressed admiration for both Zobel and Fayed. What mattered ultimately to him, he proclaimed, was the Sultan, Princess Mariam and the future of Brunei. While Mamaji translated, the Swami spoke eloquently about his mission for world peace and his desire to learn from His Majesty what steps he would advise be taken and what role he might want to play. Sensing quickly the Sultan's lack of interest, he stopped, raised both arms in the direction of Princess Mariam and did his number.

The Swami might have had superior skills in astrology and a 'third eye' to read the thoughts of others, but he rarely got non-Indian names straight. He consistently called Tiny Rowland 'Tony' and muddled the name Thatcher, pronouncing it 'Takur'. In the same way Nelson Rockefeller addressed most men whose names he could not recall as 'fella', the Swami found safety in 'brother'. Just about everyone was his 'brother'.

Moreover, once the Swami met a powerful person, they were joined at the hip. When he was unable to be with them, he telephoned daily. This addiction was a source of absolute horror to those whose homes or offices he entered. The telephone bills left behind were astronomical.

Just as all important men were the guru's 'brother', the Princess was his 'sister'. He was confident that the Princess and he had known each other in another life. He sympathetically responded to a kindred spirit, and immediately proclaimed her 'a spiritual woman'. Further, the Swami knew she had been mistreated by the royal family. Naturally, he was greatly saddened by their behavior. All of this bitterness, he surmised had been caused by disloyal men in the Sultan's court.

Methodically, the Swami outlined the practical and spiritual counsel he had provided to other world leaders. Dropping names like Madame Gandhi, President Marcos, and the Vice President of the United States, George Bush, he detailed his service and strictly confidential relationships with them: 'When they are uncertain about someone near them, I can know in a matter of minutes what to advise. All of them trust my judgment. When President Marcos was about to die, my prayers saved him.' The Swami told me he concluded with the added zinger: 'You call President Marcos. He will tell you I saved his life!' In fact, he had no real relationship with Gandhi or Bush. He had come across Madame Gandhi on a few public occasions, but had never met Bush.

He then segued smoothly into his mind-reading performance. Not only did he articulate the Sultan's three written responses to the 'name, number, wish' question flawlessly, he spoke the answers in Malay, a language he does not know. Taken aback, the Sultan began to listen seriously to what the Swami had to say and agreed to see him whenever possible as well as to speak by telephone on a daily basis.

The Swami retired to the quest house at the conclusion of his royal audience where he revealed to Zobel that the Sultan's friendship with Fayed had been poisoned and that Zobel's position at court would soon be restored. Zobel had to be patient for a few months, but the Sultan had recognized the necessity of banishing Fayed as soon as possible. Zobel had every reason to believe that the Swami had everything under control.

The day after meeting the Sultan, the Swami called from Singapore. Like most Americans in 1984, I had never heard of Brunei. 'What?' yelled the Swami, 'The Sultan is the richest man in the world! He is now my disciple. I will make you friends.' From that day forward he talked of virtually no one but the Sultan.

Princess Mariam, from all outward indications, began to see the Swami as her lifeline. There was never any doubt in her mind that the Sultan was devoted to her, but Brunei was filled with rumors that she was filling the bank accounts of her family with royal money and that she might cost the Sultan his throne. The former Sultan, now called the Paduka Seri Begawan felt she had lured his son away from his royal duties. The old man was reputedly plotting with his second son, Prince Mohamed, to oust the Sultan. It was a troubling and confusing time for both of them, but especially for the Princess.

The Sultan had no desire to enter into an open conflict with his father and brother, but he needed to know who in his court might seek power at his expense by encouraging his father, and who he could trust to protect his throne. Princess Mariam pleaded with her husband to employ the Swami's insight and spiritual powers in His Majesty's tests of loyalty. She truly believed the Swami had special powers that granted him the ability to identify anyone disloyal to the Sultan at once. Before the Sultan could think, she looked at him lovingly and whispered, according to the Swami: 'His Holiness has promised that I will have a male child within a year'. Whether the Sultan knew it or not, the Swami had cornered him for the moment.

While Mamaji took pictures of this seminal meeting, the Swami discoursed on his recent haircut. Swamiji had allowed his hair to be cut for the first time in seven years as symbol of devotion to the gods. The ritual would not be repeated for another seven years.

The Sultan was a man of very few words, but one could certainly forgive him for lacking a comment at this moment. It was another of the Swami's ego trips. The holy man had once inquired if his bath water should be saved, but discarded the notion when everyone was consumed with laughter.

# – 9 –

# Money Makes the World Go Round

*'Young men have strong passions, and tend to gratify them
indiscriminantly ... While they love honor, they love victory still more,
for youth is eager for superiority over others, and victory is one form
of this. They love both more than they love money, which indeed they
love very little, not having yet learnt what it means to be without it.'*

Aristotle, Rhetoric

Washington has been home for twenty years and while I would not
wish to live anywhere else, it is an environment somewhat different from other American cities. In Boston you are judged by your
genealogy, in New York by your wealth, and in Los Angeles by the
make of the car you drive. In Washington, it is who you know that
counts. Considerations of wealth, genealogy, and other status symbols
are minimized because they are undemocratic. Everyone begins on an
equal footing in the nation's capital. The Rockefellers must dine with the
new Congressman from Boonsville and ignore his lack of sophistication.

The former chief of staff to President Carter is famous for allegedly
complimenting the wife of the Egyptian Ambassador on her pyramids
while staring down the front of her dress at dinner. Those who needed
to know the White House chief of staff, including the Ambassador,
pretended nothing was ever said. If an unknown prince or sheik sponsors

an exhibition of art at the National Gallery, it must be overlooked when he passes wind at lunch.

The wife of the Ambassador of Canada, Sondra Gotlieb, simplified the situation graphically in a syndicated column. Her husband, Mr Ambassador, would entertain and cultivate Cabinet members, Important Jobs, and wives of Important Jobs.

Money is not a topic for discussion in proper Washington society. Most Washingtonians are, rather astonishingly, shocked by frank comments on or questions about an individual's wealth. It is generally understood that in a society of equals, people are meant to be judged by higher standards than their net worth. Of course, everyone in the nation's capital understands the importance of money in the complicated world of politics and international relations. It is simply considered bad form to openly acknowledge that people of great wealth are different from the rest of us.

Spending time with Khashoggi, the Swami and especially the Sultan of Brunei shattered all of my prior conceptions about wealth. Rich had always described a life in which money was no problem. What I visited was a world in which rich is a noun. It meant billions of dollars, not millions, bank accounts the size of gross national products.

The *Fortune* magazine list of the richest people in the world starts at net worths of $5 billion and heads north. The Rockefellers and the Vanderbilts are no longer there, European royalty seldom make the bottom line, and traditional fortunes like the Gettys have been broken up among squabbling relatives. Dynastic oil fiefdoms and multinational business portfolios are the only real source of major wealth as we know it today.

Two established members of this modern club are King Fahd of Saudi Arabia (worth about $20 billion) and Sheik Jabar el Sabbah of Kuwait ($5 billion). The rest are nearly all conglomerate kings with interests in real estate, media or service industries. Men like the discount retailing czar, Sam Walton ($8.7 billion), and Canadian newspaper tycoon, Roy Thompson ($5.5 billion).

*Forbes* magazine, which publishes a similar list, chose the West German Brunninkmeyer family and a number of Japanese, including property developer, Taikichiro Mori, and Yoshiaki Tsausukmi, who owns more than $15 billion in hotel and transportation investments. Not to be overlooked, of course, is Queen Elizabeth II, who tops the list of women at $8.7 billion.

Altogether there are only twenty to twenty-five people with net worths of $5 billion or more. At the top of the list is the only person who could

64

afford to buy out the King of Saudi Arabia (and probably old Midas himself), the individual who by any calculation is far and away the richest man in the world: His Majesty the Sultan and Yang Di-Pertuan Negara Brunei Darussalam.

Brunei is a small country, 200 miles north of the equator, on the island of Borneo. It is the only Muslim state in Southeast Asia and its citizens are intensely religious. The capital of Brunei, Bandar Seri Begawan, is a dreary, mosquito-infested provincial town on the bank of the Brunei River, surrounded by a swamp forest of nipah palms and mangrove trees. It is entirely dominated by the gigantic, gilded palace of the Sultan. The palace, which is 10 per cent larger than the Vatican, cost over $600 million to build and boasts 1788 rooms. When I last saw the Sultan, he was contemplating an addition to the family quarters for the Crown Prince.

The incomprehensible wealth of the country can be summed up in two rather staggering statistics. Brunei has an income of $3,775 million per year and a population of just over 170,000. The people of Brunei are better off materially than any other country in Southeast Asia. The per-capita income is second only to Kuwait. There are no taxes.

A brief history of Brunei will better explain the point.

In the fifteenth century, the Sultans of Brunei ruled a trading empire which covered half of the South Pacific, from Java and Sumatra to the Philippines. Their deep-water junks carried jungle produce such as bird nests, camphor and behoar stones, to southern China, and returned laden with metals, pottery and textiles. The trade was profitable and the Sultans grew rich.

In 1519 the Spanish launched an expedition under Magellan to find a route to the Indies via America. Magellan himself was killed in the Philippines, but the expedition limped on and two of his ships reached Brunei Bay. The first white men stepped ashore in 1521.

They were amazed to find themselves in an impressive water city, built on piles like Venice and housing more than 25,000 families. The Sultan lived in a palace, guarded by a cannon and grandly illuminated by candles in silver chandeliers. The court was rich with silks and brocades, and the Sultan's treasure ran from elephants to jewels – among them, according to legend, two pearls the size of pigeon eggs so perfectly formed they could not lie still on a flat surface.

The country was as wealthy and sophisticated as any in Europe. The centuries that followed, however, were a story of fading glory. Brunei's empire gradually diminished. It would be 450 years before Brunei again became a power, but the legend remained and the sultanate continued.

By Victorian times, the island of Borneo was owned and run by the British Empire and was known as the North Borneo Company. Its history follows the pattern of most extensions of the Empire. The chief administrator of the North Borneo Company was James Brooke. He appeared on the island in 1839 and soon became known as the 'White Rajah of Sarawak'. In essence, Brooke fended off the outside world and, with the connivance of the British, shaped the future history of Brunei.

The Sultans were quite happy with British occupation. They continued to enjoy their privileges and maintain their traditional court while tedious matters such as foreign affairs were taken out of their hands. If the British were obsessed with abolishing slavery and headhunting, they also put down the pirates which had plagued the South China Seas for centuries. It was a reasonable trade-off. Above all, the British presence guaranteed that Brunei was not entirely swallowed up by its neighbors. And when there was a rebellion, as happened in 1884, it was useful to have a British gunboat sail up the Brunei River to quash it.

So it was that the medieval court, with its aristocratic rituals, drifted into the twentieth century almost untouched by modern life and unaware of other cultures.

The event which broke the spell was the discovery of oil off the coast in 1929. The British Malay Petroleum Company, a subsidiary of Shell, had been drilling for nine months and was about to give up when crude oil was struck at 900 feet in the southern coastal town of Seria. It proved to be there in commercial quantities and over the next sixteen years a small field was developed, producing about 17,000 barrels a day.

Overnight, Brunei was transformed from a distant, backwater protectorate into a strategic target. The Sultan's importance grew with his wealth (it was never considered the country's). Foreign visitors began to schedule Brunei as an important port of call. The country was late emerging from its long sleep and unequipped for the modern world. It needed peace, stability and time to adjust. Unfortunately, it got none of these.

During World War II the thirty-eight oil wells were destroyed by the British, rebuilt by the advancing Japanese, destroyed again by Allied bombing, rebuilt, and finally blown up once more by the retreating Japanese. Also during a brief period of occupation by the Japanese, the Sultan was forced to work and conduct himself like a common man. The royal family has never forgiven the Japanese for this insult. In the same way Queen Elizabeth blamed Mrs Simpson for the untimely death of King George VI, the royal family considered the Japanese responsible for the death of the twenty-seventh Sultan at the early age of thirty-five, in 1950.

This accident of history produced a remarkable and wily new leader. Sir Omar Ali Sarfuddin, brother of the late Sultan, was elevated to the throne.

Sir Omar recognized his lack of experience and understanding of the outside world and immediately set about to inform himself. He traveled around the world to meet with other heads of state and spent a great deal of time in London establishing the terms under which his country would be ruled and protected by the British. His goal, in short, was to obtain as much power for his family as possible, to protect the dynasty, and move his country forward under British rule. The last thing Sir Omar wanted was full independence. Democracy is a luxury a Sultan of Brunei cannot afford. His ability to manipulate the British by agreeing to their demands and then doing exactly what he deemed necessary is a marvelous example of the failure of Western governments and cultures to create and define Eastern countries in their own image.

At the end of World War II, Her Majesty's government was under great pressure from all sides to grant independence to its colonies. So in 1959 the British informed the bemused Bruneians that they could now hold the first democratic elections in the country's history. Internal independence was intended to be the first step toward ending British rule. UK forces would continue to defend Brunei, its foreign policy would continue to be decided in Whitehall, and the dynasty would remain, but the balance of power was to be shifted toward the citizenry.

The Sultan looked on with dismay as the election was held and the popular People's Party (PRB – Party Ra'akyat Brunei) won an overwhelming victory. The PRB advocated immediate independence from the UK, a close alliance with Indonesia, full democratic rights, and, of course, the abolition of the dynasty.

Sir Omar was not amused. He refused to summon an assembly and blocked the fledgling nationalists at every turn. Angry and exasperated, the PRB launched an open revolt in 1962. Their North Kalimkantan National Army was equipped with nothing but small arms, the promised support from Indonesia did not materialize, and most Bruneians missed the point. Sir Omar, however, was quick to act. He reminded the British that under an agreement signed in 1959, they were obligated to intervene. A battalion of Gurkhas was immediately dispatched to put down the insurrection. The Sultan declared a 'state of emergency' which has been in force ever since and banned the PRB whose Chairman, A M Azahari fled to Singapore to avoid going to jail. The country reverted to an absolute monarchy, lacking other options, the British began to lobby Brunei's neighbors to press the Sultan for reforms.

As a result, various coups were plotted. Malay agents even invaded the capital, then called Bandar Brunei, and freed several dissidents from jail. These rude actions, however, strengthened the Sultan's resolve. He ordered the Gurkhas to take control of the internal security of the country and recruited an elite squad of 600 Gurkhas to act as his Praetorian guard.

In an attempt to appease the British, Sir Omar agreed to another election in 1965. To put it mildly, it was somewhat less than democratic. The PRB was excluded and few people bothered to vote. A legislative assembly of sorts was formed with ten elected representatives and ten appointed by the Sultan. When the Sultan's royal ministers were told they would be held accountable for their actions and subjected to questioning by commoners, they resigned. Within weeks the assembly was suspended by royal order.

This time, however, the elected representatives appealed directly to Her Majesty's government for help. Responsible individuals in Whitehall had finally lost patience with Sir Omar and threatened to withdraw the Gurkha regiments unless he began to conform. It looked like the final showdown for the royal family. To everyone's amazement, however, the Sultan out-maneuvered the British by abdicating in favor of his son in 1967.

Faced with an entirely new head of state, the British eased the pressure for democratic reforms. The internal opposition, which was never well organized, became less so with the startling news of Sir Omar's abdication. Brunei's neighbors also decided to give the young ruler time to tackle his new role. Sir Omar had bought another reprieve for the royal family.

To commemorate the occasion, he adopted the title Paduka Seri Begawan Sultan (Noble Former Sultan) and renamed the capital after himself. Bandar Brunei (Brunei town) became Bandar Seri Begawan.

At the age of twenty-one, Hassanal Bolkiah was suddenly directed to leave school and return home to become the twenty-ninth Sultan. It is fair to assume that the new monarch was totally unprepared for such a turn of events.

The twenty-ninth Sultan, Hassanal Bolkiah, had always been kept out of the limelight by his father. He had been educated at English speaking schools in Malay and in 1966 was sent to the Sandhurst Military Academy with his younger brother, Mohamed. The abdication forced him to leave school several months before he was to complete his studies. At Sandhurst he was considered a less than average student.

Sir Omar always had favored his second son, Mohamed, who was said to be more intelligent and diligent. Tradition, however, directed that the eldest son become his successor, and Sir Omar was not only a believer in tradition, he intended to perpetuate it.

The former Sultan intended to use his son as a figurehead and was convinced the weak-willed young man would do as he was told. Sir Omar expected his son to attend public functions and then vanish when serious business was to be discussed. Ten years passed with virtually no conflict or change in the country. Sir Omar got the breathing space he desired. What he failed to comprehend was that the sultanate was sitting on a time bomb of money, not anarchy.

Events in the Middle East caused the value of Brunei crude to soar three to four times its previous market value, and it was now being produced from the Seria wells at the rate of 170,000 barrels a day. Soon natural gas was discovered in massive quantities. The reserves seemed inexhaustible.

Most of the gas which passed through Brunei's massive cooling plants went to Japan. The oil was exported to Singapore and other Southeast Asian countries or sold on the world spot market. The country's energy income had reached a level of $6.6 billion per year and continued to grow. The national reserves soon grew to over $40 billion.

This incredible amount of money was controlled, of course, by the royal family. Bread and circuses were given to the populace when necessary. Color television was introduced and free television sets were provided for every citizen in 1975. A massive road-building program was completed in 1976. Earth satellite links were constructed and a national telephone system was installed in 1980. Government employees were given interest-free housing loans for housing and cars, per capita income swiftly became the second highest in the world, and the government cheerfully subsidized the holy pilgrimage, or Haj, to Mecca for employees who were expected to earn the title Haji. Income tax was never considered. The people of Brunei happily accepted the mandate that only the royal family could own and drive a Rolls-Royce motor car. A Mercedes in every *kampong* (household) was not all that bad.

Never mind that there was no university and no modern hospital, that political prisoners were incarcerated for up to twenty years without a trial, that housing for the stateless Chinese, who comprised thirty per cent of the work force, was inadequate (and that they had no rights whatsoever), or that the country was being polluted at an uncon-

69

scionable pace. The sultanate had been preserved.

Most of the world, especially the leaders of the Commonwealth, found the situation in Brunei increasingly offensive. Malaysia and other Third World countries began to speak out against the Sultan in the United Nations.

Brunei was not only an anachronism for the British government, it was expensive as well. The cost of maintaining a small Gurkha army there was difficult to justify in the face of military cut-backs at home and the increasing publicity about the country's inconceivable wealth. Whitehall, under heavy criticism by the press, was more than ever determined to force Brunei to accept independence.

After a series of intense diplomatic maneuvers which involved Brunei's closest allies, it was announced on 30 June 1978 that Brunei would become an independent nation on 1 February 1984. The Gurkha troops would be withdrawn in September 1983, and the Sultan's government would assume complete responsibility for its own affairs. As usual, these negotiations were conducted between the British Government and the former Sultan. The Prime Minister of Singapore, Lee Kwan Yew, made a greater effort than any other head of state on behalf of the British to assure Sir Omar that Brunei would not be bullied by the other ASEAN nations, and that the dynasty would continue. He also promised a grateful father that he would act as a mentor to the young Sultan.

His Majesty was now thirty-two years old and becoming increasingly independent. He had authority and control over the country's billions and, as independence approached, told his father he planned to make his own decisions on investment matters in the future. Sir Omar would live to regret that he had not paid more attention to the son for whom he saved the throne.

# – 10 –

## His Majesty the Sultan and Yang Di-Pertuan Negara Brunei Darussalam: Troubles with Father

---

There is an air of Joseph Conrad or early Graham Greene about Brunei which is typified, among other examples, by the story of Ponniah Rajaratnam.

Rajaratnam was a retired deputy commissioner of the respected Singapore police force. He had once headed the corrupt practices investigation bureau in Singapore and his credentials were impeccable. Prime Minister Lee Kwan Yew urged the Sultan to enlist the help of Rajaratnam in ridding Brunei of at least some of the corruption now rumored throughout Southeast Asia to be everywhere. Always somewhat in awe of Lee Kwan Yew and in the midst of a major feud with his father in 1984, the Sultan called in Rajaratnam for help.

It took little time for Rajaratnam to uncover the appalling amounts of corruption in the civil service, the banking industry, and among many members of the Sultan's court. His investigations began to lead to members of the Sultan's family, and he actually revealed this to His Majesty, while complaining about the lack of official cooperation and the constant threats he had been getting from royal cousins and in-laws.

On the morning of 22 July 1984, the crusty old whistle blower was

71

found floating face down and fully clothed off the beach at Maura. The local police records listed him as 'missing' for several weeks. Finally, the official explanation given to his family and the Prime Minister of Singapore was that he had 'an accident while swimming and had drowned'.


Brunei in 1984 was not the country Sir Omar had envisioned when he abdicated in favor of his first son, Hassanal Bolkiah, in 1967. The old man did his best to control the destiny of Brunei and to shape the life of the new Sultan, but the age-old vices of greed and lust played a major role as well.

Few observers of Brunei at that time would challenge the fact that the Sultan had too long been manipulated by his father. His Majesty had been on the throne for over twelve years. In less than four years, Brunei would become an independent nation. Like it or not, the supreme executive authority over literally every public and royal decision resided in the Sultan. It was inevitable that he would become impatient with his father's attitude and strike out on his own. What resulted was a state of affairs the skillful managers of the British Empire would never have allowed. It was a lesson learned at an incredible cost. Had the old Sultan understood what he was forced to learn later, men like Mohamed Fayed, Adnan Khashoggi and the Swami might not have mattered.

At his father's insistence, the young Sultan had married his cousin and Sir Omar's favorite niece, Saleha, in 1965. She was well suited to become the Raja Isteri (Queen) given her royal blood and sensible ways. There seemed little excitement in their relationship, but she gave him six children, including his eldest son and heir, Al-Muhtadee Billah. The Raja Isteri, who had been raised in the strict Muslim fashion, happily performed her duties and cared for her children without regard to the outside world. When the Sultan traveled to other countries, as he had begun to do with greater frequency, she preferred to remain at home.

Still a young man, with few responsibilities and a vast amount of money at his disposal, the Sultan was tempted by the lifestyle of the ultra-rich. He began to visit London often where his wild spending sprees were reported in the gossip columns. He frequented nightclubs and learned to enjoy champagne, gambling and other forms of entertainment not allowed in Brunei and frowned upon by the Muslim religion. News that he had lost over a million pounds sterling in one night at Aspinall's casino eventually found its way back to Brunei. One joke at the time was that it was impossible to buy a new Rolls-Royce since the Sultan bought them by the dozen. The palace in Brunei houses 800 cars in the royal garage.

In the years before the Sultan was persuaded to buy a custom designed 727 airplane for his exclusive use, he would summon, on short notice, an Air Brunei plane to transport him and his party to his favorite haunts. Many ticketed passengers were delayed by this royal diversion, but no one dared complain.

It was on one of these flights that His Majesty met a striking Air Brunei stewardess and fell hopelessly in love. Her name was Mariam Bell. The Sultan is allowed four wives under the rules of the Muslim faith.

The royal family, however, was against Miss Bell: Mariam was a commoner and part Japanese. Bruneians, and especially the royal family, will never forgive the Japanese for the occupation of the sultanate during World War II. She also struck Sir Omar as too aggressive and, for a combination of all these reasons, unsuitable to marry his son.

The Sultan did not heed the advice of his family. In 1980, Mariam Bell became Her Royal Highness Pengiran Isteri Hajjah Mariam. It may have been the first time in his life that the Sultan defied his father on a matter the Paduka Seri Begawan Sultan considered of ultimate importance, but it certainly would not be the last.

The Sultan and Princess Mariam seemed extremely happy and almost inseparable. She loved to travel with him and enjoyed her contacts with the jet set. The Raja Isteri now was seen with the Sultan infrequently and only at official functions.

Not only was Brunei moving toward full independence during this period, but it appeared that the Sultan intended to exercise more control over his life as well. It angered him that his father and family did not approve of Princess Mariam. She, too, was well aware of the royal family's attitude and did her best to distance the Sultan from them whenever possible. She encouraged him to seek out his own advisors and to make whatever royal decisions he wanted. She insisted their marriage herald that the time had come for his father and family to acknowledge his superior position in the country.

The Sultan devoted a great deal of time to the sport of kings, polo. It became his passion. The Jerudong Royal Polo Club, which the Sultan founded, had some of the best horses in the game. They were bred solely for polo and transported around the world for the Sultan's use. At one point, His Majesty even agreed to purchase a 747 airplane as transport for the horses. Wiser heads prevailed and the purchase agreement was

73

canceled, but the horses lived, despite this setback, in luxury not known to many humans.

The polo club is indeed something to see. It offers three polo fields, grandstands, a swimming pool and an adjacent golf course as well as air conditioned stables for 200 horses. It cost the Sultan about $17 million.

Word soon flashed around his world that polo was the certain entrée to the world's richest man. Statements approved by the palace touted polo as the means by which His Majesty had become friendly with the sultans of Malaysia – who were not always regarded as friends – and with the Prince of Wales. It was no accident that the British High Commissioner sent to Brunei in 1983 was said to be skillful in both diplomacy and polo. Between chukkers, alas, other men befriended the ingenuous Sultan.

On the polo field, the Sultan met Enrique Zobel, a businessman of Spanish descent with great ambitions and great problems at home. Zobel had been feuding with other members of his family over control of their corporate flagship, Ayala Corporation, based in Manila.

Off the polo field, Zobel became the Sultan's close friend and advisor. An easy-going relationship developed between them and the Sultan began to rely on Zobel's knowledge of politics and finance. Enrique could describe the complex power struggles of Southeast Asia in simple terms. In addition, he understood the construction business and the problems of building modern facilities in Brunei. In that spirit of friendship and trust, they entered into commercial banking, and began other projects at a dazzling pace. Zobel was one of the first outside advisors to initiate a joint venture with the Sultan. The Brunei-incorporated Island Development Bank (IDB) was established in 1980 as a 50–50 partnership between them. Enrique saw the Sultan and IDB as a way to skim off some of the more solid assets from the Ayala stable, and rid himself once and for all of his cousin, Jaime Zobel, and other tiresome members of the family.

With the help of the Sultan, Zobel brought the Bank of the Philippine Islands into IDB, and later the Dai-Ichi Kangyo Bank of Japan. Soon, with Zobel as chairman, IDB opened two commercial banking branches in Brunei and installed his son as the manager.

Of the nine commercial banks represented in Brunei, seven are branches of foreign banks. The only other Brunei-based bank, besides IDB, is the National Bank of Brunei. It was managed by another friend of the Sultan's, Singapore hotelier Khoo Teck Paut. A major scandal erupted when it was reported that the National Bank of Brunei had made several billion dollars in loans to projects ultimately owned by or benefiting Khoo Teck Paut. Records indicate that the royal family, primarily the Sultan, had invested a great deal of money in the bank. When the Sultan learned that virtually all of the loans were in default and unlikely ever to be repaid, he ordered his friend's son put under house arrest indefinitely. The matter is still pending.

None of Zobel's projects in Brunei was more extraordinary than the building of the Istana Nurul Iman. The *Guinness Book of Records* had to revise its 1984 statistics to put the Istana at the top of its list as the world's largest palace. Cost estimates on the construction run from $600 million to infinity. Zobel headed the management team that built the palace and made certain it was completed for the celebration of Brunei's independence in February 1984.

The gigantic monolith overlooks a shantytown on the Brunei River. As I walked from room to room on my one and only visit to the Istana, I tried to imagine what had motivated His Majesty to build such a monstrosity. There must have been a better way to prove to his father and family that he would no longer be manipulated.

One enters the palace through ornate iron gates operated by a central computer. Inside the palace grounds, the entrance leads to a mammoth marble courtyard with lagoons, waterfalls, and fountains on either side of three grand archways of carved Philippine hardwood. Surrounding the courtyard are a royal dining hall, a ceremonial hall, audience rooms, sitting and conference rooms and a prayer room. Further down, the courtyard ends at the entrance to the privy council chamber, its main wall paneled with slabs of red Moroccan onyx. When the final block of Moroccan onyx for this room was quarried from the last onyx mine in the world, the mine was declared exhausted and was closed.

From the ground floor, guests are carried by escalators to a reception hall on the second floor. The hall can easily accommodate 1000 people. Through great Moorish arches of gold leaf, one enters the throne room. Twelve two-ton Viennese chandeliers, which cost $1 million each, grace this room which seats 2000 people comfortably. Everything is covered in 22-carat gold including two enormous domes on each end of the palace, the canopy which hangs over the dais in the throne room, and at least half of the 82 feet high walls in the public rooms.

Buckingham Palace is one fourth the size of the Istana; Versailles is about one half as large. The private area of the palace has a total of 944 rooms and the public area has 844 rooms for a grand total of 1788 rooms plus 44 staircases. Plush carpets cover 240,000 square feet of floor area. Over 4500 laborers, engineers, designers, craftsmen, and managers worked three years to complete the palace in time for the celebration of Brunei's independence in 1984. Every detail was under Zobel's supervision.

World press reports on the palace were uniformly critical. *House and Garden* magazine's story may have been the most flattering. '"Restraint" is a word that is unlikely to figure in any description of the interior', it read. 'It is impossible not to be reminded of *The Wizard of Oz* as one approaches the golden mosaic triple arch that surrounds the doorway to the throne hall . . .'

To make matters worse many of the high technology features failed to work. The escalators malfunctioned, and the air-conditioning in the throne room caused the million dollar chandeliers to rattle so loudly it was impossible to hear anyone speak. The Sultan began to think he had been made to look a fool and, not unreasonably, blamed Zobel.

Clearly hurt by the reaction to this first enterprise, when the Sultan built a second palace for Princess Mariam, the Istana Nurulizza, he did not employ Zobel and refused to allow any press or photographers inside. It is totally different from the main palace. It is grand while not being imposing or cold, and set in the forests away from the capital. His Majesty spends most of his time there with Princess Mariam when in Brunei. The Raja Isteri has been left to reign over 'The Palace for the People', as the Istana is called in government publications.

My own stay at the palace came in late August 1985. Zobel was not with us, but it was clear at once why he had lost the Sultan's trust and why he had enlisted the Swami to bail him out. It almost worked.

This brief visit also confirmed the rumors about the Sultan's predicament. He may have had good reason to be angry at his father and family, but it was evident that he was unworldly, vulnerable, and seemingly out of control. This impression was formed to a certain extent not by what was said, but more palpably by the looks and responses to my innocent questions. No one in Brunei dared talk about it, but all knew the old Sultan was critical of his son's rule and up to something.

Within months it emerged that the battle royal often verged on the ludicrous. In a moment of rage at his son's behavior, the Paduka Seri Begawan told the government-controlled television station to announce that he was once again the ultimate ruler of Brunei. Disarmed by the former Sultan's decree, the station managers sought confirmation from the palace. The Sultan immediately countermanded his father's order.

Watching the evening news, Sir Omar became furious that his edict had been omitted. Summoning his gold plated Rolls Royce, he ordered his driver to take him to the station, where he stormed into the studio to demand that his pronouncement be broadcast in the next installment.

Unable to resist Sir Omar in the flesh, the commentator did put out the statement. This particular broadcast, as fate would have it, was in Malay. Sir Omar's words were delivered in English, making his pronouncement not only inappropriate but incomprehensible to the majority of the viewers. The incident only served to fuel speculation that a palace coup was in the works.

Hassanal Bolkiah understood the time had come to act. In a matter of hours the army and police, led by British officers, came forward and declared themselves for the Sultan. Sir Omar finally realized he was no longer in control.

The Paduka Seri Begawan died in September, 1986. Friends report that father and son embraced each other in the last year of the old Sultan's life and that the Hassanal Bolkiah is no longer the troubled man I encountered in 1985.

# – 11 –

## The First Non-Billionaire Appears

Brunei became an independent nation on 1 January 1984, under the terms of the agreement reached with the United Kingdom in 1978. The nation's fate had been placed in the custody of the British in 1906 at the Sultan's urgent request. The UK received little or no thanks for its efforts in preserving this tiny sultanate which Asian colonial expansion or democratic reforms most certainly would have eliminated. No country resisted leaving the empire more vigorously than Brunei, and few countries were as wealthy. Yet, the issue of whether or not Her Majesty's Government would continue to fund Brunei's defense and pay for the Gurkhas was a sore point in the 1978 negotiations that neither side can forget. The Brunei government publishes a 'facts and figures' brochure which glumly reports: 'Brunei Darussalam became a British protectorate, accepting in 1906 a British Resident, whose advice had to be followed in all matters except the Islamic faith and Malay custom.'

On the resumption of independence, the Sultan declared Brunei 'a sovereign, independent, democratic, Muslim monarchy, according to Sunni belief'. Luck and the Sultan's timing saved the populace from pondering the royal decree. 24 February 1984 had been made the national day of celebration. Heads of state from around the world had been invited to attend and participate in the independence festivities. A great deal of work had to be done.

While those 4500 individuals labored to complete the palace on schedule, the rest of the citizenry pulled weeds, scrubbed the sidewalks, hung flags, rehearsed dances, organized meals, and dealt with hundreds of other details necessary to transform their country into a showplace. By 22 February they were ready to roll out the red carpet and welcome envoys from seventy-one countries.

An enormous crowd gathered at the airport to ogle and welcome the distinguished guests. His Royal Highness The Prince of Wales, caused the greatest excitement. The Prince was center stage during the entire visit. Another impressive figure was the King of Tonga. The affable king was so enormous that a custom made chair had to accompany him to all state functions. No one in Brunei had ever witnessed such a procession of kings, sheiks, presidents, prime ministers, princes and other potentates.

No doubt thinking that they had seen it all, the onlookers journeyed back to the center of Bandar Seri Begawan. Suddenly, the Bruneians began running toward the river. They were galvanized by the arrival of what appeared to be a floating palace at the royal dock. As the 282 foot yacht set anchor, the curious onlookers tried to guess which head of state had arrived.

The yacht was the *Nabila*, named for the beautiful daughter of its owner, Adnan Khashoggi. Always a master of the moment, Adnan had arrived in a display of wealth and sparkle none of the seventy-one designated representatives of the world community could match. His wife, Lamia, and daughter, Nabila, were positioned by his side. It was obvious few could compete with the beauty of the Khashoggi women either.

Out of courtesy, the Sultan went aboard the *Nabila* to greet his guests. His Majesty was annoyed with Khashoggi for what he had been persuaded were exorbitant commissions taken on his purchase of a 727 jet and jewelry, but it was not a time for bad feelings. Besides, the Sultan could not wait to see the yacht.

Not only did it have its own laser lit discotheque and private pool surrounded by bullet-proof glass, it also contained a helicopter and landing pad, an operating room for medical emergencies, eight staterooms, six guest suites, and more electronic gadgets and telephones than the White House. One almost had to have seen the palace in Brunei to appreciate what Time-Life's *The Luxury Yachts* called the 'most opulent modern yacht afloat'.

Adnan Mohamed Khashoggi was born on 25 July 1935, in Saudi

Arabia. Three years before Adnan's birth, King Abdul-Aziz had won a hard fought battle with the sheikdoms and wandering tribes that lived on the land between the Red Sea and the Persian Gulf. In 1932, Abdul-Aziz declared himself to be the King of the Islamic nation of Saudi Arabia. Fortune smiled on both the King and Khashoggi.

In 1938, oil was struck at Dammam on the Persian Gulf elevating the Saudi royal family to billionaire status in short order. Khashoggi happened to be born the son of one of the few doctors in Saudi Arabia, Dr Mohamed Khaled Khashoggi. At about the same time that the royal family hit the oil lottery, Dr Khashoggi was appointed the court physician by the King. In this capacity, he acted as an advisor and traveling companion to the King as well as his doctor.

Dr and Mrs Khashoggi brought six children into the world: Adnan, Samira, Adil, Essam, Assia, and Soheir. As the eldest, Adnan had a special relationship with his father whom he idolized. Dr Khashoggi took Adnan with him whenever possible and Adnan, with his jocular style, quiet voice and sparkling brown eyes, soon became a favorite of the Saudi royal family.

In this period, Egypt was the cultural and intellectual center of the Arab world. Among other young men whose fathers intended their sons to be the future leaders of that world, Adnan was sent to Victoria College in Alexandria at the age of eight. At Victoria, a boarding school that taught all of its classes in English, Adnan excelled in his studies. He also became friends with classmates destined to lead their countries such as Hussein, the future King of Jordan, and Hisham Nazir, the future minister of planning for Saudi Arabia.

After graduation in 1952, Adnan went into the importing business in Saudi Arabia with his cousin, Anas Yassin. Even at the age of eighteen, this was too limited a universe for him. Within months, AK was off to America to become a petroleum engineer. He enrolled first at Chico State University in California where he lasted three semesters. Engineering and geology courses bored him, but more important, he had discovered a new social climate in which women and men were free to dress, dance, drink, and conduct themselves as they pleased. The California party scene was considerably more interesting than homework.

Moreover, like the Swami and Fayed, AK preferred to live by his wits. Adnan admired his father, who had studied over a decade to become the physician to the King, but he desired to live the life of a King. A college degree was no help, he had a better way.

His experiences in Egypt, and during this short period in America, taught him that his innate skills as a dealmaker should be developed.

Constantly traveling between the US and Saudi Arabia, he became an interpreter of the US commercial ethos to the royal family.

The death of King Abdul-Aziz in 1953 gave Adnan the opportunity to help persuade his successor, King Saud, that he must lead Saudi Arabia into a new era of growth and development. In that context, AK requested permission to form joint ventures with foreign companies and individuals to build factories and import Western technology. In less than two years the King had given him the franchise to build a brick factory, a tire-recapping factory, and an exclusive fifty-year franchise with National Gypsum Co to produce the gypsum boards used in the construction of most new houses. Commissions paid on these deals may or may not have made Adnan a millionaire, but certainly made him hungry for more.

The turning point in Adnan's fortunes came in 1962 when a civil war broke out in Yemen on Saudi Arabia's southern border. The struggle in Yemen was a classic conflict between the dynasty that had ruled since 1918 and revolutionaries in the army seeking to overthrow the Iman Badr (king). Egypt was supplying Soviet made weapons to the revolutionaries which made it awkward for the Saudis to openly back the royalists. On the other hand, the royal family viewed this insurrection as a preliminary attempt by pro-Soviet factions to take control of the Arab states. Motivated by self interest, King Saud instructed Crown Prince Faisal to do whatever he deemed necessary to help the royalists, but to make certain that the royal family's efforts were conducted as discreetly as possible. The Al Saud name could not be directly linked to aid to the anti-revolutionaries.

The Crown Prince immediately offered Khashoggi his first major assignment as a covert agent for the royal family. Faisal entrusted him with a bank draft for £1 million which he used to purchase arms from Great Britain and supply to the royalists. The mission was a success. The newly armed royalists defeated the insurgents and the King praised the Crown Prince for his handling of the matter.

True or not, Adnan informed Faisal that he had taken no commission on the arms deal from the British and wanted none. It was the kind of skilled performance Khashoggi often employed. Faisal must have assumed Adnan had received a commission, but was impressed by the fact that he did not try to profit from both ends of the deal, especially his end. It was a critical signal. Over the next ten years Khashoggi did virtually anything the royal family requested and they agreed to do business with companies that retained him as their agent.

In the aftermath of the civil war, Khashoggi and others convinced the royal brothers that closer ties with the United States would strengthen the Saudi position against the advancement of pro-Soviet movements. A new direction in foreign policy was established which, although somewhat diminished, remains in place today.

The civil war in Yemen did much more than launch AK, it opened Faisal's eyes to the need to both build up the country's defenses and improve the quality of life of his subjects. Working with Prince Sultan and Prince Fahd, Faisal persuaded the King to ban slavery and implement an aggressive modernization program to upgrade health, housing, education and transportation.

The decision of the Saudis to build roads, houses, hospitals, and to buy arms was great news for the world's entrepreneurs, but the correspondent foreign policy tilt toward the United States doubled the heartbeats of American business executives. In board rooms across the nation, corporate presidents were asking the same question: 'How do we break into the lucrative Saudi market?'

Needless to say, Khashoggi did his best to provide the answer and brokered many deals on behalf of US companies. His client list included a number of major conglomerates, but consisted mostly of corporations such as Lockheed, Raytheon and Northrop. The press soon began to refer to him as the 'Saudi arms dealer, Adnan Khashoggi'.

Exactly how much money Khashoggi earned during this era of Saudi largesse is impossible to calculate. Court records and US government documents disclose his commissions from Raytheon over the ten year period totaled $100 million on $1.5 billion in sales. All told, he probably made upwards of $500 million before the bubble burst. Most brokers or middlemen would have denied pocketing such an enormous amount in an attempt to low-key their coveted positions and protect their contacts. Not Adnan.

Khashoggi took the adage that 'you have to spend money to make money' more seriously than any man on earth. Over the years he acquired twelve lavish homes around the world, three commercial-sized private airplanes, yachts, jewels, limousines, children and wives that by any calculation had to have cost most of his fortune. In addition, he made business investments in real estate and development projects from the Sudan to Florida that amounted to several hundred million dollars.

Adnan had almost never experienced defeat and had always lived for the moment. Even after 1975, he lived and spent money with the abandon of a man possessing infinite wealth. His living expenses alone were said to be over $200,000 per day. He did everything possible to promote the myth that he was a multi-billionaire. A reasonable man had to conclude that Khashoggi was either on the level or a madman. People seemed to want to believe the myth.

As already mentioned, Khashoggi and I had met in the south of France on several social occasions. It pleased the Swami greatly that Khashoggi had called to ask for an audience. Swamiji loved playing the role of power broker and relished even more the fact that by asking for a meeting, the Saudi billionaire was confirming his influence in the Sultan's court. Within hours of my introduction, the two men were enchanted with each other. Few match-makers have had this kind of success. Obviously, they were kindred spirits in more ways than I could have imagined.

Knowing virtually nothing about Khashoggi but what I had read in the papers and heard from others, I was especially intrigued by him. To watch him operate was not only instructive, but often flabbergasting.

Khashoggi was impossible to dislike on a personal level. He was soft-spoken, gracious to a fault, and gave the impression of being intensely interested in the conversation or the person at hand which, of course, made him seem interesting. It was as if he had been trained to be a king. Whatever the occasion or departure time, he always arrived last, surrounded by key aides. Once critical decisions were made and he had changed from a business suit into a more comfortable thobe (a floorlength white shirt), he would greet everyone with warmth while maintaining a proper distance. Adnan never seemed impatient and never lost his temper in public. If others began to argue, he would leave the room. Cared for by a retinue of doctors, therapists and servants, his physical appearance was never less than perfect. He did have a tendency to gain weight, but suits of various sizes were always ready to camouflage his girth. A guest could have no wish which was not granted in record time.

A great deal has been written about Khashoggi's excesses and his flamboyant lifestyle. There really was nothing like it. To board the DC-8 and fly around the world with him was magic. On one trip in December 1985, we flew from New Delhi to Madras, then on to Riyadh, Saudi Arabia, for a brief stopover to meet with Prince Sultan. The next day we were to fly to Amman for a meeting with the King of Jordan, and then to Paris. At the conclusion of our meeting with King Hussein, Adnan looked at me and said: 'You have never been to my home in Marbella! Why don't we go there for a day?' The crew sighed (each probably had made a date for the evening in Paris), but instantly changed the flight plan. Within four hours, we had arrived in Marbella via helicopters and Mercedes limousines at the 5,000-acre estate Khashoggi called home. Fires were burning in each fireplace, servants attended to our every need, a lavish dinner had been prepared. As I retired to my room I was given a list of over 200 video films available on call. The villa had a communications control room which provided any film or music imaginable by dialing a specific number. Another number summoned a masseuse. The possibilities were endless.

In less than twenty-four hours we had left Marbella and flown to Paris. Obviously, I was meant to have been impressed by this enchanting stopover, but more than anything, I was bewildered. Why would he want to spend $50,000 on such a diversion?

Certainly no one attending the independence celebration imagined that Khashoggi was in deep financial trouble, least of all the Sultan.

The Sultan spent a great deal of time on the yacht and rumors quickly spread that Adnan hoped to marry his daughter to the Sultan, making Nabila his third wife. This gossip became a minor flap in the press which Adnan rather enjoyed. Nabila, still believing her father's fortune to be intact, was outraged by the insinuation that her father would try to marry her to the Sultan in exchange for money.

Adnan's up-front purpose for the Brunei trip was to smooth over past misunderstandings. His hidden agenda was to sell the yacht. It was a time in the Sultan's life when he wanted to own everything that fascinated him. He was on the *Nabila* less than ten minutes before he offered to buy it. Adnan, the professional gameplayer, replied that the yacht was not for sale. It was his most cherished possession, he told the Sultan. Then he turned to His Majesty and confessed he could not refuse a friend. 'Your Majesty,' AK announced, 'We are honored to be guests on your yacht.' Everyone assembled cheered!

At the appropriate time, AK told His Majesty the price for the *Nabila* was $90 million. Adnan could not state a price without adding a 300 per cent markup. The Sultan paused for a moment, then told Khashoggi he would give him $50 million as a deposit and the additional $40 million once he was certain that everything worked and that it met his needs. Adnan gladly agreed, and departed the next day with the check for $50 million aboard his DC-8.

The deal was to become one more arrow in the bow of his former brother-in-law, Mohamed Fayed.

# − 12 −

# Mohamed Fayed and the Sultan

Gossip about the Sultan's ongoing feud with his father, his anger at Zobel over the bad press on the palace, and the growing corruption in Brunei spread quickly among the rug-traders and jet-setters. Millionaires who fancied becoming billionaires aggressively pursued an introduction to His Majesty. They reasoned that while the Sultan was isolated from virtually everyone who was not a member of his court or a head of state, he was obviously less cautious than people might expect and clearly not listening to his father or unbiased financial experts. After all, he had bought jewels and an airplane from Khashoggi, and he allowed Zobel to construct a $600 million palace. With over $40 billion up for grabs, fortune hunters around the world followed the Sultan in the same way that sharks follow blood.

While the jewelry salesmen and financial experts in hot pursuit of the Sultan cooled their heels at the bar of the Sultan's newly acquired Royal Holiday Inn in Singapore, an unquestionably clever Egyptian, who liked to be called Mohamed Al-Fayed had a better idea. While he had met the Sultan in London on social occasions, Fayed had not been successful in cultivating His Majesty or becoming a financial adviser.

Fayed had made no secret of the fact that he wanted to become a key member of the Sultan's court. He had approached Tiny Rowland in early spring 1984, exhibited a page torn from the brochure of the

85

Swami's to Tiny and, seeking his advice, said the Swami had offered to recommend him as an adviser to the Sultan for $2 million. Fayed later told Tiny that he had obtained the Swami's endorsement for a mere $500,000. Fayed subsequently denied the Swami had persuaded the Sultan to trust him and work with him, and began to make disparaging remarks about the Guru. Not until June 1985 would Fayed regret his intemperate remarks and seek out the Swami to smooth over past differences because he had concluded he needed the guru's help with the Sultan once again.

Fayed's ties with the Maktoum family of Dubai had always been overstated. Outside of Dubai, he told people he was a close friend of Sheik Raschid and a part owner of the trade centre. Both statements were false, but the Maktoum family never bothered to dispute these exaggerations because Fayed always entertained many of the younger family members in London, and often acted on their behalf as a discreet local agent in difficult moments.

Fayed, it turns out, was clever enough to gain access to the one man on earth the Sultan truly admired, Prime Minister Lee Kuan Yew of Singapore, through his Dubai connections. Without divulging his real purpose, Mohamed casually asked his younger friends in the Maktoum family to arrange a meeting with Lee Kuan Yew. Fayed often had managed to convince men in high places that he had come from a background of wealth and privilege in Egypt. He told the story of skilfully side-stepping President Nasser's nationalization programme by investing the family fortune abroad, thus creating a vast business empire. Mohamed was keenly aware that the Prime Minister was worried about the situation in Brunei. Mohamed persuaded the Prime Minister that he had the confidence of the British government and that he could encourage the Sultan to pay more attention to matters of state. Also, he promised to push aside men like Zobel and Khashoggi. His most appealing statement to the Prime Minister was that, the only reason a billionaire like himself wanted to become involved in Brunei was to help his adopted homeland, England, and to nurture a Muslim brother.

Distraught over the shocking death of his former Deputy Police Commissioner and worried that Brunei was on the verge of chaos or civil war, Lee Kuan Yew welcomed Fayed's interest. He agreed to encourage the Sultan to follow his advice.

Khashoggi and Zobel had greatly offended the Sultan, but the easy-going ruler tended to avoid unpleasant encounters and had preferred to simply reject any future proposals instead of confronting them about the past. Fayed had learned of a few major missteps by AK and Zobel that had not only angered His Majesty, but also had pained Mrs Thatcher and Lee Kuan Yew. He exploited their mistakes with skill. In no time at all he pushed aside Zobel and Khashoggi becoming the Sultan's closest advisor.

For over twenty years the British Crown Agents had managed Brunei's multi-billion dollar reserves. The Crown Agents is an idiosyncratic state-owned British institution acting as buyers and investors for foreign governments. By July 1983, at a point when he was riding high in the Sultan's orbit, Zobel had convinced the Sultan to fire the Crown Agents and entrust the Brunei billions to Citibank and Morgan Guaranty in the US and the Japanese securities houses, Nomura and Daiwa. It was a crushing blow to the Crown Agents, but more important a slap in the face to the British Prime Minister, who was struggling to keep the pound from dropping to parity with the dollar. Fayed made his concern over this affront known at Whitehall.

Zobel's status began to decline the following February when the palace was unveiled to the world and received bad reviews. In addition to the negative press, it was soon discovered that much of the workmanship on the Istana Nurul Aman was sub-standard, causing repairs to begin almost immediately. The Sultan felt betrayed. Even Zobel must have realized that he had overplayed his hand. For the next few months he was hardly seen in Brunei, explaining to friends that he had to attend to business in the Philippines.

Khashoggi's mistakes had been less dramatic, but had the same effect. In the late seventies, he had befriended the Sultan in London where they often met at the Belfry Club. A world-class expert on after hour pleasures, Adnan introduced the young monarch to London's nightlife. One can imagine Khashoggi laughing with the Sultan when he lost a million pounds at Aspinall's at one sitting, and comforting him with stories of his own greater and more frequent losses in Monte Carlo.

During the late seventies to the early eighties, Khashoggi did more than amuse the Sultan. He brokered sales of jewels, rumored to have been over $700 million, for the royal wives and sold him a custom built 727 jet.

Khashoggi observed at an early age that the indirect sales pitch was more effective in dealing with high profile men. Rather than appear to be a sales agent, he offered His Majesty the use of what he described as one of his personal planes for a return trip to Brunei. Soon after landing in his homeland, His Majesty told Adnan he wanted to buy the 727. AK had just bought the plane but realized he could make a large profit by a quick sale to the Sultan. An employee of Khashoggi's who traveled with the plane to Brunei, complained to the Sultan he had been unfairly treated when the sale was finalized, and asked for $1 million commission. Startled and somewhat angry, the Sultan, none-the-less, gave him a check for that amount. When His Majesty expressed dissatisfaction about the messy situation, AK fired the man, but did not offer to return the $1 million. The money did not matter, of course, but the Sultan began to dislike Khashoggi's style and distrust him. Enter Mohamed Fayed.

When Fayed first became a powerful member at court, the Sultan had just advanced $100 million to Jet Aviation, the company owned by Carl Hirschmann in Geneva, to purchase and customize a 747-SP for the royal flight. In spite of the fact that Hirschmann had bought the 747 for $34 million and made substantial commitments to sub-contractors to convert it, Fayed persuaded the Sultan that the plane would be a public relations disaster and gained his approval to cancel the contract. Unpleasant litigation resulted in which Fayed acted, for the first time on the public record, on behalf of the Sultan. Court documents describe Fayed as the Sultan's 'financial advisor and general attorney'. It was a crudely managed affair, but Fayed did get $86 million back from Hirschmann. Hirschmann was forced to settle for $10 million in damages, but the real damage was done to his working relationship with His Majesty. Jet Aviation's contract with Brunei to manage the royal flight was subsequently canceled.

Fayed's strategy was first to gain the confidence of officials in Mrs Thatcher's government and Lee Kuan Yew. They supported him in large measure because of his ability to push aside men like Khashoggi and Zobel. He indulged the Sultan in much the same way Adnan and Zobel had, but he did it less openly and, from his vantage point in London, with a greater appreciation of the world view of his patrons.

At the same time that Fayed spoke to Lee Kuan Yew about broadening the Sultan's involvement in international business and ending the corruption which surrounded His Majesty, he convinced the Sultan that Khashoggi was asking too much money for the *Nabila* and had taken usurious commissions for the jewelry purchases.

In a similar vein, while convincing the Thatcher government that he could persuade the Sultan to return the Brunei billions to British banks, Fayed encouraged the Sultan to banish Zobel by fingering him for exploitation over the building of the palace.

Finally, the Sultan felt that at last he had found someone on whom he could rely. He gave Fayed virtually anything he asked for, including control over a vast sum of his money. Fayed was convinced no one could stop him.

Similar actions convinced the Sultan that Mohamed was acting in his best interest and that he no longer wanted to be involved with Adnan and Zobel. So when Fayed suggested they open a joint bank account to facilitate quick and quiet business transactions, His Majesty agreed. Obviously, Fayed argued, the minute it became known the Sultan was the principal in any proposal, the price doubled. His Majesty needed only to be reminded that he had paid Khoo Teck Paut twice the market value for the Holiday Inn in Singapore.

The Sultan agreed to the joint account with Fayed, and transferred about $1.5 billion into it. He also signed two letters granting Fayed full authority to act on his behalf in matters of mutual business interest. And, at almost the same time, signed another document giving Fayed the ability to utilize funds from the Sultan's account with Credit Suisse, Zurich. By late 1984, Fayed virtually had a blank check on accounts at Swiss banks which generally had a balance of $5 billion. To quote Fayed himself: 'I have power of attorney. You ask His Majesty. I have power of attorney, I can do anything, anything on earth, right, I can go to the Bank. I can have 10 billion dollars if I want. You can ask him.'

Once these financial arrangements were finalized, Fayed entered into negotiations in London to purchase the Dorchester Hotel, giving every appearance he was making the offer on his own behalf. The hotel was managed by Regent International, a part owner with a consortium of other investors. Fayed proposed an attractive price, said to be £88 million, and the offer was accepted.

A few days after the deal, the press reported the actual buyer was the Sultan. Fayed insisted he had been acting for himself, but when the Sultan expressed a keen desire to be the owner, he acceded to the wish of his royal friend. Always the romantic, Mohamed revealed that the Sultan's parents had spent their holidays at the Dorchester and that His Majesty was conceived at the hotel while his parents were on their honeymoon. In what was to become a consistent pattern, the Sultan paid double the price Regent had paid six months before.

Imbued with the Sultan's confidence and an ever improving reputation in the City of London, Fayed made his boldest business move yet. This time, acting solely for himself and his brothers, he tendered £615 million in cash to purchase House of Fraser.

# – 13 –
## The Harrods Saga

An improbable series of events allowed Fayed to take control of Harrods.

Tiny Rowland had met Sir Hugh Fraser in 1977, at a moment in Fraser's life when he had decided to sell his last major asset: the controlling shares in Scottish and Universal Investments, the holding company for House of Fraser (HOF). His father had willed him the controlling shares in HOF and Sir Hugh had survived as chairman of the board more out of the board's regard for his father than his talent as a businessman. Under his leadership, the company had become unaggressive and pedestrian.

Advancing with Sir Hugh's blessings, Lonrho was able to buy 29 per cent of the stock in HOF and developed extensive plans to acquire and expand the company.

Without rehearsing all of the complications and setbacks, Lonrho's takeover aspirations were three times referred to the Monopolies and Mergers Commission for reasons which I doubt can be recalled today by the responsible ministers. Lonrho did not own other department stores so there was no monopoly issue. In addition, it was a public company with substantial funds on record so there was no question of the source of funds to be proffered or the ability to sustain and improve HOF. Five years of inquiries passed in which Lonrho honorably disclosed whatever the Commission requested. Yet, the Government made no final determination and actively prevented Lonrho from making a bid to the HOF shareholders. In late 1984, a frustrated Rowland began to consider other options.

Merrill Lynch, Hambros, and other banking firms had made unsolicited offers for the Fraser stock. Nonetheless, Tiny turned them down in favor of the bid from a little known Egyptian, Mohamed Fayed. Rowland liked the Fayed bid because he continued to hope that the Office of Fair Trading's opposition to Lonrho's takeover was grounded in some sort of logic not bias. When Mohamed Fayed first approached Tiny to buy Lonrho's shares, he explained he had the necessary funds from the Maktoum family who rule Dubai. The Fayed acquisition seemed the perfect way to place Lonrho in a position to regroup and, thereby, be released from the undertaking extracted by the Government preventing a bid. Tiny knew Fayed had no experience in the retail business and assumed he would never be deemed qualified to own House of Fraser. He also knew Mohamed was in no financial position to buy the company, so he considered it a 'safe' tactic. Fayed bought Lonrho's 29 per cent interest on 2 November 1984.

On 14 February 1985, the Monopolies and Mergers Commission finally sent their report to the Secretary for Trade and Industry, Norman Tebbit, recommending the Government back off and allow Lonrho plc to bid. Inexplicably, the Secretary of State did not act on the report. Shortly thereafter, on 4 March 1985, Fayed announced his offer to buy the remaining 61 per cent of shares in HOF, and the Fraser Board simultaneously issued a statement of support for his offering. The press notice from the Department of Trade and Industry on 14 March, stating the Fayed bid would not be referred to the Monopolies and Mergers Commission, revealed the deal had been sealed for the Fayeds. In ten days, the relatively unknown Egyptians became the owners of HOF, the most famous asset of which was the world renowned Harrods. Only after the fact did Tebbit act on the Commission's report and inform Lonrho that the restrictions against them making a full bid were withdrawn.

In the aftermath of this inexplicable development, many questions were asked. Some have been answered in this book, many are impossible to address. For example: (1) Was the political and financial establishment in the City of London so disdainful of Tiny that it prompted the Fayed bid for HOF more out of petty feelings about Tiny than an intelligent evaluation of the facts? (2) Given that Lonrho's bid had been at issue for seven years and the Monopolies and Mergers Commission had recently recommended the Government's restrictions be lifted, why would the Secretary for Trade and Industry act in such a cavalier manner?

The safe decision for Tebbit would have been to request a referral of the Fayed bid to the Commission. Had he been ordered not to make the referral? By whom? (3) We now know that virtually every claim made by Kleinwort Benson on behalf of Fayeds was false or inflated. Why would a director of Kleinwort Benson comment publicly that: 'I have got no statement of their consolidated financial position' in one breath, and state in the next: 'Their net worth from what I know is several billion dollars'? (4) Even more confounding, why would the British press, indeed the world press, accept information circulated by a public relations firm without any verification? What enabled Fayed to hypnotize the press by his publicity campaign? His generous gifts to the right charities? (5) Had Mrs Thatcher been told to instruct her ministers to look the other way in order to reclaim the Brunei billions for British banks?

Most of the old guard tried to dismiss Tiny's interest in HOF by telling each other he merely wanted to own Harrods for the status it would give him. Far from coveting Harrods, however, Rowland saw in House of Fraser an opportunity to acquire a sleeping giant. Ironically, it was Fayed who wanted only the status and had no real interest in the larger picture.

Tiny Rowland is one of the most impressive and most irascible men I have ever met. The name, Tiny, has been with him from childhood and must mislead those who have never actually seen him. He looks the image of the chief executive of a major corporation. At the age of 71 his hair is near-white, he is over 6 feet tall, trim, perfectly dressed, gruff while polite, and always in command. In his early days as head of the London-Rhodesia Mining Company (now Lonrho plc), he ruffled many of the traditional feathers in the City of London by his bold style and a willingness to deal with Third World leaders his competitors preferred to ignore.

One needs only to consult any of Lonrho's 50,000 stockholders to learn that Roland W (Tiny) Rowland made the company one of the most successful and profitable in England. To his stockholders and to many others, Tiny is a hero. Had he chosen America as his base of operation instead of the UK, he would have become a scion of American business society in a league with John Hay Whitney, J Irwin Miller, and

David Rockefeller. In the City of London, however, he was always regarded as an outsider.

Few men of Tiny's intellect and wealth are unfailingly congenial, but Tiny often seems to be intentionally off-putting. Perhaps because he was British by birth, but half educated in Germany, and certainly because he could grasp a myriad options and crunch them into a plan of action, some members of the British establishment felt uncomfortable in dealings with him. He had no difficulty advocating his position in a few precise words, but rarely couched his remarks with the niceties others used to avoid being brusque. Many felt he was disdainful of their considered views.

In addition, Tiny was free of the school ties, the social obligations and the business debts most other leaders of the City of London had to consider. He was not willing to make a poor business judgment for social reasons. Rather than sitting back in his boardroom chair and pondering a problem, he would instantly argue for a plan of action. The more successful he became, the more the old guard resented him.

Such attitudes were a minor irritation, and did not stop Rowland from becoming one of the wealthiest men in England. He bought the London *Observer* from Robert O Anderson in the late seventies. Skeptics had to eat their words when the paper became profitable!

Kleinwort Benson, the distinguished investment banking firm often engaged by the British Government in various privatization programs, represented the Fayeds in their bid for Harrods and elevated them to billionaire status with conviction. Norman Tebbit seems also to have taken the Fayeds' statements at face value in spite of evidence proffered by Lonrho. The press regurgitated the Fayed hype without any reference to a second source. And Mrs Thatcher said she was 'batting for Great Britain' when asked if there was any tie between the return of the Sultan's billions and the swift approval of the Fayed takeover of House of Fraser.

Tiny Rowland's past success, perceived arrogance and enemies in the City of London, combined with the illusion which Fayed had created of his wealth and power, not to mention the return of the Brunei billions to banks in the UK, canceled objective thought.

Also whether Tiny will admit it or not, he was being too clever by half. He took Fayed at his word and unwittingly opened the door for him to push Lonrho aside and pluck the jewel from the commercial crown. Rowland was regarded by those who truly knew him as a man of unusual ability, insight and intellect. Many thought him obstinate, but few disputed he was a man of his word. Fayed was not.

Fayed, however, underestimated the reaction and turmoil his crafty maneuverings would inspire. The City of London became obsessed with talk of the takeover. Fair-minded people began to wonder if the seemingly unexamined and startlingly sudden purchase of one of England's best known corporations by the mysterious Egyptians had been properly handled. Many old curmudgeons paused over their whisky at Whites to observe that while they might not think much of Tiny Rowland, the turn of events seemed a bit odd.

Fayed had anticipated that questions would be asked and had retained the public relations firm, Broad Street Associates, to deal with the press. The senior man at Broad Street, Brian Basham, was ready with answers to all questions. Channel 4 put forth the best summary of the press reports at that time in a recent program on the Harrod's sale, on 24 July 1988:

'Mohamed and his brothers, Ali and Salah, have climbed a commerical and social Everest since their great-grandfather, Ali Al Fayed, founded the family fortunes a century ago by growing cotton on the banks of the Nile and exporting it in his own ships to the mills of Lancashire. The origins of their wealth go back to 1876 when their grandfather began business in Egypt shipping cotton to Liverpool. The family's link with Egypt was abruptly ended when President Nasser nationalized their business. Fortunately their grandfather had begun investing in Paris and Switzerland 80 years ago and there was a major fleet of ships, Nasser got only two, carrying pilgrims and cargo around the Gulf. He delights acquaintances with recollections of an English nanny and an Egyptian education based on the British model, complete with canings.'

This was a completely false picture.

What the directors at Warburgs said about him mattered little to Tiny, but the confidence and support of his stockholders was important. For seven years he had led Lonrho's effort to acquire House of Fraser. A great deal of time and money had been spent in evaluating and planning the future of the company. Tiny felt betrayed and, in turn, felt Lonrho's stockholders had been cheated. He pressured hard for an unbiased examination of the Fayeds' claims.

Another motivation, of course, played a part in Tiny's relentless inquiry. Just as the demon of greed plagued Fayed, the demon of vengeance captured Rowland. It gave him the necessary determination to continue when almost everyone was against him.

*The Times* described what followed as: 'Tiny Tedium'. Channel 4 said that he: 'launched an increasingly obsessive £12 million campaign'.

Too often responsible observers have asked, in frustration, what difference does it make whether Fayed used his own money or not? The answer is found in UK company law and in the process which governs all takeovers in the UK. The same standards which the Government employed to prevent Lonhro from purchasing HOF should have been applied to the Fayeds. They were not.

The Fayed bid for HOF was first considered by the Office of Fair Trading (OFT). This office was established by Parliament to advise the Secretary of State for Trade and Industry whether to refer a bid to the Monopolies and Mergers Commission or to allow it to go forward. There are few specific laws on takeovers, rather, those involved must abide by an honor code which provides that no relevant information can be withheld, and that all parties to a takeover must exercise special care not to make any statements or claims which may mislead the shareholders or the market. The OFT relies on outside advise from financial firms and a full and honest disclosure from all concerned in making its recommendation to the Government.

Such scrutiny is necessary because the Government has a duty to protect the economic stability of England's major corporate entities in order to insure that jobs are not lost and that the stockholders are not unfairly compensated for their investment.

Until recently the Government had had to rely on a variety of 'toothless' sanctions to enforce any significant abuse of the process of self-regulation proscribed for mergers and acquisitions. After the highly publicized misdeeds of Ivan Boesky on Wall Street and similar less jolting revelations in the UK, the British Government recognized more enforcement powers were needed and created the Serious Frauds Office. Now, when honest disclosure and self regulation appear to have been violated, the matter is referred to the Serious Frauds Office which has well-defined statutory powers.

Mohamed Fayed and his investment bankers, Kleinwort Benson, were under an obligation to adhere to these principles in all information provided to the OFT and any other party to the transaction.

In brief, Kleinwort Benson made two essential representations about the Fayeds: (1) The money to be used in the takeover was entirely their own. (2) They had several billions of pounds at their disposal which resulted from inheritance and a vast business empire.

Mohamed's brothers, Salah and Ali, are always mentioned in public as key players in the Fayed empire. The brothers are close. Mohamed, however, is the unquestioned ruler in all matters.

Based on these crucial details, the Fayed bid for Harrods was not referred to the Monopolies and Mergers Commission. None of the claims made to the British Government was true, but it has taken a considerable effort on the part of Tiny Rowland and others for the truth to be officially investigated and publicized.


In response to Lonrho's unrelenting determination to fight on and the extensive media coverage that predictably followed, Fayed spent millions on a public relations campaign intended to inculcate his fabrications of wealth and history into the collective opinion of the British public. While professing that he valued his privacy above all else, he spent a fortune getting the 'right' mentions in the gossip columns and cultivating opinion leaders in every segment of British society.

Fayed promoted an image of his lifestyle as more English than the English. Among other things, he understood that the flamboyant Khashoggi style was disdained in London. In a society increasingly tense about Middle East oil money buying up all of its treasures and clogging Park Lane with gold Mercedes, Fayed appeared to be a 'gent'. He began to systematically contribute large sums to charity, especially those favored by the London establishment. All were impressed that he sought no recognition for his contributions. His public relations firm, of course, quietly mentioned his good deeds to friendly reporters who unfailingly publicized his generosity.

Once again, the man who told the biggest lie seemed able to confuse his family, his friends, his bankers and the press. As late as April 1988, *Town and Country* magazine was propagating the Fayed billionaire myth. Consider this: 'It is known that the Fayed family were successful cotton growers in nineteenth-century Egypt who prospered by owning the ships on which they transported the cotton to English mills.' Or this: 'Why did the ruler of Dubai give me $3 billion of business? Because he trusted me.' (A Fayed quote taken from the *Wall Street Journal*). And finally: 'British curiosity about the Fayeds' undisclosed billions rose to fever pitch when the impeccably established board of House of Fraser, plc, announced in March of 1985 that it had accepted Mohamed al-Fayed's bid to purchase the company's several hundred stores and its flagship Harrods for £615 million. The cash was available immediately. CASH? gasped the City.'

Long before the glow of the public relations blitz had begun to fade, investigative journalists returned from Egypt to report that Fayed had been born and raised in modest circumstances in Alexandria. His father was a good man and a dedicated schoolteacher, but he was not at all wealthy nor had he been remotely involved in commerce or business. Even more devastating were the well researched reports on his financial empire: (1) The Fayeds had no fleet of ships. (2) 75 Rockefeller Plaza was, predictably, owned by the Rockefeller Group, not Fayed. (3) Not only had the Ritz Hotel in Paris lost money every year since Fayed bought it in 1979, but his claim of revenues, earned from licensing the name Ritz, was laughingly denied by the makers of Ritz crackers and others as preposterous. (4) The Fayeds' 10 per cent shareholding in National Bank Shares Corporation of Texas was valued by analysts at no more than $20 million (now, of course, it is worth a good deal less). (5) No extensive interests in oil exist to support Fayed's billionaire status.

Even more troubling information was disclosed by the Fayeds' accountants: (1) When the Fayeds purchased House of Fraser in 1985, the total debt of the company was £109 million. (2) As of May 1987, hardly two years after the takeover, the debt had increased to £826 million. Simple logic dictates that an immense amount of money had been borrowed for some purpose, and in light of Kleinwort Benson's submissions, begs for an explanation. The answer is painfully obvious: there was no family money and no business empire generating billions of dollars in revenue. The Fayeds had to borrow the money to buy Harrods.

By April 1987 virtually every statement made by Kleinwort Benson on behalf of the Fayeds had been convincingly challenged by investigators and journalists examining the Egyptians' categoric statements. A general election was approaching and the new Secretary of State for Trade and Industry, Paul Channon, prudently appointed Inspectors to look into the takeover.

By the usual odd set of circumstances, I was a witness before the Inspectors looking into the matter of the Harrods takeover on 6 October 1987. I appeared, under oath, before Henry Brooke QC and Hugh Aldous, and explained the circumstances by which the tapes of a conversation between Fayed and the Swami were made.

The tapes disclose that Fayed used the power of attorney granted him by the Sultan of Brunei to borrow the money to purchase Harrods. They also offer a unique glimpse of the methods of the men I profile. How the tapes came to be made is discussed in Chapter 16. A transcript is reprinted in full in the Appendix.

The Inspectors' 15-month investigation produced a 750-page record on the Fayeds and the takeover. On 23 July 1988 the document was forwarded to Lord Young, and almost immediately referred to the Serious Frauds Office.

As late as 16 September and on many prior occasions, Lord Young stated the Inspectors' report would be published as soon as possible. Then on 25 November, a full four months into the six month statutory period the law allows for a referral to be made to the MMC, Young announced the takeover would not be referred and that the report would not be published.

Lonrho had watched months pass with only vague promises from the Government to press ahead. Unwilling to let years of hard work be cavalierly brushed aside, Lonrho initiated proceedings for judicial review of the Government's actions.

On 17 January 1989 Lord Justice Watkins of the High Court, the second ranking criminal judge in the United Kingdom, ordered Young to refer the takeover to the MMC and to reconsider his decision not to publish the report immediately. 'No reasonable Minister could have reached the decision which he did,' stated Lord Justice Watkins.

Inevitably, the Fayeds and Lord Young appealed the decision. On 20 January the Court of Appeal reversed the decision of the High Court, but let stand the final appeal to the House of Lords thus preserving the MMC referral if upheld by the Law Lords. This book will be published before they have handed down their decision.

Reading the opinions of the two courts on the HOF takeover, causes this American writer and lawyer to believe there has been a coverup. It is impossible not to speculate that the British power structure is determined to keep the truth of the circumstances which allowed the Fayed takeover from being publicly acknowledged and acted upon by the Government.

In overturning the ruling of the High Court, Lord Justice Dillon of the Court of Appeal stated: 'The mere fact that there was fraud in the course of a merger operation might require in the public interest that the fraud be punished, but it would not necessarily follow that the creation of the merger situation had operated or might be expected to operate against the public interest.' Never before has a distinguished judge suggested that fraud might be in the public interest. It is tantamount to stating that it is necessary to punish the criminal, but the rights of the victim are not important.

Mr John Mummery, Counsel for Lord Young, told the Court of Appeal the present system of references to the MMC would break down if the High Court's ruling prevailed. 'Instead of only 11 out of a possible 260 cases in 1988, if there had to be 250 references, the system just would not work,' he argued. Such reasoning must encourage and instruct those who wish to engage in corporate mergers intended to harm the public. Can he be advising sinister foreign interests to wait until at least twelve referrals have been made before they push ahead in their bid to monopolize and corrupt certain sectors of the British economy?

The specter of the Director General of the OFT, Sir Gordon Borrie, looms over this entire matter. He has been at the center of the dispute from the outset. Since his advice has been followed from Lonrho's initial involvement with HOF in 1977 until the present, at great expense to the Treasury and the credibility of the Government, one has to wonder why Lord Young did not ask him to step aside after receiving the Inspectors' report. They had given the matter a fresh examination and found substantial undisclosed material facts. Would it not have been sensible for Lord Young to seek advice from someone whose career status was not grounded in past judgments and might offer an unbiased opinion?

Finally, few in Great Britain have not heard the allegations against the Fayeds. ITV's Channel 4 ran a devastating 30-minute documentary disputing every claim they made to the Government. The *Observer* and countless other media outlets have published articles about the Fayed deceptions. Tiny Rowland's book, *A Hero From Zero*, documents the Fayed lies in great detail and has been read by over 100,000 people. Even the Sultan was reported to have said he thought it possible Fayed used his power of attorney to further his own business interests.

How could publication of the Inspectors' report interfere with the work of the SFO?

Whatever the Law Lords call it, in my mind it will always be called **Harrodsgate**.

'Followers of the House of Fraser marathon will doubtless be puzzled as to why the innocent Pharoah of Harrods, Mohamed Fayed, and his brothers are so keen to see the DTI report into their 1985 takeover published that they went to court to support the delay imposed by Lord Suit, upheld by the Court of Appeal, while it is considered by the Serious Fraud Office.

It may also not be immediately apparent why the Fayeds, who deny any wrongdoing, have demanded 72 hours' advance notification of publication and have protested about the inspectors exceeding their remit.

It is no doubt entirely unrelated to those perfectly justified responses that the normal DTI policy – courtesy of Cap'n Bob's distressing experience all those years ago – is for the inspectors to provide those they intend to criticise with an outline or draft of their proposed criticisms prior to finalising their report.'

*Private Eye*, 3 February 1989

# – 14 –
## An Audience with the Sultan

By the beginning of 1985, the Sultan had become a personal reference point in much the same way aspiring to the presidency had been in my earlier years. I was excited by the prospect of representing him in America. He was young, he was new on the world scene, and he had the financial freedom to do virtually anything.

The Swami had always attributed his relationship with the Sultan to the visit I had arranged with the Marcoses in Manila where he had met Zobel. He had promised to deliver the Brunei account as compensation for my time and effort on his behalf.

In late March 1985, Mamaji rang from Delhi to convey the encouraging news that the Sultan had requested a meeting. As usual, Mamaji overstated the situation, but none the less, the bottom line was what mattered. The details had been worked out, and I was to join the Swami and the Sultan in Singapore the following week.

The possibility of becoming the Sultan's representative appeared within reach, and the excellent travel arrangements seemed further indication that His Majesty meant business. The journey, however, did not proceed as planned.

Before I could unpack my suitcase and settle in at Singapore's Royal Holiday Inn, I was hustled into a waiting limousine. Within minutes I was on another Singapore Air flight to Djakarta. Mamaji apologized

101

for the sudden departure (we were late for the plane) and explained that the royal meeting had been delayed for a week during which time we were to rest in Bali as the Sultan's guests.

After an uneventful night in the capital of Indonesia, we departed the next day for Bali, the 2,220 square-mile island in the Lesser Sundas of East Indonesia. On arrival, we were whisked by waiting cars to the Nusa Dua Beach Hotel, Bali's grandest.

One week at the Nusa Dua in Bali is hardly punishment. On the other hand, spending a week with the Swami, Mamaji, Ernie, and two Indian disciples was hard work.

During the course of our 'holiday', the Swami managed to traverse the island like a candidate for office. With our group in tow, he called upon the Governor, made several speeches to school groups, and participated in an enormous Hindu festival at the top of Bali's highest mountain. The point of all this was lost on me, but the Swami seemed to have a terrific time and everyone in Bali seemed glad to see him. At our departure, the Swami disclosed the Governor had formulated plans to build an ashram for him in Bali where he would reside for two or three months a year offering prayers for the citizens. Swamiji seemed more than enthusiastic about the idea and, for all I know, the Governor was serious as well.

En-route back to Singapore, we were required to change planes at the new international airport in Djakarta. The stop-over, scheduled for thirty minutes, took ten hours.

President Suharto had just ordered all air traffic to be directed to the newly constructed airport. He had insisted it be opened months before it was ready, because several leaders of Third World countries were to arrive for the Non-Aligned Nation's Conference of which he was the current chairman. Nothing worked.

Every eye followed an Arab with four wives and at least twenty children, respond to the gate changes. Their flight was scheduled to depart from gate 20, then gate 40, then gate 32, and finally canceled because the plane had obviously been lost on the runway. At every announcement, the attentive father would round up his wives and children and herd them to the next area. All were dressed in the pale blue chowdars and chattering at an increasingly higher pitch.

In the midst of all this confusion, Ernie and I exchanged our first civilized words. Jokingly, I remarked that if the Swami had his own jet, we would not have been in this predicament. Ernie looked at me with great interest and inquired: 'How does owning your own plane work?' It was a notion that clearly had never before occurred to him. Casually,

I explained what was required and offered to put him in contact with a dealer in the US. I have a vague recollection of Ernie calling my Washington office a few weeks later, and remember flipping through the files to give him the name of a friend who brokered the sale of private airplanes, but beyond that I gave it little thought.

Within months, the Swami was traveling the world in a Falcon 50 jet. The plane was managed by Ernie, but was always at the guru's disposal. The Swami never waited ten hours for a commercial flight again.

Another two days passed in Singapore before the meeting with the Sultan actually took place. I was instructed not to leave the hotel because the Sultan might arrive any minute and I must be prepared whenever the call came. Never before or since have I had such a perfect suntan. Finally, on the third day, Mamaji rang to announce that bin Isa, the Sultan's top aide, was coming to escort me to the Sultan's quarters.

Proper names in Brunei read a bit like a 'thank you' speech at an awards dinner. They include a reference to everyone in the individual's genealogy. Bin Isa's proper name was always listed in official documents as: Pehin Orang Kaya Laila Setia Bakti Di-Raja Dato Laila Utama Haji Awang Isa bin Pehin Datu Perdana Menteri Dato Laila Utama Haji Awang Ibrahim.

Bin Isa had been a close advisor to His Majesty for years and looked every inch the careful manager of royal affairs. He had a slim build, appeared middle-aged, and wore wire framed glasses. He always wore a communications' plug in his ear which enabled him to interact with the master security control. Isa greeted me with the aloofness I now associate with everyone near the Sultan, and asked me to accompany him. From my room on the tenth floor, we took the elevator to the lobby, walked across the hall and, after a special key had been inserted in the elevator door and the communication system had flashed various clearance messages, we entered the Sultan's elevator. The doors parted in seconds to allow entry to the royal quarters on the third floor.

The guest rooms and public rooms at the Royal Holiday Inn are green – Holiday Inn green – green walls, green carpets, green chairs, and green bedspreads. Suddenly, I found myself in an exquisite, luxury apartment decorated in beige, salmon and gray. I had an instant flashback to Happy and Nelson Rockefeller's apartment at 812 Fifth Avenue. This was a classy piece of interior design where no expense had been spared.

Bin Isa motioned toward the main sitting room. Upon entering, I was summarily introduced and invited to sit on a sofa adjacent to His

103

Majesty. The Sultan was wearing what I came to refer to as his 'royal Ralph Lauren' attire, a polo shirt and designer jeans. He never really looked me in the eyes, nor did we seem to connect in a personal way. Yet, I had the odd feeling that he felt more relaxed in my company. The Swami and Mamaji had a heavy, unrelenting aura about them in the presence of a VIP. They labored at being men of stature and wisdom. The language barrier, too, lessened any real chance for glib repartee. Whenever I teased the Swami or restated his often doctrinaire phrases in simple English, the Sultan's eyes twinkled. His response gave me a glimmer of hope that we might become friends.

As usual, the Swami or Mamaji did most of the talking. The Swami told His Majesty I was a powerful Washington lawyer with friends of great influence around the world. Mamaji then interjected that I was anxious to help better the Sultan's image in America, and that both the Swami and he recognized I was an expert in public relations. They seemed to be saying I had done a great deal of work for the Sultan already, implying it was just a matter of his consent to continue an effort well underway.

When I tried to put their comments in perspective by explaining that nothing had been done as yet, the Swami interrupted by saying: 'His Majesty does not want to hear these modest words, he wants your support and your help.' I remember giving the Sultan a frustrated, round-eyed glance to which he responded with a 'don't worry' hand gesture.

Before the meeting, Mamaji had warned that the Sultan was likely to offer a gift of great value and that it must be refused. This gesture would demonstrate I was not interested in his money, but truly wanted to be a friend and advisor. Since I had been sunning by the pool before being called to the Sultan's quarters, I had forgotten to wear my wrist watch. Remarking on this, the Sultan removed what looked to be a classic Piaget watch worth about $100,000 from his arm and insisted I take it and wear it. As instructed, I declined his generous gift by saying it would not be right to accept such a treasure at our first meeting. Both of us were impressed by my lack of greed.

Nothing of consequence was said in this first meeting. After twenty minutes, it was over. The Sultan's final words were: 'You must visit my country before long.'

Returning to my green room, I waited and waited until Mamaji rang after three hours with his report. Mamaji never spoke rapidly and rarely expressed excitement or anger. In his usual, frustrating style he monotoned: 'His Holiness is still with His Majesty. They are both thankful you were able to be with them. His Majesty is impressed with your sincerity. He requests that you return next month for another meeting. We will inform you of the details in two weeks time. His Holiness understands you have been neglecting your work in Washington and has instructed that you may now return on this evening's flight. The hotel has made all of the necessary arrangements. All has gone very well. You have His Majesty's gratitude and His Holiness's blessings. Good bye.'

I returned in the same grand fashion: first class on Singapore Airlines to London and Concorde to Washington. While I had been treated royally, the audience was frustrating. Nothing of substance had been discussed. In the end, a good client rightly wondered why he was paying my fledgling firm a retainer when I was off chasing a pot of gold and terminated his contract.

Many is the night I did not sleep pondering this coveted opportunity the Swami had orchestrated. I was aware that others had sought and been denied such a moment.

Suddenly, the office telephones rang with strange requests for an appointment. Proposals for business deals turned up in the daily mail with promises of large commissions if the Sultan could be persuaded to invest in them. Even local Washington friends invited me to lunch to request assistance in a matter they hoped would be of interest to His Majesty.

Less enjoyable was the negative campaign initiated by men like Fayed who wanted to limit the Sultan's circle of friends. I chose to ignore the weird telephone calls and threatening letters. They increased my determination not to give up.

Months before this sojourn, appointments had been scheduled in May 1985 with the directors of ITC Ltd (The Indian Tobacco Company) to formulate plans for ITC to participate in a joint Indo-US commercial venture. A group of American doctors of Indian origin had agreed to finance an Indian restaurant in New York which would be designed, staffed and managed by ITC. The doctors were all disciples of the Swami's and he had suggested I be retained for the project. ITC is a well-regarded corporation in India with interests not only in tobacco, but in luxury hotels among other holdings. It was the first tangible retainer I had landed out of my efforts on behalf of the Swami and it was reassuring to know that his recommendation had been taken seriously.

The ITC meetings in Calcutta and in Delhi went well. This was my first foray in India without the Swami and Mamaji hovering about. The trip was strictly business. I arrived on 29 April and was planning to return on 1 May. By this time, I had become an expert at traveling around the world on a day's notice and managing to shuffle appointments in Washington in a way which made it seem I had never left.

Three hours before the scheduled departure from Delhi, an emissary of the Swami asked to meet in the lobby of the Moraya Sheraton. He brought news that His Majesty had requested a meeting in Singapore the next day. The Swami and Mamaji would expect me at the appointed hour. All of the necessary arrangements had been made, he whispered as he handed me a schedule and the plane tickets. I did not even bother to ask the man his name or to inquire further. It was not that he seemed particularly mysterious, but I had finally learned these messengers were never told or dared to ask the purpose of their assignment.

Once again, I checked into the Royal Holiday Inn never really seeing or sensing anything of Singapore. Happily, this meeting with His Majesty took place as scheduled. On 2 May, bin Isa appeared and directed me to a tightly guarded suite on the tenth floor. There was no explanation for this change of venue, but I guessed the royal floor was occupied with children or other guests. At any event, His Majesty, the Swami, and Princess Mariam were waiting inside. This time, the atmosphere was more open and relaxed. And when the Sultan expressed his gratitude for my efforts on his behalf, I knew he was referring to a recent proposal on Brunei's involvement with the ASEAN nations I had prepared after our first meeting.

The Sultan was about to become chairman of the ASEAN nations (it is a rotating position) and I had hoped to convince him of the importance of his leadership, especially in aiding the non-communist forces loyal to Prince Norodom Sihanouk. The freedom fighters in Kampuchea would have been encouraged and sustained by his financial support. Further, his world image could have been enhanced by tilting toward Sihanouk and away from the dreaded Khmer Rouge guerrillas led by Pol Pot.

Within minutes, it was clear I had lost the attention of everyone present. The Swami changed the subject with an odd reference to Rajiv Gandhi. Pictures were taken. Once again, I departed totally confused and, this time, discouraged.

The Swami and Mamaji appeared in Washington the following week. For the first time, Mamaji disclosed the roster of the key players and the other critical elements involved in the contest for the Sultan's favour.

From their vantage point, Mohamed Fayed was the major obstacle. He had succeeded in limiting Khashoggi's and Zobel's access to the Sultan. Naturally he was worried that the Swami sought to usurp his position. As evidence of his malice, Mamaji warned that Fayed had begun to spread rumors and lies about me. The Swami rocked in his chair and commented: 'Yes, terrible man.'

The Swami's advocate at court was Princess Mariam. Whenever Fayed or another detractor made scurrilous remarks about us to His Majesty, the Princess did all she could to redress the balance. As far as I could tell, the Sultan still regarded the Swami as his brother and continued to speak with him on the telephone daily. Mamaji said that the next few weeks and months would be critical.

At that, the Swami entreated: 'You must get me an appointment with the Vice President tomorrow!'

As diplomatically as possible, I explained that such an appointment required weeks to secure. The Vice President saw no one from a foreign country without routine background checks on their credentials with the Department of State and the National Security Council. And, even without these formidable obstacles, I was hamstrung. The central question any appointment secretary asks is: 'What is the reason for your request?' Maa Goddess Bhagwath herself could not have prevailed upon the Vice President's staff for such a meeting.

Giving the Swami bad news was pure misery. 'No, no, you must make this meeting for tomorrow,' he mumbled, frowning. Again, I summarized why his request was out of the question.

After an aching silence, he groused: 'You told me you could introduce me to Bush.' To my honest, stern reply: 'Now, Swamiji, you know that is not true. *You* told me that I could introduce you to the Vice President. I never made such a statement,' the guru rose and stormed out of the room.

Finally, Mamaji expressed my dilemma to the Swami in Hindi with my apologies and the reminder that even the meetings I had been able to arrange in the Philippines and elsewhere had taken weeks. 'Now you know what cannot be done, let me tell you what can when we meet tomorrow,' I sighed. With that, I beat a hasty retreat. The hotel suite was jammed with people waiting to see him.

The prevailing atmosphere in the Swami's room the following day was totally different. The Swami never expressed regret at his temper tantrums, but at least they passed quickly. His interest had been drawn to what could be done to strengthen his hand and convince His Majesty that Fayed was merely being vindictive.

For months I had been touting the need for an association of Americans and Americans of Indian origin to promote better relations between India and the United States. The Swami had shown passive interest, but demonstrated little real enthusiasm. Finally, however, he began to appreciate the enhanced stature he would gain by directing his influence and his disciples toward this goal. A knowing look suffused his face when I explained the immediate value of the project. 'Very good,' he said. 'I understand. You know that this is what I have wanted all along. Tell me what you need and I will take care of it.'

To his credit, the Swami kept his word and persuaded his followers to support and fund the initial work of the Council on Indo-US Relations.

The Fayed chicanery, however, demanded action. While my first impulse was to ignore the falsehoods, I recognized the Sultan needed something positive from the Swami. So I decided to organize a few courtesy calls on friends in the higher levels of the US Government to demonstrate I was not *persona non grata* in Washington.

The Swami and Mamaji took to this idea at once and agreed to the ground rules: (1) no hocus-pocus, (2) no requests for another, in-depth meeting, (3) no mention of the Sultan, and (4) no more than 15 minutes.

The vision of the black-haired Swami in white robes, walking with a cane, Mamaji in his Gandhi topi hat and chudi dhar trousers, and me in my sincere blue suit leading them down the halls of Congress was unforgettable. The expressions on the faces of Senator Claiborne Pell (the chairman of the Senate Foreign Relations Committee), Senator Donald Riegle (a ranking member of the Senate Banking Committee), and John Block (the Secretary of Agriculture at the time), were priceless. God only knows what they said as we walked out the door.

# – 15 –

## A Critical Period for the Con Men

---

While the Swami was glad-handing the great and the near great of Washington to prove to the Sultan he had friends in high places, Khashoggi was winging his way to Brunei to see His Majesty, hoping against hope to save his crumbling financial empire. At about the same time, Fayed had purchased HOF and had become the owner of Harrods. Under constant attack by the media, he categorically denied he had used the Sultan's money to make possible his astonishing coup. In less than two years, Khashoggi would be undone by his commercial adventurism, Fayed would find himself under investigation by the Serious Frauds Office, and the Swami would trip over his own feet in his climb to the top, but, for now, each was still 'going for the gold'.

Khashoggi founded Triad America in Salt Lake City in 1974. The name Triad refers to the three Khashoggi brothers who owned the company world-wide, Adnan, Essam and Adil. Essam eventually was made the chairman of Triad America and moved to Santa Barbara, California, to run the company on a day to day basis. Unfortunately, Essam was basically uninterested in managing the business, and allowed himself to be dominated by Adnan. Adil, Adnan's smart younger brother, was born in 1936. He lives primarily in Riyadh with his wife Aida, and left Adnan years ago to start his own business.

By an improbable turn of events in March 1986 the Swami and Adnan persuaded me to spend three weeks at Triad America in Salt Lake City. It was a moment of crisis for Triad. The assignment was to do a 'quick and dirty' examination of the company's problems. No one was to know the real purpose of my mission, I was not empowered to make any decisions, and by this time I knew I would be lucky even to be reimbursed for my expenses. But the assignment was irresistible. It seemed a perfect opportunity to finally piece together how Khashoggi managed to parlay millions into billions.

In a matter of days, the answer had become obvious. Khashoggi had come to Utah heralded as the Saudi billionaire with a special affinity for the Mormon Church. Working closely with the community, AK proposed a plan to build an international trade center adjacent to the Salt Lake airport and a multi-purpose skyscraper with twin towers in an area of the city which badly needed rebuilding. He pledged over a million dollars to charity, made significant investments to other projects in the city, and, in short order, overwhelmed the people of Utah with his wealth and generosity. The city fathers were thrilled to work with this billionaire who cared about their 'promised valley'.

AK did invest several million dollars in downpayments on land and seed money for Triad projects in Utah. Triad America was launched with great fanfare in 1974.

In the first few years, Adnan kept his promises. The international center was built and the first tower of the Triad twin towers was completed. The Triad Center was the largest development ever undertaken in Utah. The compound housed retail stores, an outdoor amphitheater, an ice skating rink, five theaters, restaurants, skywalks, plazas and parking. Countless trusting people mortgaged their homes to lease space and open a restaurant or retail store in the new building. Contractors committed millions to procure steel beams and other equipment necessary to build the second tower.

Basking in the glow of what was touted as another billion dollar investment, Khashoggi systematically borrowed money from major banking and insurance institutions pledging Triad America assets. Travelers Insurance, First Boston Financial, and others never doubted for a moment that Mr Khashoggi's word alone was sufficient collateral, but were pleased with the added security of the Utah properties.

The money from these loans barely passed through Triad. Adnan drained every million possible for other purposes. It all happened so fast that routine audits did not matter. Creditors, suppliers, contractors and employees were left holding an empty bag.

Even as Triad declared bankruptcy under Chapter 11 of the US Code in early 1987, Khashoggi initiated a scheme to transfer Edgington Oil, the only solvent asset remaining in Triad, to a Canadian corporation out of the jurisdiction of the US Courts. The stock transfer was blocked by a watchful Utah judge, but he could not alter the damage done to Salt Lake City or to the countless numbers of small investors in the Triad debacle.

Not only did the Salt Lake City development include the International Center, a business and industrial park west of the airport, and the downtown Triad Center, in addition Triad purchased 900 acres of commercial property, including the Sheraton Hotel, a small trolly company, and half ownership of the NBA, Utah basketball team. Outside of Utah, Triad America owned properties in Texas and Florida, Edgington Oil Company in Long Beach (a heavy-products refinery), Triad Aviation (an aircraft refueling company), and Agrifuels Refining Corporation (a synthetics fuel plant in New Iberia, Louisiana).

Adnan did everything imaginable in Salt Lake City to live up to his legend. Even when Triad was at a particularly low ebb in June 1984, facing disgruntled creditors, less than 30 per cent occupancy in the downtown office building, and constant complaints that construction on the second tower, announced in 1982, had not begun, he continued the bluff. Seemingly unaware of impending disaster, Khashoggi flew in friends from around the world to be present when he announced plans for even greater expansion. Eyes filling with tears, he also disclosed his intention to donate $1.2 million to the LDS Hospital for the construction of an international center for medical education in honor of his father.

All of this commotion brought Adnan time to try to find investors willing to keep Triad America from going under.

Although Fayed had advised the Sultan against allowing Adnan into Brunei, His Majesty consented to receive him and other Triad officers in late March 1985. After all, the Sultan had known AK for years and retained fond memories of their carousing about the clubs of London. Fayed's heavy handed attitude toward anyone who came near the Sultan may have begun to annoy His Majesty.

The Sultan knew the two men loathed each other. He may have relished the chance to toss a little sand in Fayed's face by seeing Khashoggi. Entering into a joint business venture with Adnan was another matter, however.

As best he could, Khashoggi pitched a deal in which he and the Sultan would own Triad America as equal partners in return for the Sultan's investment of $300 million. Triad executives, led by Emanuel Floor, a

111

Utah native and an experienced administrator, gave an intelligent if somewhat optimistic appraisal of the company and its potential. The Sultan was pleasant, but definitely not interested.

When the two were alone, the Sultan quizzed Adnan on a recent report from his accountants which revealed Khashoggi was long overdue on the interest payments negotiated upon his return of the *Nabila*.

As mentioned above, the Sultan tentatively purchased the yacht during the independence celebrations in February 1984 for $90 million. Six months later, he informed AK he did not want it. Fayed and others had convinced him the price was three times the worth of the yacht. Unable to pay back the $50 million, Adnan persuaded the Sultan to agree to allow him to pay interest only for two years and then refund the down payment. By this time, however, Adnan's situation had deteriorated to the point where he could not even make the interest payments, and the Sultan had begun to tire of his excuses. Finally, His Majesty repossessed the *Nabila* and entrusted it to Fayed to sell. Few people could afford or would even want such a white elephant. In the end Donald Trump bought it for $29 million and he named it the *Trump Princess*.

Unquestionably it was not Adnan's day. He never saw the Sultan again after that summit, although it was not for lack of trying.

The story of Triad America is the story of Khashoggi in lurid red. He used the company to enhance his billionaire image and as a vehicle to eclipse his increasingly desperate financial plight from his family, his friends and creditors.

Audited reports on Triad America indicate that during the period from 1972 to 1984, Khashoggi put $117 million in cash into the company. During that same period, he withdrew $90 million which he either invested elsewhere or squandered. It is also a matter of record that he pledged stock in the company to borrow an additional $53 million. His net investment, therefore, was several million short of his withdrawals and loans. None of this includes unpaid fuel bills to Triad Aviation (the bills often went over $3 million per month) or funds purportedly moved out of Edgington Oil.

Khashoggi also used Triad America to take advantage of the US Government's program which offered incentives to corporations engaged in the production of synthetic fuels. The Department of Energy, in a competitive review, selected the Triad Agrifuels Refining Corporation's application over several others and guaranteed a $73 million loan to the company. Headlines like 'US Government Loans $73 Million to Saudi Billionaire' caused quite a stir in the halls of Congress, but soon faded as terrorists bombed civilian targets in Lebanon, took innocent people hostage, and threatened them with death until the free world responded to their demands. The loan guarantee to Triad may have been the first time Khashoggi made the US Government a laughingstock. But as Irangate proved, it would not be the last.

As noted, Triad America filed for bankruptcy under Chapter 11 of the US Code in January 1987. This section of the bankruptcy law provides that all of the company's assets are placed under the control of a judge and his appointed trustee allowing the company to either reorganize and start over, or to work out a settlement with the creditors once the assets have been liquidated. Adnan, of course, tried every ploy imaginable to side-step the law. By this time, however, his creditors had exploded the Khashoggi myth. Not only did they persuade the court to block an ingenious exchange of stock with a Canadian company intended to move Edgington Oil out of the jurisdiction of the court, but the trustee also sued Khashoggi for $1 billion in California after he accidentally discovered that Northrop had finally settled a claim Khashoggi had filed against the company in 1976.

At the peak of Adnan's financial success, the Saudi ministers became fed up with stories in the world press about the outrageous commissions paid to foreign agents. On 15 September 1975, Saudi Decree 1565 was issued which essentially ended Khashoggi's and countless others' seemingly limitless incomes. The decree outlawed commissions paid on the sale of arms to Saudi Arabia and stated unequivocally that the Saudis would not deal with foreign corporations who paid them. Northrop wanted to continue to do business with the Saudis and also saw the decree as an opportunity to stop payment on fees owed to Adnan from pending contracts. An agreement to perform an illegal act is not a contract enforceable by the courts. Northrop executives told Khashoggi the party was over.

Khashoggi had filed suit against Northrop in 1976, seeking commissions due him for houses and airplane parts he had brokered to the Saudis. He argued the money was still due since it did not result from arms sales. The matter languished in the courts and in arbitration until July 1988, when a $47 million settlement was finally mandated by the judge.

The Utah trustee in bankruptcy moved quickly to petition the California court to freeze the $47 million and prevailed. Adnan was forced to bargain. The Triad creditors were well served. Secured creditors will get 90 cents on the dollar, unsecured creditors will get 40 cents. It must have pained Adnan to be forced to even partially honor a debt. Normally that money would have been used to pay loans made against his personal holdings such as the DC-8 or the villa in Marbella.

For a man who had always been lucky, Adnan had to deal with a series of brutal set-backs. The overthrow of President Numeiry of Sudan prevented him from brokering the country's natural resources and cost him $50 million. His old school chum, the King of Jordan, no longer spoke to him after learning he had tried to exploit their friendship. The Triad offices in Beirut had been irreparably bombed. A Federal court in New York recently indicted him on obstruction of justice and racketeering. The allegation was that AK forged documents to claim buildings owned by former president Marcos had been sold to him before the President was exiled. And, now he had lost the Northrop money.

The LDS Hospital in Salt Lake City did receive $300,000 on Khashoggi's pledge of $1.2 million, but was left in the lurch when the other funds were not forthcoming. The sign reading: 'The Dr Mohamed Khaled Khashoggi Center For International Education', has been quietly removed.

# – 16 –
## The Secret Tapes

Working with Swamiji, Mamaji and Miller was an impossible challenge. They never planned ahead, had no understanding of organization or protocol, and, if a decision was made, nothing prevented them from reversing it the next day. I tended to chalk this behavior up to cross-cultural differences. My staff always referred to them as 'those flakes'.

Soon after I had met the Swami, we had discussed the formation of the Council on Indo-US Relations. The Swami promised to help raise the funds necessary to float the Council from his disciples. My task was to put the group together and publish a magazine tribute to Indian Prime Minister Rajiv Gandhi to commemorate his first State visit to the US on 12 June 1985.

The founding members of the Council included Senator Charles Percy, Zubin Mehta, Senator William Cohen, Zbigniew Brzezinski, Senator Donald Riegle, Paige Rense, Ambassador Robert Goheen . . . and others of influence who cared about India. The magazine, *India*, was taking shape nicely. I had been invited to the State Department lunch for the Prime Minister and to the White House the night of the President's dinner. The Festival of India exhibition was to open at the National Gallery of Art, and the director, J Carter Brown, had asked for the names of the members of the Council to be included at the official reception, also attended by the Prime Minister.

The full extent of Fayed's deceptions was not known to me in June 1985. What information I had on Fayed had been given to me by the Swami. In my mind he was a vague figure seeking to keep us from working with the Sultan.

Suddenly, on 3 June, Swamiji rang to advise it was essential I come to London to meet with His Majesty. The last thing I needed at this moment was a trip to London. There simply was too much to be done in Washington. The Swami, as usual, was adamant.

I had been told the Sultan was paying for the trip, but later discovered Ernie Miller had pre-paid the ticket. The Swami was always doing this kind of thing. I recognize now it was to reinforce my impression of him as a 'man-of-god-without-worldly-goods'. While I was beginning to have my doubts, I continued to see the good in these adventures. After all, who else would have introduced me to the richest man on earth?

5 June was a bright morning. I walked over to the apartment the Indians had rented at 1 Carlos Place, across the street from the Connaught Hotel. To my surprise, it was an elegant two-bedroom flat with a large sitting room. The Swami informed everyone the Sultan was picking up the tab for this spacious pad, and all who entered were duly impressed. The public room was filled with about twenty of the Swami's disciples and servants, but at least in this flat one could breathe, and the smell of curry was not omnipresent.

Swamiji and Mamaji were talking to one of his most loyal disciples in England, Yogesh Mehta. Mehta was a prosperous middle-class businessman, the owner of a moving and storage company in north London. Like most of the non-resident Indians who became disciples of the Swami, Yogesh was ambitious and went out of his way to accommodate the Swami. He saw Swamiji as his ticket to fortune. No doubt he was promised a future deal with the Sultan as well. Dr Reddy from Madras also was present. Later, I learned that Dr Reddy had actually rented the flat.

Whenever I entered a room like this, the Swami would introduce me to everyone as his 'brother' from Washington. Each person had a son who desired acceptance at Harvard, a daughter with a visa problem, or some other US-related concern. The Swami promised I would take care of it. I explained I could make no promises, but would try. After the introductions, we would seclude ourselves in his room to go over whatever he felt important at the time.

Once alone, the Swami handed me a photocopy of a letter from Washington addressed to Fayed. He said Fayed had given it to the Sultan who had, in turn, given it to him. The letterhead had been blanked out and I had heard it all before from the Swami, but it still made chilling reading. Apparently Mohamed Fayed, fearing he might lose control of the Sultan, had commissioned a report on my background. As they were unable to dig up any real dirt, they had invented quite a list.

The report repeated the assertion I was Jewish. Obviously this was Fayed's way of putting me down before the Sultan who is very pro-Palestinian. It was stupid of Fayed, however, because while he may be anti-Semitic, the Sultan is not. Further, His Majesty knew I had been born and raised a Christian, and had on one occasion questioned me about the Mormon Church. The second paragraph said I had been arrested for criminal activities and was about to be disbarred.

The entire document was so transparently ridiculous, I told the Swami to drop the matter. But then, I began to wonder. Would the Sultan take it seriously? Knowing what I did of His Majesty's attention span and isolation, I became increasingly worried. He might not double check the facts. The usual nonsensical discussion rambled on between the Swami, Mamaji and me over what to do about the letter until we were interrupted by the ringing of the telephone.

I was standing nearest, so I answered and, to my utter amazement, a voice on the line identified himself as Mohamed Al-Fayed. In a low, raspy voice, he asked to speak to the Swami or to Mamaji. The room became silent as I handed the telephone to Mamaji whispering: 'It is Fayed. What does he want from us?' Mamaji spoke for about three minutes, hung up, and with the greatest of glee announced that Fayed wanted to meet with the Swami. An appointment had been arranged at the Carlos Place apartment the following day.

'Aha! You see!' chortled the Swami, with his hand on my shoulder. 'Your friend, Fayed, the man who says these evil things about you, is now coming to see me. He knows I control the Sultan and he needs my help. This very good for us! You may go now, but you must be here tomorrow before Fayed arrives. I will introduce you and make you friends. Good news for us!'

I was flabbergasted by the entire episode. The Swami had met Fayed and his brothers, Salah and Ali, several years earlier. He even displayed a rather shabby photograph of them in his ever present photo album. From what I know they were not, however, closely allied or even in frequent contact.

The Swami spent several hours daily on the telephone conferring with his friends and contacts around the world. One could be kept waiting for hours while he took telephone calls from P V Narasimha Rao, at

117

that time the Defense Minister of India, or placed a call to the (now deceased) Chief Minister of Tamil Nadu, M G Ramachandran. They would talk endlessly in their native Hindi language, and afterward, the Swami would comment (usually while belching or farting, which he did with great regularity): 'Very important disciple of mine, very important person.' Clearly this was done for the benefit of the assembled followers, but it also substantiated his claim of influence over the faces in the photo album. Fayed had been removed from his call list. I had been warned that Fayed considered the Swami a crook. To the best of my knowledge, this was the first time the Swami had heard from Fayed in over six months.

From various sources, Fayed learned the Sultan and the Swami were meeting frequently. A young head of state who controls over $40 billion has few secrets. Every move he made, everyone he saw, everything he did, flashed like an electric shock around his world. Current intelligence among the jet-setters and rug traders suggested the Swami now controlled the Sultan.

Fayed's call confirmed that the Swami had managed to put himself in the middle of the international incident centering around the Sultan, Fayed, Tiny Rowland and the Thatcher government. As previously discussed, the Sultan was young, inexperienced, and going through a difficult period with his father, brother and wives. The poor man could not walk out of his $600 million palace without someone trying to take him on a million dollar ride, as with Khashoggi's yacht or the 747 jet. The Swami maintained he was not like the rest. He was not interested in money. As the Sultan's spiritual advisor, he would counsel on whom to trust and whom to avoid. He also had promised the Sultan that Princess Mariam would give him another male heir . . .

The Swami made much of this with the people close to the Sultan, with Zobel, and with his own followers. True or not, at this moment in June the key players believed the prediction.

Fayed had made a bold business coup in his takeover of HOF, but he had failed to estimate the degree of public and press reaction that would result.

The Sultan hates negative publicity of any kind. When stories began to appear about the palace, mentioning not only its technical problems but the excesses, he dismissed Zobel from his inner circle. Now he was furious over the constant press about his alleged involvement with Fayed in the purchase of House of Fraser.

If Fayed and Mark Thatcher had cleared the plan with His Majesty in Brunei, they would have had to have promised to keep His Majesty out of the matter, especially out of the press. Fayed feared his world might be shattered.

Fayed's request for a meeting with the Swami and Mamaji made them dizzy with anticipation.

Mohamed was coming to the mountain.

The Swami wanted me to be present when Fayed arrived at Carlos Place in order, he said, to introduce me and, thereby prevent the spread of any further disinformation. The situation seemed awkward at best, but it did raise intriguing possibilities.

The first surprise next day, upon entering the crowded Carlos Place apartment, was to be introduced to Enrique Zobel. I had, of course, heard of him from the Swami and knew of his relationship with the Sultan, but we had never met. He presented an amazingly normal figure in that he dressed, spoke, and acted like the chairman of a bank. Now, of course, I realize it was the Swami's method of demonstrating power. No doubt when he reported to the Sultan on his meeting with Fayed, he also informed His Majesty that Zobel and Martindale were in the next room awaiting his instructions.

When Fayed arrived, Mamaji hastily bundled us into the second bedroom. 'You must wait in here,' he said in an urgent whisper. 'Fayed must not know you are here until Swamiji feels it is right. He will make us all allies, do not worry. He will take care of everything.'

The door closed and we were left alone. The chatter in the living room died away as Fayed was greeted by the Swami and ushered into the other bedroom. Then the household seemed to freeze.

Although we had never met, Zobel and I knew about each other and had many people in common. This and our mutual curiosity enabled us to carry on a desultory conversation. I tried to engage him in a discussion about the building of the palace in Brunei, saying how truly remarkable it looked. He was suitably modest about his achievements. Finally, Zobel nodded off, and I read a book as the minutes stretched into hours.

After two claustrophobic hours, Mamaji opened the door and invited us into the Swami's room. Finally we were going to meet the great Fayed. As we entered, however, it became clear that he had just left. The Swami, Mamaji and Yogesh were literally jumping up and down with excitement. The Swami said: 'Listen, listen to your friend, Fayed, we taped everything. The Sultan will never speak to him again!'

To repeat, Fayed was introduced to the Sultan by the Prime Minister of Singapore, Lee Kuan Yew. Fayed's inflated description of the work he had done in Dubai had impressed the leader of Singapore. He hoped Fayed could convince the young Sultan to build a similar trade center in Brunei. Lee Kuan Yew wanted to focus the Sultan's attention on international business and away from girls, polo ponies and jewels.

As I listened to the tapes, I sat in stunned silence.

Tape recordings? Mother of Jefferson Davis! What crazy scheme were they up to now? But, sure enough, Yogesh Mehta came in with a small cassette recorder under his arm, following a wire that led along the skirting to a microphone hidden under the bed. He put the tape into the recorder, plugged it in, and we settled down to listen to the most indiscreet conversation of Mohamed Fayed's life.

There were two cassettes in all and the conversation was riveting. Fayed was obviously desperate for the Swami's help with the Sultan. The two met again the next day for an hour. That conversation, too, was recorded.

These are the tapes Tiny Rowland bought for $2 million. The tapes are a key part of the evidence being considered by the British Government in the matter of Fayed's purchase of House of Fraser. They provide other personal insights as well. In much the same way as the Nixon Watergate tapes informed us of the clumsy and criminal efforts by the White House staff to stop those investigating the Watergate scandal, and provided a startling picture of Richard Nixon and his staff, these tapes are immensely revealing.

In the process of analysing the tapes, it is important to note the difficulty of dissecting a conversation between a Hindu speaking in his native tongue (as interpreted by another Hindu, Mamaji), into a passable but imperfect English, and an Egyptian whose English is equally difficult to follow. Also, half of the conversation is body language, hand movements, and knowing looks and grunts. Even after three years of participating in meetings with the Swami and Mamaji, I still found it difficult to know what was being said a great deal of the time.

Thanks to Tiny Rowland, we have the transcripts of the tapes (see Appendix). At first blush we learn, in part, of Fayed's use of the Sultan's money to take control of House of Fraser, but in the end the story is told of Fayed's takeover of the Sultan himself.

At the beginning of the meeting, Fayed obviously has given the Swami money. In response, the Swami remarks that he only seeks Fayed's love, affection, and confidence. He repeats over and over again that while he is grateful for the money, his real interest is Fayed's faith in him. He then segues into his universal religion speech: 'My religion is humanity and its vestments are love and affection, and I respect the Muslim's Koran equally as I respect the Hindu's Adjunta or the Bible.' Becoming more expansive, the Swami explains how grateful he is for the friendship shown to him by the Muslims. Attempting to win over Fayed's confidence, the Swami tells Fayed he regards the Muslim religion as first among equals. Of all the religions of the world, he tells Fayed, the Muslims have treated him the best. While this seems an obvious ploy, the Swami, as a Hindu holy man, does it convincingly. Both laugh uproariously to Fayed's response to this speech on universal religion: 'Not the Jews! Not the Jews!'

Mamaji always described himself as a lawyer experienced in cross examination. Here, he proved it. Edward Bennett Williams could not have extracted more information from Fayed. Obviously because of the crisis precipitated by his purchase of House of Fraser, Fayed needed the Sultan's support now more than ever. Also, he knew how whimsically the Sultan could behave. Mohamed was gambling the Swami could put things right between the Sultan and himself. In turn, the Swami, as created and interpreted by Mamaji, flattered Fayed into his confidence. Overstating by far his influence over the Sultan, and with a clever use of insider knowledge, he tricked Fayed into an amazing process of admission and self incrimination.

Fayed is told that the Swami meets with His Majesty frequently, and that the Sultan has asked the Swami to give him guidance on those around him. Mentioning others in the Sultan's orbit such as Zobel, and powerful members of the Sultan's court like Ibnu and bin Isa, the Swami promises to be supportive of Fayed. Mamaji phrases all of this in the most selfless way possible, but the bottom line is simple: you scratch my back and I'll scratch yours.

Fayed becomes relaxed, and puts his cards on the table. First, he acknowledges the Sultan is 'not strong' and that he is 'sinking in corruption.' He further agonizes over the much talked about conspiracy against His Majesty by his father and brother. Finally, he points out that everyone around the Sultan – except present company, of course – is bad. Bin Isa, Ibnu, Zobel, and Khashoggi, according to Fayed, are all corrupt. Fayed even reports a representative of the Prime Minister of Singapore sent to Brunei to help clean up the government had been murdered by one of the Sultan's ministers while the Sultan looked the other way. (This was the first time the tale of poor Ponniah Rajaratnam had surfaced, as it were.)

Next, Fayed explains that the Thatcher government is keenly aware of the problems surrounding the Sultan. The British government is opposed to Zobel, he says, because it was Zobel who advised the Sultan to take billions of pounds from the British Crown Agents and place the money in American and Japanese banks.

Fayed then explains to the Swami his position of influence with Her Majesty's government. His unfortunate use of words were: 'Mohamed Al-Fayed up there inside Prime Minister.' Later, he states he has taken the Sultan to meet Mrs Thatcher three times at 10 Downing Street. He also brags that it was he who convinced her to stop in Brunei on her recent tour of Southeast Asia in April 1985.

Just when I was beginning to think I had heard it all, Mamaji asks Fayed about the power of attorney from the Sultan. 'Yes,' Fayed responds, 'I have a power of attorney. I signed it, he signed it, and I gave a copy to bin Isa. Bin Isa then gave a copy to Zobel.' As the conversation continued, he states he can get $10 billion if he wishes. Further, he brags that his money and the Sultan's are often commingled in his bank accounts. It is, therefore, virtually impossible to know whether, for example, the money Fayed had Hirschmann return to the Sultan ever left his account for Brunei. Never mind, one thing is clear. Fayed was operating with the Sultan's money and borrowing by pledging the Sultan's money as collateral. The funds he had used to buy Harrods were not his own.

The plan was to meet His Majesty at the Dorchester the next day at 10 am. I left Carlos Place confused, and concerned that 'my guys' were overplaying their hand. But the Swami said: 'Go! Relax! I know His Majesty will now work only with us. Fayed is out forever!'

At the Dorchester we were ushered into a suite the Sultan was occupying for business meetings, and asked to be seated in the waiting room. The Swami, alone, was taken into the Sultan. They spoke for about ten minutes, then a security guard invited me to enter.

The Sultan, dressed in his polo shirt and Levis, and the Swami were sitting on the bed laughing. His Majesty thanked me for leaving Washington at such a crucial time (The Swami had, obviously, told him I was working on the Gandhi visit) and then, fell silent. I had always known him as a man of few words, but this was unusual even for him.

Breaking the silence, the Swami said: 'Tell His Majesty what is being said about him in Washington.'

The correct response would have been to say that, outside the Department of State, virtually no one had heard of Brunei or the Sultan. However, not knowing exactly what to say, I launched once again into remarks I had prepared on the importance of the ASEAN nations and the role the Sultan should assume in leading them. Without comment, the Sultan stood up and thanked me for my thoughts. In ten minutes the meeting was over.

The Swami gave me a knowing look, and said something which implied he knew I had to return to America at once. 'The Sultan and I need your help in Washington!' he said. 'I will remain with His Majesty for a few days, then I will join you and my Prime Minister.'

The critical meeting had ended, and I was able to catch the 1 pm Concorde home. Luckily, the flight took only three hours. Had it been longer, I would have gone crazy asking myself over and over: What was that all about? Did the Sultan hear the tapes? How can he be so uninterested in world affairs? Why was I needed? What can the Swami possibly talk to him about for hours on end?

It would be months before I was able to answer any of those questions.

# – 17 –

## The Royal Club

The urgent trip to London turned out to be another confusion. Did the Sultan want to establish himself as a world leader of stature and substance or not? When I discussed the matter with the Swami by telephone, he agreed that His Majesty needed direction. 'Give me a plan of action,' he said. 'You must tell me how to transform him!'

Reflecting on the Swami's request, I decided to press ahead. 'Allow me to introduce the Sultan to other members of the Royal Club,' I suggested to the Swami. 'He needs to meet people who share similar responsibilities, others who have been born into positions of power and learned the duties that follow.' I proposed introductions to the Prince of Monaco and the Prince of Liechtenstein.

A few weeks later, the Swami was on the telephone to say that the Sultan approved the plan. The Swami had been appointed his official representative to orchestrate his entry into the Royal Club.

Unfortunately, I had underestimated the Indian's appetite for intrigue. The Swami had not contacted Brunei and the Sultan knew nothing about the proposed trip. Far from being his ambassador, the Swami was planning to impress him with a *fait accompli* when he returned to Brunei. In the meantime, he was relying on his wits and piety to see him through.

For the next three weeks I was hard at work in my Washington office

124

making the necessary arrangements. These were complicated because, although I knew the royal families of Liechtenstein and Monaco, it wasn't easy to explain why they should receive a Hindu guru from India representing a Muslim head of state. However, I received a sympathetic response and, by the beginning of August, the schedule had been organized.

We were due to fly out from New York on 10 August, and I traveled to New York at dawn to meet the Swami and his party. They were staying at the extremely expensive Lowell Hotel on East 72nd Street. The departure was scheduled for 11 am, which meant leaving for the airport at 10 am. Always the advance man, I turned up at about 8.30 am, to make certain everything was all right.

On entering the suite, I was assailed by the heavy aroma of their breakfast curry. It was a smell that was to pursue us for the next few weeks, as the Swami always traveled with a cook to prepare his meals. This was partly to cater for his vegetarian diet, but the cook also acted as his food-taster. The byzantine nature of Indian politics had left him with a continued fear of being poisoned.

The apartment began to swell with people, including the Swami's servants and disciples; Asha Putli, who was to accompany us on the trip; Mamaji and Ernie Miller. On this trip, Ernie had volunteered to handle all of the administrative and financial decisions.

It appeared that Ernie spent his days investing in the Canadian and American stock markets. When he was around, it was impossible to make a telephone call. He monopolized the phone and could always be found screaming: 'Buy!' or 'Sell!' at some poor broker.

Rich or not, Ernie lacked style. Like the Swami, he was about one hundred pounds overweight, but as he dressed in flashy Western clothes, his bulk was more obtrusive. Even though he was about six feet two inches in height, his frame could not conceal a stomach that would have made Santa Claus blush.

Ernie insisted we take taxis to the private terminal at Teterboro, New Jersey, where the Sultan's jet was standing by. Having graduated from the 'Rockefeller for President School of Travel and Advance', I attempted to explain that we were about to depart on a major mission, that the schedule was very tight, and that Teterboro Airport would be difficult for a cab driver to find.

When I suggested to Ernie that he organize limousines instead, he walked over and, unintentionally, pressed his large belly against mine, and looked me straight in the eye. 'No!' he said. 'When I am calling the shots, I call them. We will take taxis.'

125

Because of the size of the entourage, three cabs had to be hailed on the corner of 72nd Street and Madison. In the spirit of a team player, I jumped into the front seat of the lead cab. As the cab pulled away from the curb, I looked around to find the back seat was occupied by Mamaji, the cook Nataji, and a redheaded woman of about thirty whom I had never seen before.

The three were chatting away happily as I pushed back the protective divider to introduce myself. It seemed reasonable to be polite as this woman was apparently going to be part of the group for the next several weeks.

The woman said her name was Jane and that she was the stewardess for our flight. The comment inspired laughter because we had just been joking about needing a stewardess when we were leaving the hotel. The Swami was surrounded by a constantly changing group of disciples. So I assumed she must be a devotee who had been invited on the trip. At least, I reflected, she seemed to have a sense of humor!

The taxi transporting Swamiji and Ernie got hopelessly lost. But, just as everyone had come to terms with the possibility that they must have broken down or had an accident on the freeway, their cab arrived. Both Ernie and the Swami were shouting loudly and berating the driver for his incompetence. It was such a relief to see them, I did not bother to say: 'I told you so.'

By now, we were running over an hour late. Trying hard to suppress my growing concern, I urged everyone to board the plane as quickly as possible. The Swami and I were last. As we walked across the tarmac, I inquired about his new disciple. The brown guru went pale. 'What woman?' he asked. 'What disciple?'

No one had thought to question Jane. She was now comfortably seated on board our plane. Everyone had assumed the woman was with someone else and, with mounting hysteria, each of us denied any knowledge of her. The Swami, fearful of attempts to assassinate him, went into a state of shock. Mamaji and Ernie called for the police.

Airport security officials eventually arrived and removed our stewardess who wasn't. The fire department was alerted for a possible bomb threat and dogs were brought in to check the plane for explosives. Each piece of luggage had to be emptied and searched, while the terrified stowaway was questioned by the police.

There was no plot, of course. It turned out that she was a mad woman, one of the homeless who haunt the streets of New York. She happened to be walking down 72nd Street, saw our group departing, and – understandably – assumed that she would fit right in.

Our departure to Monaco had now been delayed by about eight hours. After discussing the matter with the pilots, they calculated that, if we left immediately, it would still be possible to reach Monaco on time for our appointment. Once informed, the Swami instructed everyone to board the plane at once.

At precisely that moment, the telephone in the airport waiting room rang. It was Ernie's wife, Kim, calling to say she had experienced a terrible premonition about the trip. She insisted the trip be postponed until the next day. This was the last straw. As forcefully as possible, I pleaded with the Swami to take no notice of a bad dream.

It was a considerable honor for the Swami to be granted an audience with the descendant of the oldest dynasty in Europe. To accommodate our schedule, Prince Rainier had agreed to return early from a yachting trip.

Premonitions were as critical to the Swami's flight plans as the right weather forecast. And of course, Ernie was 'in charge'. Suddenly, three limousines – not taxis – were summoned and we were transported to a nearby hotel for the night. The Swami threw his arms in the air and said: 'What can I do? Ernie is my most devoted follower. How can time be so important?'

For me it was a sleepless night. But once we were safely on our way, I felt better, even though the Falcon 50 airplane was not particularly spacious. It accommodated twelve people, and although the group numbered only ten, we were strapped in thigh-to-thigh. There was barely room to stand upright in the cabin and the lavatory was oddly situated at the front. One emerged to an audience of expectant faces looking ready to applaud. However, the television videos were fun, the catering was good, and we were, after all, on a diplomatic mission for the Sultan in his private jet. Life at the top wasn't all bad.

It was a surprise to learn the pilots came from Mexico, and I remember wondering why a plane provided by the Sultan of Brunei should have Mexican pilots. Mamaji explained they had been employed because of their knowledge of Western air traffic patterns. After all, Brunei is a small country ...

I discovered later that the plane was not the Sultan's at all, but registered to Ernie Miller in the Cayman Islands. The story was just another subterfuge to indicate that the mission had the Sultan's official approval. I subsequently discovered that the plane had been purchased by Ernie from the Bank of Mexico and had been brokered by an agent I had recommended. The joke was on me.

It was a long flight, but as the plane began to descend over an iridescent sea to land at Nice Airport, the whole of the Cote d'Azur seemed to be on show for our benefit.

To my relief, the whole group was cleared through customs instantly. This is very unusual when traveling with Asian Indians. Airport officials tend to take hours making certain that they have no plans to emigrate.

Instantly, two helicopters sent by the Prince appeared. Things were moving smoothly now.

We landed at the foot of the huge walls of the Grimaldi Palace, dominating the 200 foot cliffs overlooking the harbor. Beside the heliport was a rose garden the Prince had ordered constructed and dedicated to the memory of Princess Grace. Asha's eyes filled with tears when she realized it was filled with the favorite roses of the Princess, many of which she had bred and nurtured. We paused briefly in the garden to admire the blooms. It wasn't quite the Taj Mahal, but it was certainly a moving tribute to a beloved wife.

Within minutes sleek limousines arrived to take us to the Hotel de Paris. The hotel is owned by the government of Monaco and managed by a director designated by the Palace. The Swami was ushered into the Royal Suite. The furnishings were luxurious and the windows opened to a dazzling panorama of the city. The beam on the Swami's face was a clear sign that he, too, felt the trip was off to a good start.

The Hotel de Paris' windows offer a spectacular view across the square at Monte Carlo's famous Casino. It had been constructed long ago at the behest of another actress who had married into the Grimaldi family, HSH Princess Caroline of Monaco. She may have given the principality its Victorian flare, but it was HSH Princess Grace who endowed Monte Carlo with culture and beauty. Gambling now accounts for only about 3 per cent of the principality's income and the Casino is a ghost of its former glory, but the hotel is still one of the grandest, and most expensive, in Europe.

The palace courteously suggested the meeting be delayed for an hour so we could relax. Refreshed and happy, our group crowded into two Mercedes limousines which had been waiting to drive us around the harbor, up the Rampe Major, through the sixteenth-century gateway and into the Palace Square. Full of excitement, my eyes turned away from the fantastic yachts in the harbor to the Palace Square with its piles of cannonballs and ceremonial guards in tall shakos (a military dress hat with a metal plate in front and a plume).

We were shown immediately to the royal family's private quarters in the southern wing. Before her untimely death, Princess Grace had personally organized this room around a large solarium shielded from the sun by a screen of pine trees. It was jammed with comfortable, almost homely furniture. In the center of the room was a recently commissioned bust of the Princess.

Ten years before, I had been invited to tea with her at the request of a mutual friend. On that occasion, Princess Grace had apologized for the formality of the traditional rooms. But her personal beauty had dominated the formal room. I felt her presence once again.

Seconds after our arrival, the Prince entered. He was wearing his traditional blue tie which brings out the startling blue of his eyes. He looked healthy and happy, and welcomed our party with great charm, chatting to each of us briefly. Then the Prince, the Swami and Mamaji retired to one of the private meeting rooms. Asha, Ernie and the rest of the group waited outside for over an hour. When the discussion was over, they returned in high good humor. The Prince seemed to be enjoying their company.

Suddenly, Princess Stephanie arrived wearing a simple white dress which emphasized her sun tan. She looked absolutely radiant and said she had just returned from water-skiiing. I had heard she was shy and rather withdrawn. But at this moment she was bubbling over with fun, even to the point of laughing at one of my jokes. After greeting us, she was taken aside by the Swami, who asked to have a private word. They disappeared into the den for what I assumed was his usual getting-to-know-you, mind-reading routine.

While they were away, Prince Albert joined us. The Crown Prince looked elegant and handsome in a white suit. It was evident he had inherited his mother's features. Asha wasted no time in making herself agreeable. The three hours spent in the Palace were relaxed and informal. The Prince even apologized for the absence of Princess Caroline, who was on holiday with her husband.

The royal family took the time to extend our tour round the palace gardens, including a walk around the upper wall of the compound which looks out over the entire principality. Standing on the ramparts, looking down on the Condamine, it seemed as if not only Monte Carlo but the whole world lay at our feet. The Prince could not have been more gracious. When we departed, he asked us to return the next day. We left on a complete high.

As the limousines threaded their way back through the streets of the old town, we were blissfully unaware of the storm clouds gathering on our horizon.

Diplomacy of the kind we were attempting must be unobtrusive. The cavalcade of limousines, with the white-robed figure in the back seat, was impossible to miss. We were stared at wherever we went. In the lobby of the Hotel de Paris, several people even approached the Swami with a slight bow. They figured he had to be somebody important!

It didn't take long before the Swami was besieged by strangers wishing to obtain an introduction to the Sultan. His suite was full of people who had flown into Monaco just 'to pay their respects to His Holiness'. The Swami loved all of this attention, but it made me very nervous.

Our lives were also tormented by Manfredo Horowitz, who ran the Harry Winston jewelry store in the lobby. He literally chased me up and down the corridors of the hotel begging for an entrée to the Sultan.

Manfredo paid a great deal of attention to Asha, figuring she might be more easily seduced by the jewels, and invited her for a day on his yacht in the harbor.

Asha is a naturally friendly and trusting person. She accepted without suspicion and told Horowitz everything we had been doing, who we were seeing, and about our future plans.

Manfredo, unknown to all of us, had been a close business partner of Adnan Khashoggi. Over the years they had sold the Sultan upwards of $700 million worth of jewelry. Both allegedly had earned extremely large commissions on the sales. Manfredo was unlikely to be allowed back in Brunei, but did not seem to be aware of that. He immediately contacted Khashoggi and several others with a rundown of our movements. The Swami and I were particularly concerned that a distorted version of events should not get back to the Sultan.

One morning, Mamaji introduced me to a blond man in his late thirties named Carl Hirschmann, Jr. He was, said Mamaji, an associate of Zobel and had once sold the Sultan a 747 jet. When I glibly commented that I could not imagine why the Sultan would want a 747, Carl gave me an unpleasant look and responded: 'It would enable him to fly his polo horses around the world and not have to smell the shit.' Properly rebuked, I went for a walk around the hotel pool.

Hirschmann was an ally of Zobel. This meant for the time being he was on our side in the shifting alliances which surrounded the Sultan. Hirschmann said he had come to accompany us on the next leg of our journey and would organize the limousines and accommodations in Liechtenstein. Ernie seemed pleased to have Carl along. It meant he would not have to pay all the checks.

We arrived at the palace the following morning in excellent spirits. The group had been reduced to the Swami, Mamaji and myself because the others were bored with the endless hanging around in outer rooms. It was just as well, because this time the Swami, Mamaji and the Prince were closeted together for more than two hours.

When they eventually emerged, the Prince called for some refreshments and asked if I would join him in some 'iced tea'. An iced tea laced with vodka appeared discreetly at my side. When I thanked him, he gave me a sly wink to let me know he understood my predicament. Swamiji insisted no alcohol be consumed in his presence.

On the way back, Swamiji revealed the Prince would entrust us with a formal letter to the Sultan inviting him to Monaco. The Prince even asked where he could obtain the flags of Brunei to fly for the occasion.

At the hotel I quickly changed into a swimming suit and settled down to enjoy the sun. I needn't have bothered. A porter rushed to the poolside with the news that the Prince's secretary, Mr Napier, was calling. I was summoned to the palace. Napier expressed sorrow at interrupting my brief moment of relaxation, and I replied laughingly: 'Please sir, I never say no to royalty. I will be there at once!'

There was barely time to dress before a limousine appeared. I was swept back up the hill and taken directly to the Prince's private office in the northern wing of the palace.

The Prince was looking for reassurance. 'Tell me more about the Swami, the Sultan, the point of all this,' he said. As best I could, I attempted to answer his questions. He seemed quite happy with the idea of the visit. I emphasized the importance to the Sultan of having him as a friend, and also expressed the hope that the Sultan and Prince Albert might spend time together. He seemed especially pleased to know that we were going to visit the Prince of Liechtenstein for the same purpose.

After a long discussion, the Prince summoned Mr Napier and dictated a letter to the Sultan which he signed in my presence. The content of the royal message was quite simple and straightforward: 'Your Majesty,' he wrote, 'I have enjoyed very much my conversations with His Holiness, Shri Chandra Swamiji, over the past few days. It would be a great pleasure to welcome you to Monaco as my guest at the Palace. I would be most grateful if you would have your chief of protocol be in touch with mine to arrange the time of your visit. I look forward to having you in my country.' He signed it, 'Sincerely'.

Letter in hand, I journeyed back to the hotel confident the mission had been a success. The Swami's strange coalition of gods, however, had saved their best throw until last.

Early the next day our group assembled in the lobby of the Hotel de Paris, before our journey to Liechtenstein. But when Ernie presented his American Express card to pay the bill, it failed to clear the computer. This seemed odd as American Express has unlimited credit and their cards are always honored unless the holder has not paid his bill in the last 90 days.

Ernie insisted they repeat the procedure and, once again, the plastic bounced. The staff was firm. The bill, they politely informed Miller, was $12,000 for the three night stay. Ernie was red-faced and becoming more enraged by the minute. The rest of us retired a discreet distance to let him sort it out.

Discretion, however, was not Ernie's strong point. Soon we heard him from across the lobby shouting at the cashier. Were they idiots? Did they not realize we were the personal guests of the Prince? Eyes bulging with rage, Ernie began to pound on the reception desk.

Once again, my carefully planned schedule was delayed. We were running over two hours late, and our appointment with the royal family in Liechtenstein was in jeopardy.

The entire lobby stopped to listen. Heads appeared around doors. Finally, when it was impossible to ignore the scene any longer, the Swami sailed to the rescue. By then, everyone had become so worked up he had difficulty making himself heard. The Hotel de Paris was soon in an uproar of Hindustani, French, and English.

The Swami suddenly abandoned the argument and returned to the waiting room. Mamaji was dispatched to settle the matter. The little man pushed his way through the crowd, opened his briefcase on the counter, and to the astonishment of all, solemnly counted out $12,000 in cash from an enormous stack of bills.

In the limo on the way to the heliport, the air was thick with indignation. Incredibly, it had been assumed the Prince would pay the bill. No one seemed to fault Ernie. It was the French who were to blame. Such treatment was outrageous. The Swami had never been so insulted. He would never, the Swami declared, *never* come back to Monaco again.

Not even if the Prince asked him!

# – 18 –
## On to Make Friends

The next stop on the itinerary was the principality of Liechtenstein. (I have often wondered of late if our New York, Monaco, Liechtenstein, Gibraltar, Bahrain, Singapore, Brunei, Saipan, Marshall Islands, Honolulu, Los Angeles, Toronto excursion was ever before contemplated, let alone carried out.)

Liechtenstein differs in almost every way from Monaco. Situated in central Europe between Austria and Switzerland, it is the epitome of quiet beauty and Prussian discipline. The Bank In Liechtenstein operates throughout the world with discretion, profits and clout envied everywhere. With a population of 26,000 and only 62 square miles within its borders, there are few civic problems and fewer surprises. There is absolutely no way to become a citizen of Liechtenstein unless born of parents who are citizens. The principality is governed by democratically elected representatives who, in turn, elect a Prime Minister. They are fiercely independent. As far as I know, the Prince has not been granted permission by the parliament to purchase the land required to build a gallery in which to display one of the most outstanding collections of art in the world. Like Brunei, Liechtenstein does not need tourist income.

I had met Prince Franz Joseph and Princess Gina years ago at a dinner given by Senator and Mrs Claiborne Pell in their Georgetown home. At the end of the evening, the Prince had politely suggested a visit if I were ever in Liechtenstein.

On holiday in Europe in 1978, I found myself in Vaduz, the capital, quite by accident. With innocent zeal, I telephoned the castle to say hello. That is the way it worked in Pocatello, after all. In spite of the fact that it was the National Day and that the royal family did not have a free moment apart from their official engagements, Princess Gina instructed the secretary to extend an invitation to tea.

Schloss Vaduz graces the principality at the lower base of the beautiful Liechtenstein mountains high about the city. An ancient caretaker lifts the gate to permit entry to the royal estate. Once inside, a winding dirt road which crosses an ancient wooden bridge over the moat leads to the fifteenth-century castle. Behind a creaky door in the main hall is the armor room replete with swords, shields, spears, and other family treasures. The castle is an historic jewel.

Entering the family rooms, it began to dawn on me that I might as well have called Buckingham Palace to ask the Queen if I might stop by for a drink. The expression on my face must have revealed my thought.

Her Serene Highness Princess Gina behaved impeccably. I was introduced to the royal family, invited to the National Day celebration, and made to feel at home. At tea, Princess Nora, the second child of the royal family, reported she was planning to spend the next year in Washington working for the World Bank.

On my return to Washington, I received a well-deserved scolding from Senator Pell for my lack of manners, but eventually all was forgiven. This time serendipity was on my side.

In many ways, Prince Hans Adam was perfectly suited to introduce the Sultan to the Royal Club. His father, Franz Joseph, had recently abdicated in his favor and lived in a dignified, quiet way secure in the knowledge that his son was more than prepared to assume his royal duties. The Sultan and Hans Adam were the same age and, though they were worlds apart in most respects, my instinct was that they would like each other. The Crown Prince was a good friend of the future Emperor of Japan (who ascended the throne after the death of his father, Hirohito, on 5 January 1989), and had spent considerable time in the Far East. The Prince and Princess of Wales had become special friends of Prince Hans Adam and Princess Marie. The future King of England and his Princess now spent their annual skiing vacation in Liechtenstein hosted by the royal family. What better friend could the Sultan have?

The Swami had never heard of the Grimaldis or Monaco, let alone Liechtenstein. What had impressed him, however, was Prince Rainier's positive reaction when Swamiji revealed his next stop was Vaduz.

Our plane landed in Zurich where Carl Hirschmann, Jr, was standing by with two Mercedes limousines to transport us to the castle. Prince Hans Adam stood outside the formal entrance to greet us and escorted our group to the reception room. After the introductions and preliminary conversation, Mamaji and the Swami retired to the family rooms with the Prince and Princess Marie while, at his request, I took Asha and the others on a tour of the chapel and the armor room.

We left after a three-hour visit, the Swami wreathed in smiles. The Prince, it appeared, had confided that he planned a trip to Japan in the Fall and would be pleased to include Brunei in his itinerary.

On arrival at Zurich Airport to commence the trek east, a teary eyed Asha suddenly appeared outside the gate. I tried to go to her, but was stopped by the Swami. Apparently she had to return to New York. There wasn't time for any goodbyes because she was late for her flight. Once inside the plane, Mamaji revealed another side to the story.

It made little sense at the time, but the Swami blamed Asha for the Sultan's increasingly negative reaction to our mission. Asha's conversations with Manfredo Horowitz in Monaco had proved to be a major indiscretion. The Sultan had berated the Swami over her comments, which had been relayed to him by Horowitz and Hirschmann. To put things right, Asha had to be sent home. The only hope was that the Swami would be able to put the matter in perspective when he got to Brunei. There was nothing I could do for Asha, although I would miss her company.

In less than an hour, we were to land in Gibraltar.

Seven months before, Sir Eldon Griffiths MP, had helped organize a conference in London for the Gibraltar Heritage Society. HRH The Duke of Gloucester chaired the meeting and opened my eyes to the wonders of the Rock.

At the conference, I had a talk with the Chief Minister of Gibraltar, Sir Joshua Hassan. Sir Joshua had been at the forefront of Gibraltar's political life since 1946. When I rang him from Washington, he volunteered that he would be pleased to welcome the Swami, and that Gibraltar had a large population of native Indians whom he knew would be thrilled to have a Hindu holy man in their midst.

Gibraltar's history can almost be defined by a series of sieges which began with the Moorish invasion in 711 AD. The fifteenth and last siege began in 1969 when Generalissimo Franco closed the border between Gibraltar and Spain. Franco opposed Britain's sovereignty over the Rock, which it has claimed since the Treaty of Utrecht signed in 1713. Ten years after Franco's death in 1975, the frontier was re-opened. Gibraltar was now bustling with tourists.

The frontier border is also the airstrip for the Rock, which meant that traffic had to be halted for our plane to land. Doubtless few private jets land in Gibraltar. Seas of cars stood honking their horns and a crowd began to gather as the plane touched down. We disembarked to be welcomed by polite applause and an official escort organized by the Chief Minister.

The Swami was in his element among the devout Hindus, and Sir Joshua seemed to score some useful points with his Indian constituency. After a pleasant two day holiday, we departed for Bahrain, then on to Singapore. (I do not recommend Bahrain in August. The heat was so intense that even when wearing socks and shoes my feet were burned while walking on the cement pavement.)

The day of our arrival at the Royal Holiday Inn, the Swami came to my room for a talk. The look on his face betrayed bad news. Awkwardly, he poured his ever-expanding body into a green chair, and rehearsed his version of the Sultan's attitude about our ambassadorial efforts. Never, of course, admitting that he had undertaken the trip without royal approval, the Swami confided that the Sultan was in a rage. The purpose of our trip had been distorted alarmingly. Horowitz and Co had reported that we were imploring the Prince of Monaco to become a caretaker to the half-witted Sultan of Brunei. It also appeared that Fayed had been telling tales, saying I had portrayed the Sultan as a hopeless womanizer and drug abuser.

I sat in stunned silence as the Swami rose with the words: 'HM was so angry he told me not to come. But when I talk to my sister (Princess Mariam), she said I must come tomorrow to explain. You and I will go tomorrow, no one else. With the help of my sister, HM will understand. This very bad for us, very bad.'

I had never seen the Swami in such a state. He was trembling, and mistakenly walked into the closet thinking it was the door to the hall. When I offered to see him back to his room, he practically collapsed on my arm with a sigh of relief.

So it was that on 21 August 1985, the Swami and I boarded an Air Brunei flight to Bandar Seri Begawan. Still tense and ill at ease, the Swami was overjoyed to see the Minister of Interior standing at the gate to welcome us. Instantly our passports were stamped with the required visas and we were comfortably seated in our brown Mercedes limousines for the short trip to the palace. The Swami's spirits lifted again when we approached the guest house His Majesty had said would always be kept exclusively for him. Inside, the staff stood waiting to prepare his special meals, an extra set of white robes and sandals had been placed in the closet, and the smell of his favorite incense was everywhere. 'We did not need to worry,' he said. 'This is still my home. My sister has made certain everything is OK.'

After a brief rest, a royal Rolls-Royce appeared and the Swami cheerfully departed for his session with His Majesty and Princess Mariam. As he walked out the door, he explained that I should stand by for the car to return. 'Don't worry,' he said. 'I will explain everything to HM and then request you join us. I have the letter from the Prince of Monaco. HM will be happy with our work.'

After six hours, the Swami returned to the house in a state of utter despair. He was too exhausted to explain what had transpired, but said we were to leave the next day. In an offhand way, he explained that His Majesty had a full schedule tomorrow and regretted he could not see me. Then, as he closed the door to his bedroom, he added: 'HM and I had a bad fight. It was not possible to ask him to see you. But, I promise he understands the good work we have done. My sister is with us. Fayed's power is finished. I will see you tomorrow.' I shall always remember his pathetic smile as he retired for the night.

The Swami spoke little on the return flight to Singapore. He looked a defeated man. I remarked that it would not be the end of the world if the Sultan turned his back on us.

Swamiji's reaction to this half-hearted attempt to be cheerful was telling: 'You must never tell anyone that HM is angry with me!' he said. 'No one must know, not even Mamaji. Say nothing!'

Setbacks and defeat were never openly admitted by the Swami, Fayed, or Khashoggi. Whatever the truth of a situation, they managed to carry on with bravado and conviction. The further Khashoggi blundered into debt, the greater were his excesses. Fayed's answer to the accusations that he had lied about his wealth and family history was to spend more money on public relations.

The Royal Club initiative had backfired. Even Princess Mariam had been unable to put things right. When the Swami bemoaned the fact that the Sultan was infuriated to learn the Swami had been representing himself as His Majesty's advisor with: 'HM must understand that I know what is best for him. *My friends, the Princes,* they will be a good influence. I told him it was never necessary to check with him first on matters I know are important. I am a spiritual man. He must trust me!', I knew the Swami was history in Brunei.

None of this, however, prevented the Swami from exploiting the Sultan's name and position at every possible opportunity. His photo album was full of pictures of him with the Sultan and Princess Mariam. The rumor mill still described him as the Sultan's spiritual advisor. And he continued to work to restore their relationship, but when it became clear this was impossible, he cultivated others of wealth and power by fabricating telephone calls and meetings with the Sultan.

# – 19 –
## Khashoggi and the Swami are One

The Swami moved into Khashoggi's guest apartment at Olympic Towers in New York two weeks after his final meeting with the Sultan and less than five days after he had met Adnan in Toronto. The two-bedroom, two-bathroom 45th-floor extension of Khashoggi's $25 million residence on the 46th and 47th floors of the Fifth Avenue building, originally owned by Aristotle Onassis, was modest by billionaire standards, but certainly comfortable. It was perfect for the Swami because it was not too lavish, yet it was evident immediately that the guru had found himself a choice location.

When rumors of Adnan's financial decline began to circulate, a friend instructed me to offer $1.5 million for the 'swami suite'. Shaheen laughed at the suggestion of a bid under $2 million. 'The view of St Patrick's cathedral alone was worth $500,000,' he insisted.

The relationship between Adnan and the Swami was incomprehensible. Never before had I been in such intimate contact with men who knowingly lied to each other, yet continued to place their lives in each others' hands.

The Swami secreted himself in his bedroom at 11 am daily to receive a call from the Sultan. Khashoggi generally dropped by at 11.30 to be debriefed on His Majesty's thoughts. For weeks the Swami instructed everyone to be ready to travel to Brunei in two days time for the crucial

139

meeting. Then, at the last moment, the date would be changed. In the midst of this performance, the Swami challenged Adnan to deliver as many of his important contacts as possible. It was a joke. AK was constantly jetting to Cairo or Saudi Arabia on a confidential mission, while the Swami spent his days on the telephone. I now believe he was talking to a dial tone.

Every other day Shaheen called to ask if the Swami could really produce the Sultan. When I told Shaheen that he probably knew more about current developments than I did, he groaned.

On 8 October 1985, Mamaji rang to say they were at the Four Seasons Hotel in Washington for a meeting with the King of Jordan. Both Adnan and His Majesty, King Hussein, were born in 1935 and both had studied together in Egypt as young men. The King no longer speaks to Khashoggi, but at that time he treated him like an old friend. Mamaji implored me to drop whatever I was doing to join them as this would be a perfect opportunity for the Swami to arrange an introduction to the King.

As the hours passed, it became clear an appointment with the King had not been organized. I do not even know if he met the Swami. Mamaji felt it was important to balance the equation of people outside the King's rooms with his advisors. The Swami was more in command when he could introduce his close friends to whomever else was waiting for an audience. Far from gaining an audience with the King, my role was that of a supporting actor on the Swami's stage.

When I arrived Khashoggi, had already gone across the hall for his meeting with the King. The Swami and Mamaji greeted me effusively, then Mamaji announced to all present that I was the Swami's closest friend in America. He made the usual overstatements about my contacts and inside knowledge. He had an annoying habit of making a speech rather than actually effecting an introduction. The names of those present were never revealed.

After the initial burst of enthusiasm, the room fell silent. The clock ticked on and small talk flickered sporadically. In the midst of this time-killing chatter, the Swami mentioned a particularly offensive remark Fayed had made in the Carlos Place tapes as a way of discounting Fayed's position with the Sultan. Trying to introduce a little levity to the exchange, I opined: 'It is too bad Tiny Rowland has not heard the tapes. He would be amazed at Fayed's indiscretion!'

With that, the Swami directed my attention to a gentleman at the end of the room with the words: 'Ah ha, you know! Meet AK's friend, "Tony" Rowland.'

The Swami

The Swami's Feet

RI. CHANDRA SWAMIJI MAHARAJ

Founder
*Sarva Dharma Sambhav Kendra*
Center of Interfaith Harmony

An international, spiritual, dedicated to
furthering the cause greater harmony and
understanding between religious traditions.

The Sultan (*Camera Press*)

The Swami, the Sultan and the Princess

The Arms Dealer with his wife and daughter (*Popperfoto*)

Adnan, Swamaji, Tiny and Mamaji

FAYED

(En capitales )

Fayed, the Alexandrian

( Nom de jeune fille )

: Mohamed Abdel Moneim Ali

( En minuscules )

e

No 1106

Passeport No. 11515

Fayed and Father
Christmas

On the street where
Fayed lived

Fayed's shop

Dictators in exile: Papa with Baby (*Reflex Picture Agency*)
and *below*, Imelda and Ferdinand (*Reflex Picture Agency*)

Concealing my astonishment as best I could, I presented myself to the chief executive of Lonrho. It was our first meeting. We spent the next thirty minutes talking about the tapes. If Tiny bothers to read this book, I want him to know the meeting was not a 'set-up'. I had no idea he was in the room.

This was the period during which Tiny was aggressively searching for evidence to corroborate his statements on the Fayed takeover of HOF. At the first mention of the taped conversation between Fayed and the Swami, he wanted to know more. Instinctively, he understood their content might provide him with the 'smoking gun' he needed.

The Swami walked me into another room to discuss the matter. 'Do you have the tapes with you?' I asked.

'Yes,' he whispered. 'But I think it is better if we tell "Tony" to meet us in Toronto tomorrow to hear them. I would rather have him on my own ground. I will tell him they are not with me. We will all go to Toronto tomorrow.' The purpose of the Swami's power play seemed childish, but Tiny agreed to fly to Canada the next day.

Imagine the following scene: into Adnan's DC-8 climbed the Swami, Mamaji, several disciples, Shaheen, Adnan's retainers, an Egyptian friend of Tiny's, Ashraf Marwan (married to the daughter of former President Nasser of Egypt), Tiny Rowland and myself. All flying from Washington DC to Toronto to gather at the home of Ernie Miller for the sole purpose of listening to three cassettes of a covertly recorded conversation between Mohamed Fayed and the Swami. Rowland had been told by Khashoggi that the tapes were proof positive that the money used in Fayed's takeover of Harrods was not his own but the Sultan's.

After a brief vegetarian lunch with the Millers, Mamaji played the tapes. Tiny sparked at once to Fayed's voice. Soon he began to pick out bits and pieces of crucial evidence.

Many months later, Tiny told me he had purchased the tapes from the Swami for $2 million. Men like Fayed, Khashoggi and the Swami rarely commit anything to paper, let alone allow their conversations to be recorded. Tiny realized that within this rambling, self-serving dialogue a grain of truth would emerge. And he was prepared to pay an enormous price for it.

On 8 December 1985 the wedding took place of the Indian Foreign Secretary's son, Siddarth Bhandari, in Delhi. His father, Romesh Bhandari, and I had become good friends and I was pleased to be invited to my first Indian wedding. The Swami had convinced Khashoggi to come too, so the three of us flew from New York to Delhi on 6 December on AK's DC-8.

It was an enjoyable flight. Adnan spoke at length about business opportunities in India and urged me to stick with him at all times, the better to sniff out a good deal. We had caviar and champagne, watched the latest movies, I slept in a king-size bed in the guest cabin, and was able to shower and dress before we touched down.

The wedding was beautiful and lavish. My crowd count was 4000. The groom arrived on an elephant. Two moments, in particular, were unforgettable. The night of the major ceremony (the ceremony goes on for days), our group was ushered into a special section where the honored guests were to be welcomed by the Prime Minister, Rajiv Gandhi. In the enclosure were the Swami, Adnan, a wide assortment of Bhandari friends from around the world and several other older statesmen. The Prime Minister and Madame Gandhi (Sonia) duly arrived to pay their respects to the groom. Surveying the group in the enclosure, the PM seemed uncomfortable. He shook my hand perfunctorily and quickly walked on. When I engaged the First Lady in Italian (her native language) and wished her a happy birthday, she responded with a spontaneous smile, but then withdrew. When we had been together in Washington six months before, the PM had been open and had expressed his gratitude for my efforts with the Council on Indo-US Relations. Something was clearly wrong now.

Before I could ask Romesh what was troubling the PM, the crowd turned toward the entrance to observe Tiny Rowland, Ashraf Marwan and Lonrho Director Robert Dunlop, entering the wedding tent. The Foreign Secretary seemed taken aback. What was going on?

The next day we left for Madras for a series of appointments the Swami had arranged for Adnan. Tiny followed us. While I enjoyed the magic of the southern sea and the people of Madras, Tiny and the Swami were closeted in meetings. Even when Adnan presented a check to Dr Reddy, founder of the Apollo Hospitals, for $250,000, I had the uneasy feeling the Swami's thoughts were elsewhere.

# – 20 –

## The Facts Begin to Stop the Con Men

Never one to turn away from an offer of money, the Swami had sold the Carlos Place tapes to Rowland for $2 million in October without regard to the damage their publication might cause the Sultan.

On the flight from Delhi to Madras, I had been asked to draft an agreement whereby Rowland would basically swear he would not cause the contents of the tapes in which the Sultan was specifically mentioned to be published. The terms of the proposed contract would allow Rowland to provide specific information to the courts or to investigative bodies only if approved in advance by Khashoggi. In short, it was OK to damage Fayed, but not the Sultan. Word had obviously reached the Swami and AK that the Sultan was furious over the sale of the tapes. How could they possibly have supposed he would have felt otherwise?

Even though I had spent hours drafting this agreement, neither the Swami nor AK mentioned it again after landing in Madras, nor was it ever proposed to Tiny.

Trying to make sense of the events of this period was difficult at best. Tiny had purchased the tapes after hearing them in Toronto with no strings attached. Khashoggi and the Swami soon realized they had made a mistake, and tried to revise the agreement. I had been told the tapes were given to Tiny for his private use only, and that he would be breaking his word if he caused statements in the tapes to be published.

Tiny also was shown for the first time a copy of a letter signed by a senior official in Brunei, Dato Ali, confirming that Mark Thatcher and Fayed had been in Brunei in October 1984. The Swami explained he had obtained the letter from Dato Ali as a gesture of gratitude. His prayers had saved the life of Ali's son. Adnan also gave his word that the letter was authentic.

At all events, Tiny returned to London after a few hours in Madras to resume the battle with Fayed more convinced than ever that the facts were on his side.

1986 was the year in which the *Observer* ran several controversial articles on the Fayeds. The most powerful piece was written by Peter Wickman entitled, 'In Search of the Fabulous Pharaohs'. Wickman was the first journalist to actually go to Egypt to investigate the background. *Stern* magazine had commissioned the article, but decided not to publish it because the story was too limited for their readers. Wickman's second choice was the *Observer*. The article explored the Fayeds' claims about family money and found them empty.

Other reporters would come to follow the path that led Fayed from Alexandria to Saudi Arabia, on to Haiti, and finally to 60 Park Lane. By mid-April of 1987, virtually every journalist who had seriously examined Fayed's statements determined they were lies. Only Ivan Fallon of the *Sunday Times* inexplicably continued to tout the Fayed propaganda.

As previously stated, under increasing pressure from all sides, the then Secretary for Trade and Industry, Mr Channon, appointed Inspectors to look into the takeover on 9 April 1987. The cost to the UK taxpayers for this investigation was over £1 million. The 750-page report was completed on 23 July 1988.

One of the more touching moments of the Fayed story came in an exclusive interview with the Sultan in Brunei by the editor of the *Sunday Telegraph*, published 29 May 1988. Fayed, no doubt sensing that the tide of public approval was beginning to turn against him and rightly concerned about the content of the Inspectors' report, convinced the Sultan to grant the interview. The *Telegraph* Editor, Peregrine Worsthorne, traveled to Bandar Seri Begawan for 'an audience' in the 'most spectacularly vulgar edifice' he had ever seen. Before the appointment, he submitted to two days of protocol briefings. Among other things, he was instructed not to cross his legs – a sign of disrespect – and advised it was mandatory to keep his hands folded on his lap throughout the interview. Presumably he had a tape recorder.

His Majesty's response to the question of his involvement, or lack thereof, with the Fayeds in one of the most publicized and controversial corporate takeovers of the century follows: 'He told me categorically,' reports Worsthorne, 'that there was "absolutely no truth" in recent claims that the money used by the Al-Fayeds' to buy House of Fraser had been swindled from him.'

What the Sultan did not say was even more interesting. Rather than categorically deny Fayed used the royal power of attorney to borrow the funds required, His Majesty said, 'He had given Mr Muhammed (sic) Al-Fayed a power of attorney ... He thought it possible that Mr Al-Fayed had found this helpful in raising money for his business dealings ...'

As told above the Swami had promised Princess Mariam her next child would be a male. He prayed with her, chanted the mantras with her, and gave his categorical word to both the Princess and His Majesty that a boy would arrive in December. A wise Dr Reddy had cautioned his guru in the early stages of the Princess's pregnancy to beware of such a perilous promise, but the Swami apparently had begun to believe his own inventions. Reddy suggested a precautionary sonogram or an ultrasound test, but that merely angered Swamiji.

As the plane landed in Madras on 10 December 1985, the Swami observed that the royal prince was due any minute and instructed everyone to seek him out no matter where he might be to let him know the happy news.

Returning to Dr Reddy's elegant home after a brief tour of Madras, I found the air thick with despair. The Swami was sitting on his bed, practically in tears, glaring at an antique wooden crib that had once cradled, according to the documents attached to it, the last Emperor of China. The impressive four-poster bed might have been a fake, but the price-tag certainly was painfully real. One glance at the Swami poking at this regal roost told the story. He had failed the Princess and given the Sultan one more demonstration of his very tenuous link with the gods.

1986 was a frenetic year for the Swami and Adnan. In less guarded moments, they admitted their hopes for a reconciliation with the Sultan had begun to fade. They intended nevertheless to encourage the gossip that the Swami remained the Sultan's spiritual advisor. They also formulated a plan to approach the Kings of Jordan and Saudi Arabia in an attempt to persuade them to intervene on their behalf. Or, at least,

145

that was Khashoggi's stated intent in meetings with the Swami and Miller.

Adnan must have marveled at his luck. Just when everything in his financial empire had gone wrong, he found himself in Toronto with two suckers controlling over $100 million. The more AK learned about the Swami's falling out with the Sultan, the more he offered to enlist his powerful friends in the battle against Fayed. To butter up Miller, Adnan often introduced him as a financial advisor to the Sultan. Nothing could have been further from the truth, but it worked. AK managed to con the two of them out of over $63 million.

On one occasion the duo flew on Adnan's magic carpet to meet with President Mubarak of Egypt, then on to Amman to see King Hussein, and finally to Saudi Arabia intending to see King Faud. The meetings with Mubarak and Hussein were cordial but uneventful. Not until Adnan debriefed the Swami on the DC-8 as they traveled to Saudi Arabia, did he confirm their royal majesties' willingness to speak to the Sultan about the Swami. Neither, of course, had been asked to involve themselves in the matter.

Out of friendship, Hussein had flown from his seaside villa to the royal airport in Amman for a meeting on 28 February 1986. According to protocol, our group had arrived first. The Khashoggi DC-8 looked enormous compared with the King's small Gulfstream III, and the King seemed even smaller standing beside the tall, bulky guru, but he exuded an authority that soon banished any thoughts of size. He spoke in a soft voice, almost a whisper, which required all present to hang on his every word.

The Swami and Adnan met with the King for about 45 minutes. Then, I was asked to join them. His Majesty focused the conversation on Jordan's current problems with the US. He felt that the Congress did not understand the impossible situation he confronted daily. He implied that American foreign policy expected him to play a critical part in negotiating a peaceful settlement in the region, yet frequently undermined his leadership. The meeting occurred at an awkward moment. The US Senate had blocked the King's request to purchase certain sophisticated weapons for Jordan's defense. Hussein said he was saddened by what he had perceived to be a lack of trust in his leadership.

As we accompanied him back to his jet, guarded by about twenty-five uniformed men armed with machine guns, I wondered why on earth he had used his precious time to make Adnan look good. Whether or not he saw the Swami again I do not know. But inevitably the Swami was quoted later in various press articles describing the King as his follower and loyal disciple.

The next stop was Riyadh. Ostensibly the purpose of this trip was to attend the opening of a furniture store owned by Adnan's brother, Adil.

Adnan preferred arriving at his chosen destination in the middle of the night, for reasons only he understood. As planned, we landed in the capital of Saudi Arabia at 4 am to be greeted by Adil and a caravan of white Cadillacs that transported us to the Khashoggi compound. I was assigned to a pleasant little cottage which had Essam Khashoggi's name posted on the door. The rest of the group were directed to a larger house and Adnan adjourned to his sprawling California ranch-style home.

Walking about the next morning, I was surprised to discover dirty, empty swimming pools, neglected gardens and broken lawn furniture. The compound appeared to have been unoccupied for years. Glancing toward the main house, I noticed Adnan peering at me from behind a veiled window. Neither of us acknowledged the moment. In less than an hour a crew of workers arrived to clean and fill the swimming pools, tend to the garden, and replace the lawn chairs. The deserted Saudi retreat suddenly began to look like the Beverly Hills Hotel.

I had never before been to the grand opening of a furniture store, let alone one in Saudi Arabia. The odds are that the Swami had never attended such an occasion either. But, on instructions from Adnan, the entire party rallied and turned up to witness the Swami cut the ribbon and give his blessings to the new enterprise.

Late as usual, His Holiness caused the ceremony to be delayed for thirty minutes. He got his rebuff, however, when the proceedings were further delayed as the audience knelt on their prayer blankets and bowed toward Mecca. The Swami had to cool his sandals until the Muslim ritual was completed. The sight of this Hindu holy man cutting a ribbon to open a furniture store in downtown Riyadh was priceless. Not surprisingly, members of the Saudi royal family were otherwise engaged.

The next day, a host of people called on Adnan and the Swami. I had no idea what was discussed. It soon became clear that the King had not agreed to receive the Swami and was sending his brother instead. The main attraction was the imminent arrival of Prince Talal. At one point, I heard Adnan whisper to Mamaji that the King had agreed to speak to the Sultan in defense of the Swami, but when Adnan caught me eavesdropping, he gave a sly wink which meant I should ignore the comment. Khashoggi must have been talking to dial tones as well. The telephone was always the symbol of power and influence, and the

147

'conversations' were practically made into press releases, but nothing ever happened.

In desperation, the duo began to focus their attention on the exiled leaders of Haiti and the Philippines.

Jean Claude (Baby Doc) Duvalier fled Haiti on 7 February 1986, with the assistance of the US government. An Air Force plane had been dispatched to carry him, his beautiful wife, Michelle, and others to a safe haven in the village of Grenoble, nestled in the French Alps near the Swiss border. No country, including France, wanted this unpopular family. They had looted Haiti and lived a life of Epicurean indulgence while the Haitian people either went hungry or were tortured by the Tonton Macoutes. The day after the Duvaliers had arrived, French government officials began to pressure the US to relocate them.

Michelle Duvalier was a youthful rival of Imelda Marcos. She was beautiful, dominated her husband, and did not mince words. Her wedding to the President of Haiti had set a record for bad taste and cost over $1 million. When the US Ambassador to France spoke to her in early March (Baby Doc does not speak English) in an attempt to induce them to leave France, she told him to 'fuck off.'

The first private individuals to call on the Duvaliers were Khashoggi and the Swami.

The television cameras and reporters stationed at the gates of their retreat in Grenoble payed no attention to the visit. The news interest was focused on whether or not the American Ambassador or a French official would call. The cherubic Saudi businessman, accompanied by a fat guru in white robes, might have been amusing, but they were not hard news.

Adnan had come to lend a helping hand. Soon after the visit, money was transferred from the Duvaliers' numbered Swiss bank account to Khashoggi's. A K then purchased a desirable villa on the French coast and, for a small fee, agreed to rent it to them for life. No government or court could possibly challenge the right of the exiled Haitians to rent a villa. They had to live somewhere. Moreover, the richest man in the world was expected to own such properties. It would never have occurred to anyone that he was merely a front man. The property and their financial investment, he promised, would be completely safe from any attempt by Haitian officials to seize it.

Michelle and Baby Doc now reside in a villa owned by Adnan Khashoggi on the Cote d'Azur near Grasse.

On 26 February 1986, nineteen days after the Duvaliers had been forced to leave Haiti, the US Secretary of State, George Schultz, approved the following statement: 'We praise the decision of President Marcos. Reason and compassion have prevailed in ways that best serve the Filipino nation and people. In his long term as president, Ferdinand Marcos showed himself to be a staunch friend of the United States. We are gratified by the dignity and strength that have marked his many years of leadership.'

The Marcoses bitterly resisted US pressure to leave the Philippines. Near the end, Imelda even telephoned Nancy Reagan to ask her to speak to the President on their behalf. The First Lady consulted the President and called Imelda back to say they would be welcome in the United States.

Neither Imelda nor Ferdinand ever grasped the finality of the situation during their last days under guard at Clark Air Base, one of the major US defense outposts in the Philippines. Marcos demanded to be flown to his home in the Ilocos, but the Joint Chiefs-of-Staff had orders from President Reagan to fly him to Hawaii.

The hasty departure may have forced Imelda to abandon 1200 pairs of shoes and 500 brassieres, but she and Ferdinand landed in Honolulu on 26 February, a bit dazed and carrying $10 million in jewels and gold. For Imelda, this was pin money.

Almost before the official portraits of the former first family had been nailed onto the walls of their modest seaside villa in Honolulu, Khashoggi, Shaheen, and the Swami had checked into the Halikalini Hotel and requested a meeting.

The Marcoses were not in the same league as the Duvaliers. They were much richer. AK and the guru understood the money at stake was billions, not millions. What they failed to grasp, however, was the anger that the Marcoses' excesses had inspired over the past twenty years and, more importantly, the intense scrutiny which would be focused on their movements.

Marcos had virtually bankrupted the country he governed. Even US officials with a mind to forgive and forget, were stunned by the reports. It probably was difficult for US officials to police Marcos's behavior as president – at least during that period, the Americans could pretend to believe they had no control in the matter. Now, suddenly, at the acquiescence of the government of the United States, Marcos was domiciled in Hawaii, yet still conniving as though the rules of law did not apply to him.

The Reagan administration sent representatives from the CIA, the Justice Department and the Department of State to order him to conform to the pre-negotiated terms of his residency and cease all attempts at influencing the political machinations in the Philippines. Ferdinand listened to their rebukes and thanked them for their views. Nothing that was said phased him. All returned to Washington to report that Marcos was out of control and had to be carefully monitored.

One of the most troublesome matters to face Marcos was the new Philippine government's stated intention to recover under the law whatever it could of his ill-gotten gains. The US Congress had held public hearings to investigate the extent of the Marcoses' covert financial holdings in America months before they were forced to leave the Maiacanang palace. Considerable attention was directed toward certain properties in New York generally understood to have been purchased for the President of the Philippines.

The Congressional hearing was a public attack by US leaders on Marcos's leadership and corruption. No enforcement actions were seriously considered or were within the power of the committee. What had emerged, however, was a general acknowledgment that the Crown Building at 730 Fifth Avenue, the Herald Center at 1 Herald Square, 40 Wall Street, and 200 Madison Avenue (all in New York City), were properties the Marcoses had purchased and controlled with funds allegedly stolen from the Filipino Treasury.

In March 1986 the Philippine government initiated civil litigation in New York against the Marcoses, and obtained a court order forbidding the transfer of any properties deemed to be owned by them until the court could rule on their ultimate disposition.

Khashoggi, Shaheen and the Swami pursued Ferdinand and Imelda with remarkable intensity. Adnan's ability to think objectively had to have been clouded by the pressures of impending financial collapse. Miller also was castigating him for the hopeless situation at Triad and the financial debacle into which he had lured the Swami. But, even under these difficult circumstances, reason can find no explanation for Khashoggi's actions.

Reports surfaced in the papers that Khashoggi had filed documents with the US District Court purporting to show he had bought the New York properties from the Marcoses before the President had been forced to leave the Philippines. It strained credibility to accept that AK owned a villa in France rented to the Duvaliers (a villa in which he had never set foot, by the way), that Nabila had purchased the Bel Air mansion on Summit Drive for $7 million (it had always been rumored to have been owned by Imelda Marcos), and that he had magically acquired the New York properties valued at over $100 million prior to 2 March 1986. Did Adnan still believe the billionaire myth granted him immunity from speculation that he might engage in petty crimes? Had Ferdinand, in the fashion of a Mafia boss, asked Adnan to undertake this assignment as a test of his loyalty?

I have a vivid memory of a conversation with Karl Bock Peterson, an unindicted co-conspirator in the case of *The US Government vs Adnan M Khashoggi*. Karl was an unlikely member of the Khashoggi team. He was the epitome of a WASP: understated, articulate, well-dressed, trim. If he had had wire rimmed glasses, he could have passed for George Bush. Karl glanced at me with a tortured wince when I asked about the Khashoggi-Marcos episode in New York. Adnan had involved Karl in the court proceedings. 'He would never try to bluff on a matter like this, would he?' I asked. Karl shook his head, but did not reply.

By this time, I had no doubt that Adnan and the Swami were bad news. They articulated lofty goals, but had none. Miller, Mamaji and I argued constantly over my mistaken notion of our purpose. In Paris, the Swami had slammed the door in my face when I told him I was fed up with his lies.

Adnan, however, continued to insist I work with them. He might have harbored a slight sense of guilt over the fact that I had brought him together with the Swami and never been paid the agreed fee. He had explained that the money from Miller was merely loaned, therefore no fee could be paid. Once they began to make a profit, he promised, I would be compensated. He never wanted anyone to leave in anger.

Somehow the Khashoggi myth survived in spite of his countless indiscretions, partly because he made few enemies. A master of deception must also be a master of compromise. In 1958, Adnan had sued Mohamed Fayed, his brother-in-law at the time, for over $500,000 in unpaid debts, but dropped the matter rather than go to court. A K's first wife, Saroya, petitioned the courts for $2.5 billion in her divorce action against him. Never willing to make a public disclosure of his net worth, Adnan settled the matter out of court for less than $2 million with the understanding that he would do his best to look after her and that she would remain a member of the family. Saroya has always appeared, along with Lamia, in all official Khashoggi family photos.

No. Adnan tried to sustain my friendship because he hoped I would never wake up and do something dreadful, like write a book.

151

# – 21 –
## Follow the Money

Tracking the money is almost impossible when men like Fayed, Khashoggi and the Swami are involved. Numbered bank accounts, off-shore corporations, and small nations that have no reciprocal tax treaty with the US or the UK are the tools of their trade.

Fayed admitted in the taped conversations at Carlos Place that his funds and those of the Sultan were often commingled. The Sultan had given him three letters of authorization which empowered him to terminate several of His Majesty's prior agreements. Recall the instance the Sultan advanced Jet Aviation $100 million to purchase and customize a 747 airplane. The deal was canceled by Fayed and $86 million was returned to the Sultan, or so he thought. In fact, the money was transferred to a Fayed account at Compagnie de Gestion et de Banque Gonet SA, in the name of Hyde Park Investment Holding SA. This clever ploy by Fayed angered the Sultan when he discovered it several months later. It was, nonetheless, a part of the capital used in the purchase of House of Fraser.

The principal source of the funds used in the HOF takeover was the joint account Fayed had established with the Sultan. Never wishing to bore His Majesty with small details, Fayed neglected to explain that while it was a joint account opened in both of their names, either could operate it separately. Once the Sultan had placed $1.5 billion in their account at Credit Suisse, Zurich, Fayed began to transfer the odd millions to Hyde Park Investment Holding at Compagnie de Gestion et de Banque Gonet. The funds were then transferred to a third account in the same bank, for the use of Alfayed Investment and Trust SA. Both of these are Fayed companies incorporated in Liechtenstein and are not subject to the tax laws of the UK. The Liechtenstein companies, on orders from Fayed, instructed the bank to give the necessary assurance to Fayed's new merchant banker, Kleinwort Benson, to enable the purchase of HOF to go forward.

Such transactions happen daily in the world of high finance. It probably never crossed the minds of the managers at Kleinwort Benson that they had a duty to verify Fayed's statements. Unimpeachable bank references had confirmed the Egyptians had the money; the HOF Board had given its approval to the takeover; they stood to make a tidy sum on the sale; newspaper reports had begun to appear regularly substantiating the Fayeds' claims of vast wealth. Why was it necessary to waste time on background checks? It is understandable that an investment banking firm might have felt a bit cheeky asking a client whether the billion dollars reputable banks had confirmed available on their order was honestly earned or swindled from the Sultan of Brunei.

Kleinwort Benson might also have felt that the fundamental questions should have been asked by the Secretary for Trade and Industry. Clearly, it was the duty of the DTI to check the facts and verify the credentials of the bidder. The DTI could blame Kleinwort Benson for submitting an incorrect corroboration of the source and amount of the Fayed money. Kleinwort Benson could say they were under pressure from the DTI, and had not been given enough time to do extensive background checks. In the last analysis, none of this washes, however. Lonrho raised the proper objections from day one of the takeover battle. Quite simply, their points were never seriously considered.

Fayed had persuaded the Sultan to become his partner in various business ventures and to entrust him with $1.5 billion. Most men would have considered that the deal of a lifetime. Fayed had assets of about $30 million. With this joint venture, he should have been able to make a billion dollars. Yet, he alienated the Sultan by his ill-conceived takeover of HOF.

Khashoggi operated in much the same way as Fayed, but often with even less caution. Adnan used off-shore companies in the Cayman Islands and elsewhere, as well as numbered accounts in Swiss banks. He not only had bank accounts everywhere, but also enjoyed the cooperation of the bank managers who allowed him to kite checks with impunity. He proved again and again the old adage: if you owe the bank $10,000, they hound you to death; if you owe the bank $10 million, they will loan you another $10 million to cover their bet.

When the United States Attorney in the Southern District of New York indicted Khashoggi on charges of obstruction of justice and racketeering, the action listed two Khashoggi bank accounts which are subject to forfeiture if the government wins the case. Ferdinand and Imelda Marcos were indicted in the same action. Twenty-eight Marcos accounts were identified. Both AK and the Marcoses have numbered bank accounts not covered by the jurisdiction of the US Court in this litigation. The charges filed against them are a major step forward in international legal efforts to protect the rights of innocent victims, and, if justice triumphs, the people of the Philippines will benefit by the addition to the Treasury of approximately $103 million. But other hidden accounts contain billions of dollars that most likely will never be fingered let alone returned.

It was the Marcoses' ill-advised involvement with Khashoggi, after they were forced to leave the Philippines, that brought about the indictment. Still believing they were immune from the rule of law, Ferdinand and Imelda agreed to participate in fraudulent acts which meant almost nothing to them in hard financial terms.

The scene at the New York City court on 31 October 1988, was pure soap opera. Imelda had to appear at 11 am to be arraigned and fingerprinted. The Marcos lawyers had tried to avoid this humiliation, but the judge would not waiver. Ferdinand's doctors said he was too ill to make the trip, and the judge granted a delay until court-appointed physicians could examine him.

Imelda rose to the occasion with her customary flair. She prevailed upon long-time family friend, tobacco heiress Doris Duke, to loan her private jet. Three limousines wafted her entourage to the Waldorf Towers on Park Avenue where she had commandeered an enormous suite. The hotel lobby was a madhouse with press and supporters struggling to get near her. But Imelda demonstrated, once again, that she was not distracted by such worldly intrusions. She spent the entire afternoon at St Patrick's Cathedral lost in contemplation and prayer. The next day she entered a plea of not guilty.

The imponderable question is why the former first family would indulge in such conduct for $100 million when their net worth is estimated to be over $10 billion. Ferdinand supposedly offered the Filipino government $5 billion for the right to return home. With only a few years left to live, why would he risk imprisonment?

Another defendant in this case, Adnan Khashoggi, did not appear in court in spite of US officials' attempts to arraign him. Shortly after he was scheduled to appear, the press reported he had been stopped at customs in Cyprus where $160,000 was confiscated after his failure to report the currency on the exit visa. AK was said to be traveling to Spain on a commercial airline. According to the last report, Khashoggi had returned to Saudi Arabia at the request of the royal family. Allegedly they have agreed to provide him with a safe haven from the US Courts. Adnan both helped and humiliated them. They must have determined the smart move was to grant him protection and keep him out of sight.

On a smaller scale, the saga of the Swami and the 'pickle man' relates the same story. Rather than return the poor man's $100,000, the Swami allowed himself to be jailed.

To my astonishment, the Swami invited me to join him on a visit to the Marcoses in Hawaii on 17 August 1986. In spite of my misgivings, I could not resist. At that point, the deposed leader had given no press interviews and the situation was fascinating.

On our arrival in Honolulu, the Swami was greeted by the manager of the Halikalini Hotel as though he were the Sultan. It was obvious that Adnan and he had been there many times before. As further proof, the guards at the gate of the Marcoses' villa recognized him instantly and allowed the car to enter the compound without any security checks. Imelda and Ferdinand stood at the door with arms outstretched to greet us.

Contrary to press reports, the villa was not at all large or elegant. And Imelda was dressed in a simple silk blouse wearing black cotton slacks. Never before had I seen her without jewelry. Ferdinand welcomed us effusively and ushered the Swami into his bedroom for what turned out to be a two-hour session.

The telephone rang incessantly. Imelda answered it herself. I was seated on the terrace, gazing at the ocean, waiting for something to happen. As the telephone was just inside the door of the villa, it was impossible not to hear everything Imelda said. Still, I tried to act as though my mind was elsewhere. In spite of this, I fear she heard my laugh when she sang out: 'Christina, darling! I cannot wait to see you.'

Eventually, Imelda came out on the terrace to engage me in the most bewildering conversation. For openers, she placed a yellow pad on the table and sketched a map of the world, based on her view of politics and power. In the center of her map, of course, was the Philippines. Her discourse was very like a Birch Society lecture pitting the forces of good against the forces of evil. In summary, world communism was aggressively expanding and its ultimate success or failure depended on the independence of the Philippines.

The thrust of her argument was that unless she and Ferdinand were reinstated as the leaders of the Philippines, the world would fall into the hands of the communists. Her eyes filled with tears as she pleaded with me to return to Washington and relate this message. Her life in America was simple and uncomplicated. After all, she had almost been assassinated in her own country in the defense of freedom. Why would she want to risk her life again? With more tears, she repeated her only motivation in asking to return was her commitment to the free world. She ended this oration by mentioning that she cared about Mrs Aquino and wished her well. 'Cory is unskilled and weak, however. She will hand my country to the communists.' At that moment Ferdinand and the Swami entered the room.

The former president undoubtedly had witnessed this performance before. As though following a script, he took my hand and asked me to walk with him for a moment along the beach. Not since visiting Taiwan on a college exchange program in 1967, and hearing the youth groups describe how they intended to retake the mainland of China, have I observed anything like Marcos's routine. He looked across the sea as though looking across the room and talked of his beloved country. 'You must help us!' he said.

Later, Imelda lamented that she had entrusted over $700 million of the family jewels to the wife of the former head of South Vietnam, Nguyen Cao Ky. In the last days of their rule vast sums of gold, valuable paintings and other items such as the jewels had been placed in the custody of friends to smuggle out of the country. Apparently, the temptation was too great for most of these 'trusted' pals. If Imelda could be believed, Mrs Ky had refused to return her telephone calls and intended to keep the bounty. 'It doesn't really matter to me,' Imelda whimpered, 'but, poor Imee. These were her jewels. Now she has nothing.'

Hearing this tale, the Swami became enraged and promised to recover the gems. 'Martindale and I will take care of "cowkey",' he pledged.

This was the first trip since the Brunei foray that the Swami and I had taken without Mamaji, Adnan, or any other member of the crew. As we were about to leave the hotel for the plane, the Swami dictated a brief letter to Imelda in which I was to thank her for her hospitality and include a bank account number in Hong Kong where she was to wire $1 million. I asked: 'What for?' Shaking with laughter, the Swami replied: 'prayers'.

The next day the Swami and I motored to Huntington Beach, California to meet with Ky.

Why Cao Ky agreed to receive us remains a mystery. One of the Swami's disciples had telephoned over twenty times to speak to Mrs Ky, who was never available. Finally, the Swami commandeered the telephone to inform whoever had answered that he would present himself at 3 pm that very day on orders from Mrs Marcos.

The Ky home on Sunburst Lane was a modest split-level, suburban brick dwelling on a corner lot in the midst of hundreds of other identical brick split-levels. We were shown in by a young Vietnamese man, whom I took to be Ky's son, and seated in the living room. The room was spotless, spartan, and gray (rather like a physician's waiting room without the magazines). The Swami fell asleep after a few minutes of pointless chatter, and I fidgeted in my chair for the next hour and fifteen minutes. Finally, and without ceremony, Nguyen Cao Ky appeared at the top of the stairway. Having seen his face on television so often during the Vietnam War, it was spooky to observe him materialize from nowhere, and descend the stairs. In the manner of a funeral director discussing the preference of a coffin for the deceased, he monotoned that his wife was away for an indefinite period and, in any event, would discuss the matter only with Mrs Marcos.

Angrily, the Swami responded that he had been commanded by Imelda to undertake this mission and did not intend to leave without a satisfactory answer. He demanded to know when the jewels would be returned. Ky paused for a moment, then opened the door. 'I am sorry you have wasted your time,' he said ushering us to our waiting limousine. The cold finality of his manner prevented the Swami from over-reacting further. And I was relieved he had not pulled a gun and ended our intrusion conclusively.

Whether Mrs Ky acted for Imelda or not, and where the money or the jewels ended up, will probably never be known. Just as Imelda and Ferdinand had persuaded Khashoggi to backdate documents and falsify the true ownership of the New York properties, they had asked the Swami to involve himself in another questionable scheme. The flip side of this story, of course, is that both Khashoggi and the Swami eagerly volunteered their services.

Another haunting question. Did the leaders of the free world and those responsible for the execution of their policies use Khashoggi and the others in the same way Adnan hired prostitutes?

Adnan constantly was quoted denying he hired call-girls for his business associates and as bait for potential investors. In fact there was rarely a night when the girls were not present. They were high class, well dressed, and available on a wink from Khashoggi. This ploy, used by all con men, was especially effective with men who had matured in strict Muslim countries. They learned that whenever they were with Adnan, they could enjoy the pleasures of the flesh in luxurious secrecy. Working with Adnan and investing in his projects, it turns out, was seductive in more ways than one.

# – 22 –

# The Scandalous Chandra Swami

It will forever intrigue those who knew Swamiji that he managed to beguile so many sophisticated people. What the Swami had was Mamaji Kalish N Agerwal who was the brains behind the guru. Everything said, every public occasion, every interaction with heads of state, everything was articulated and executed by Mamaji. His supreme skill was to make it seem as though the Swami was in total command. And meanwhile he funneled over $100 million to Ernie Miller.

As noted in the introduction and elsewhere, Swamiji was arrested in India on charges of fraud, tax evasion and foreign exchange offenses. The specific allegations against the Swami came from the defamation writ he initiated against the 'pickle man'. The case was subsequently dropped, but it gave the Indian authorities their first solid evidence for action. Without a conviction, of course his arrest proves little. No date for a trial has been set, and many influential people in India continue to look the other way. The Swami has even begun to spread rumors that he has used his influence to neutralize the growing opposition to Prime Minister Rajiv Gandhi, and that he will never go to trial for this reason.

A highly placed government official, and close confidant of the Prime Minister, stated: 'It does no good to wound the tiger, he must be killed. The fear of many is that the evidence obtained by the CBI is too

159

circumstantial and that the Swami will not only be found innocent due to lack of hard evidence, but that he also will use the acquittal as proof that he has become so powerful his enemies cannot stop him. You see, by wounding him, we make him stronger.'

Tiger?

The Swami became a minor power broker in India in the same pattern as Fayed in England. He mixed the most potent ingredients into the pot – money, politics, intense personal relationships, public relations and lies.

The young Nemi Chandra Jain was not successful in his attempts to gain the backing of the Youth Congress Party, but Chandra Swami emerged as a holy man imbued with some political savvy. His skills were no better than those of a local mayor, and he was limited by his lack of any formal education, but he managed to appear skillful by employing other tactics.

Lyndon B Johnson was one of America's great presidents. In the art of politics, he had no equal. My favorite tale describes Congressman Johnson campaigning to become the US Senator from Texas in 1948. LBJ would position himself outside a factory gate in the early morning hours and shake the hand of every worker. With an intent look in his eyes, he often queried: 'How are your hemorrhoids?' This calculated remark would evoke a response like: 'Thank you, sir, I am doing better. How good of you to care.' Or, 'I will tell my brother, Fred, that you asked about him.'

Swamiji was hardly in LBJ's league, but he had learned that in the presence of a man of stature a great deal can be accomplished by taking an interest in intensely personal matters such as his wife or favorite son. A bond can be formed very quickly. The guest of honor must greet hundreds of people and inevitably finds it hard to focus attention on anyone in particular. If the Swami, or anyone like him, were to ring the guest of honor the next day, he would be placed on the call list with hundreds of others. On the other hand, if he were to ring the lonely child or the neglected wife he had charmed the night before, it would be considered courteous, and might also turn out to be extremely useful.

There was no divine intervention or tantrik power involved in the relationship between the Swami and Mariam Bell. He simply paid attention to her and made her feel important perhaps for the first time since she had married into the royal family. Instinctively, he felt her pain. It was a moment when everything, including the destiny of her husband's legacy, was at risk. His first meeting with the Sultan was cordial, but empty from His Majesty's point of view. Swamiji recognized quickly that the impatient monarch was only mildly impressed. Luckily, Zobel had told him of the Sultan's consuming desire for the Princess to bear him a son. When the Swami informed Princess Mariam that his prayers would virtually guarantee the birth of a prince and further impressed her with his psychic powers, he also managed to secure his entrée with the Sultan.

Another ploy that enabled the Swami to operate in other countries, especially Third World nations, was his ability to capitalize on his reputation in India. Mamaji frequently spoke in awesome terms about the Swami's powerful following. His claims had sufficient foundation to convince members of the press and many outside India to take notice. Even when his photo album was bulging with famous faces and he controlled a fortune, the guru cultivated new devotees, tended to his loyal followers, and impressed other swamis.

His international status was a clever fiction. The sceptical swamis became impressed with his ability to produce VIPs such as Imee Marcos, and his unworldly guests returned home convinced he was the leader of a powerful Hindu movement.

On one auspicious occasion in April 1986, the fates carried me to the banks of the Ganges, in Hardiwar, for the celebration of Kumbh Mela. I was both a witness and a participant at a significant passage in the Hindu faith which occurs only once in twelve years. I was driven to Hardiwar in the usual white Mercedes. As the temperature increased, the road narrowed, and the dust flew from dodging donkeys, two-wheeled carts pulled by camels, and millions of faithful Hindus, I was grateful for the luxury of an air-conditioned car. My pilgrimage did not impose the kind of hardships most supplicants endure.

The journey from Delhi took three hours in spite of the break-neck speed the driver insisted on maintaining. Once in Hardiwar, uniformed guards waved the car past several barricades into the encampment along the Ganges which was set apart for the celebrants. Over ten million people were in attendance and had been organized into sections according to their particular Hindu bent. All milled about under the watchful eyes of thousands of uniformed police. The day after I left, forty devotees were trampled to death because of a misstep by a disoriented and overeager octogenarian. Fortunately, because of tight security and incredible crowd control, fortunately that was the only accident.

The Swami's tented house of worship boasted the largest banner: 'The

International Conference of All Faiths Kumbh Mela'. It was scripted in both English and Hindi, painted in vivid red, and could be seen throughout the compound. Driving toward his particular section, the car was engulfed by hordes of naked monks, dripping wet from their immersion in the holy river, waving and bowing toward what they assumed was a ranking guest.

Mamaji was stationed at the entrance of the meeting hall to orchestrate the arrival. He escorted me to a stage at the head of the tent where I was seated among a host of swamis of various ages, colors and sects. My favorite were the Jains who seemed to inspire a special reverence from the assembly. The Jain swamis wore white robes and a white cover over their mouths, which looked like a six-by-five-inch plastic card. The eldest of the Jains gave a sermon which was loudly applauded by the SRO crowd. Curiosity finally forced me to leave my seat of honor for a moment to ask an English speaking friend what the holy man had said and why he wore a mask. The translation of his remarks was either incomprehensible or nonsensical, but the logic of the mask was simple enough: 'It prevents him from swallowing flies,' said my pal. By the time I left Hardiwar, I was ready to join the Jains.

One thing was certain, at this festival of festivals, Chandra Swami was top dog. The explanation, I slowly figured out, was not the power of his spiritual message, but money. He not only picked up all the expenses for the main event, he also reached out to the assembled multitude in ways calculated to enhance his reputation.

That evening after the official service was concluded, the Swami offered supper to 10,000 monks. The men had come by foot from the mountains of Nepal where they lived, as the Swami claimed he had, in trees. It was instantly apparent they rarely had a proper meal. Many were blind or crippled, and none had ever seen a doctor or a dentist. They lived a barren existence sustained by the aid of caring neighbors. The monks symbolized pure dedication to the gods and were, therefore, revered.

The Swami's guests stood waiting to file into a special encampment as soon as the gates were opened, and quickly seated themselves on the earth in rows of 100. The honored guests were then summoned to duty and asked to serve what looked like porridge and fruit on a plate of leaves. My mind flashed back to the time spent at Harvard Divinity School and my tenure as the assistant minister of the Union Methodist Church in Roxbury, just out of Boston. This experience was very much like a priest offering bread and wine during communion.

Amazingly, the simple meal was served to 10,000 men in two hours.

The monks seemed thrilled. I was exhausted. Then, Mamaji produced a huge stack of 5 rupee currency notes (US 50 cents) with instructions to give one to each of the guests. When I looked agast at this suggestion, Mamaji stifled any doubts by saying that 5 rupees would buy these monks food for a week.

The gesture seemed to please the monks, but more to the point, it impressed the millions nearby who were told of the Swami's generosity and spread the word throughout India.

The Swami had mastered the basic politics of his religion, but he had failed in a monumental way to understand the dangers inherent in too much public exposure. The article in the *Onlooker,* which was typical of many similar news reports around the world, angered the foreign leaders he described as his followers, and caused everyone of substance he had met to distance themselves.

The more Swamiji flaunted his wealth and trumped-up contacts, moreover, the greater was the incentive for the CBI in India to follow and investigate his activities. It might have been believable that Khashoggi funded his travels and enabled him to live in a manner that no other swami could imagine in earlier years, but Adnan's financial crash was known in the Third World and the non-aligned nations long before the investment bankers in Western capitals woke up. Regardless of the source of funds for the Swami's extravagant home and ashram in Delhi and the new Mercedes, the money was never properly reported to the Indian tax authorities. The Swami's renown prevented any quiet payoffs or settlements to quash the charges. The authorities were literally forced to move against him. The wonder is that they hesitated so long.

The Swami's most common tactic was to tell conflicting versions of events to his close followers in order to keep them off balance and to cover up his own lies.

As I rethink his remarks about Asha, they had to have been a lie. He needed a scapegoat at the time and made me believe that Asha's innocent remarks (instead of his failure to obtain His Majesty's prior approval) poisoned the trip to Monaco in the Sultan's eyes.

Toward the end of my time with Swamiji, I caught him asking one of his disciples to make a threatening telephone call in an attempt to silence the complaints of a woman he had betrayed. Since word of this book became public, I have received scores of threats on the telephone as well as innumerable requests for interviews from individuals who first name the publications for which they work, then explain they work

163

at home so it is impossible to verify their position in the routine fashion.

Swamiji was a world famous guru for almost ten years. He began by swindling a great deal of money from hundreds of average individuals. But the bulk of his fortune came from the Sultan, President Mobutu, and the Marcoses. None the less, if he is ever brought to justice, it will be a little guy like the 'pickle man' who makes it possible. In most instances only those who have nothing to lose appear willing to struggle for justice.

Whatever else he may have been, the Swami was a genius at living several different lives. When I was watching, he lived simply and played the part of a holy man. Never in my presence did he speak of money. Perhaps I should have surmised he did not ask for money because his third eye told him I had none. When he was with Elizabeth Taylor, he spoke to her of universal religion and showed unusual insight into her complicated life. If she had offered him money, he would have declined to accept by explaining that his brother, Khashoggi, took care of him financially. What he said to his followers after Elizabeth left the room can only be imagined. To demonstrate that he was not after her money, the Swami gave Elizabeth a $300,000 emerald necklace. Why she would accept such a gift remains a mystery.

The guru instinctively knew which people he would use to enhance his status. They were exposed to the spiritual, prayerful, playful Swami. He also knew which individuals would be impressed by his high level contacts, and buy into his schemes. They were, for the most part, naive people like the 'pickle man'.

Then, in late 1984 and 1985, he hit upon a group of major players on the world scene who were incredibly rich and, to his happy discovery, ingenuous.

Khashoggi introduced the Swami to Marchel Mobutu, the President of Zaire, shortly after his witch doctor had been killed in an automobile accident. Mobutu spoke to the Swami in French which Adnan translated into English for Mamaji to translate into Hindi. The Swami's own brand of magic worked and he quickly became a trusted advisor.

At a particular critical moment, the Swami hid behind the extravagant silk window coverings of the President's Paris apartment on Avenue Foch while two generals from Zaire's army passed by. The guru then told Mobutu which man to trust and retain and which had to be exiled. A major part of the Swami's fortune came directly from the grateful President of Zaire at least $18 million in cash and $26\frac{1}{2}$ kilos of uncut diamonds.

Mohamed Fayed, by comparison, never made the Swami's obvious mistakes. When Fayed swindled someone, he was careful to go after targets with more at risk in public exposure or legal actions. He would never have wronged a man like Patak who had nothing to lose in seeking retribution.

For example, Fayed was introduced to Khashoggi through a friend in 1953. Within months, Fayed got to know Khashoggi's young sister, Samira, and soon they were married. Mohamed and his younger brother, Ali, then got jobs with AK. Mohamed became the manager of the Saudi end of Adnan's first business venture and Ali assumed the post of AK's secretary in Geneva. It was not long before the brothers were accused of cheating and stealing from their brother-in-law. The marriage soon fell apart and Samira wanted out. The situation became so complicated that Adnan was forced to give up his civil and criminal claims against the Fayed brothers in order to obtain his sister's divorce.

As a further example, when Fayed hoodwinked the President of Haiti into one of his counterfeit projects, he knew Papa Doc considered himself above the law and would never put his position of absolute authority in jeopardy to pursue a minor-league crook.

President 'Papa Doc' Duvalier first met Fayed in 1964. Mohamed presented himself as Sheik Fayed of Kuwait. Duvalier was captivated by tales of the Sheik's youth in the Kuwaiti palace and the limitless wealth of his cousin, the Emir. Papa Doc needed experienced people to guide the economic development of his country. There seemed to be nothing Duvalier would not do for this delightful member of the Kuwaiti royal family in return for his willingness to usher Haiti into the modern world. The President made Fayed a citizen of Haiti (falsely claiming he had resided in Haiti for ten years) and commissioned him to restore the wharf as well as approving other ventures.

Once Fayed had snared the President and negotiated the crucial contracts, he used the wharf project to his advantage. There was, of course, no money from Kuwait or elsewhere. Rather, he acted quickly to transfer as much money as possible from the government account, established to renovate the wharf, to an account under his personal control.

In less than five months, Fayed fled Haiti carrying his new Haitian passport and an account book at the Royal Bank of Canada into which he had transferred over $150,000 from the wharf appropriations. In those days this was a substantial sum and one which Haiti could ill afford.

He knew that Duvalier would discover his theft at once, but would have no recourse. If the Tonton Macoutes were unable to kill him on sight, he was safe. Any dramatic action would have made Papa Doc look complicitous and foolish.

Fayed next settled in London. Overnight he became another man. Haiti was magically erased from his resumé. In this reincarnation, Fayed said he had been born the son of a wealthy Egyptian family, and, with the power of that inheritance, had created a vast business empire.

No one disputes that Fayed made a substantial income from projects in the Gulf. He had hit upon the Ambassador of the Emirates, Mahdi Al-Tajir, who was a close confident of Sheik Rasheed of Dubai. Out of friendship, Al-Tajir helped Fayed gain a new name and passport, perhaps to avoid the possibility of any retribution from Haiti: Al-Fayed of Fayedia in Dubai. Al-Tajir's support also helped Fayed earn commissions on various construction contracts. Just as Khashoggi had excelled as a middleman between the US and Saudi Arabia, Fayed acted as an agent for British firms.

By most standards, Fayed had become a rich man. His net worth in 1984 may have been about $30 million. 60 Park Lane in London became the center of his business life, and he operated from this splendid location in a grand style. On weekends he would escape with his family to a castle in Scotland, unless duty required him to oversee an important part of the renovation of the Ritz Hotel in Paris which he bought in 1979. It was an enviable existence.

Not until he overestimated the timidity of the Sultan of Brunei and underestimated the resolve of Tiny Rowland would he be forced to conform to the standards that normally define human conduct.

How Fayed imagined he could defy the laws of Great Britain in the takeover of House of Fraser must puzzle everyone. Why he was not content to live the life of a country gentleman, secured by his more than respectable fortune, begs examination.

The same must be said of Khashoggi. No matter how much money he controlled, it was not enough. At first he was driven to own more houses, more airplanes, and a larger yacht than any other man. Then, as his financial resources evaporated, he was driven to squander what fortune remained to keep those symbols of success.

The Swami, too, amassed a fortune in devious ways. If the reports of his wealth are anywhere near the truth, he could have built the most lavish ashram in India and lived like a king. But the guru who said he once slept in a tree, was not content with his untold and unearned fortune.

The Swami wanted to be Khashoggi; Fayed wanted to be the Sultan;

and Adnan wanted to be a Western god. For many years, it seemed that the extraordinary guile of their lies, and their total and utter lack of morals, might enable them to succeed.

When Adnan mentioned, at an informal lunch in Cannes, that he admired Adolf Hitler, I should have taken him at his word. The odds are that it was from Hitler Khashoggi learned the axiom by which he, Fayed, and the Swami lived: the more outrageous the lie, the less people challenge its validity.

# – 23 –
# Where Are They Now?

KALISH N AGERWAL 'MAMAJI' has returned to India and disappeared.

HIS MAJESTY THE SULTAN OF BRUNEI remains the richest man in the world and seems to have outgrown his need to befriend men like Fayed and Khashoggi. At the death of his father, he understood finally that all threats to his throne were finished. Ostensibly, the Brunei billions are now in the hands of competent investment bankers scrutinized by independent accountants. Things never seem to change, however. The Sultan purchased the Beverly Hills Hotel on Sunset Boulevard in California in late 1988 from US film and corporate mogul, Marvin Davis, for twice the amount Davis paid less than two years before. The deal was brokered by a man called Manoukian, an old London pal the Sultan had met at a nightclub. In the Carlos Place tapes, Fayed describes Manoukian as 'terrible man ... shirt maker ... he brings girls to ... (the Sultan's) ... younger brother ... He's Armenian. Armenian people worse than the Jews.'

MOHAMED FAYED continues as chairman and owner of House of Fraser Holdings. The debt of HOF last recorded at just under £1 billion has now gone over the top. The Serious Frauds Office investigation plods along, and continues to petition the court by Lonrho to require publication of the Inspectors' 750-page report on the Fayed takeover continue to be granted, along with other actions initiated to expose the truth. On 16 January 1989, the High Court criticized Lord Young for failing to cite reasons why the matter should not be referred to the Monopolies and Mergers Commission in view of the latest disclosures in the Inspectors' Report, and ordered the matter be referred. The court also ordered Lord Young to reconsider publication of the report, with the clear indication that the reason he had given for not publishing was bad. Lord Young appealed successfully to the Court of Appeal. The matter awaits a final judgment from the House of Lords.

ADNAN KHASHOGGI did not appear before the United States District Court Judge of the Southern District of New York to enter a plea in the case of the *United States of America v Adnan Khashoggi*. He has become a fugitive from justice. The Saudi royal family has granted him safe haven, as they did with former Ugandan dictator, Dada Idi Amin. Khashoggi faces legal actions in most world capitals. While the yacht, the planes, and the glorious residences have been forfeited to his creditors, he still has about $20 million stashed away. Typically, AK is pleading, pulling strings, and maneuvering to make a comeback. His wife and children live in Europe and America less certain of their future, but still loyal to 'baba'.

ERNIE MILLER has sought refuge from the Canadian tax authorities and other investigators in the Cayman Islands with his family. The Falcon 50 was sold in August 1988, after it had sat unused in a New Jersey airport for weeks. Ernie had not paid the $60,000 maintenance fee. He also sold the Black Hawk motel and mortgaged the house in Gormley for $900,000. Friends of Ernie report there is no love lost between him and Khashoggi.

TINY ROWLAND remains the chief executive of Lonrho. After years of setbacks, he seems to be winning the battle to force responsible individuals in the government, the media, and the financial community to recognize that the Fayeds and Kleinwort Benson hoodwinked them into approving a major corporate takeover that was in violation of company law.

ROBERT SHAHEEN lives with his wife, Patricia, in New York City. He apparently has severed all ties with Khashoggi. Rumors circulate that Shaheen was granted immunity by US Attorney Rudolph W Giuliani in the RICO indictments in exchange for evidence against the Chief.

SHRI CHANDRA SWAMIJI was detained in India after his arrest in 1987, and his passport was confiscated. In recent months a judge in the Indian courts ordered his passport returned and granted him the right to court approved travel. He has been seen in London and in the US. At the time of writing, his trial date has not been set. His following is virtually gone, especially among heads of state. No one listens today when he boasts, as he did to the *Onlooker* magazine: 'I have sixty to seventy heads of state who would do anything I tell them.' Whatever fortune is left has been secreted away by Ernie.

# – 24 –
# The Parable of the Richest Man in the World

*Every story should have a simple lesson. I offer this parable which, had it been told to me in my youth, might have ended any interest in joining the Swami's circus. If your children are too young to read this book, you may wish to put them to sleep with my simplified explanation.*

Once upon a time and far away in the East, there lived a young King. His father, who had ruled the kingdom for over twenty-seven years, had placed his eldest son on the throne in order to keep lesser men from plotting against the royal succession.

The wily old King never intended to give the power of his throne to his son. Knowing that his first born was unprepared for the duty that was thrust upon him, the old monarch made his son a puppet, or at least, that was his intention.

The new King was not yet prepared for this awesome task. Thus, he obeyed his father's wishes and looked to him and his brothers for counsel in all matters.

When he became the supreme ruler of his nation, the young King had a Queen of royal birth, whom he had betrothed years ago at the insistence of his father. The Queen was fertile and dutiful, but it was inevitable that the young man who became the King would long to experience emotions not fixed by his father. Soon he met and fell in love with a girl of beauty and allure from a poor family. And, as the law of Allah allows, wed her, whilst the royal family, especially his Queen, wept.

Now, the King was the richest man on earth, for his wealth was the same as that of a man luck had ordained the owner of a fertile field. Those who planted the seeds and reaped the harvest were paid for their labor, but the gold others paid for the bounty, belonged to the owner. Some said his fortune increased threefold every year. The King's riches came from a black gold found beneath his land. This black gold made him the richest man in the world; it also made him the most tantalizing target for those in pursuit of great wealth.

It chanced, though, that all was not well in the little kingdom. For position, wealth, and youth bring with them their temptations, and the King had begun to go astray. He traveled far and wide seeking the pleasures of distant countries who fear not the name Allah; spending his youth in the brightly lit halls drunk with the music of flute and drum. He loved the jewels of foreign bazaars and bought the gems that are beyond price: rubies, emeralds, lapis, and diamonds to adorn his body and that of his beloved second wife, Princess Mariam. He gave but little time and wisdom to the needs of his people.

Amongst the royal family there was anger and intrigue. First, greed filled the envious hearts of his brothers. They spent their time plotting with other members of the court to enrich their coffers, for while they lacked nothing, the King's riches were so great as to cause them to feel small in the eyes of other royal sons. Second, there was unhappiness between the King's wives. Princess Mariam sought to help her poor brothers and sisters gain positions in court whereby they might become rich as well. Away from the King's ears, there was talk of gold being stored in secret caves by the oldest brother of the Princess.

All the while, the Queen sat in anger at the palace over the King's great love for her rival. As her hate grew, so did her body from feeding her sorrow with dainties from the feast table.

Finally, the former ruler, who loved the Queen for the grandson she had borne him, despaired of his eldest son's ways, and began to take long walks by the sea with his second son to search his heart and will, should Allah command the former King banish his first-born son from the throne. The second son rejoiced in his heart at his father's words.

There came to the young King's court many men from distant lands who professed to be his friend whilst seeking only riches. Their presence in court caused the King to despair of ever having trustworthy friends.

172

In the midst of feuds with the royal family and the empty words of men who cared not for him but for his treasure, the King honored not the duty of his throne. Nightly, he sat alone in the palace and prayed that Allah would send him faithful courtiers.

And so it was that three men appeared at court in the King's hour of need and isolation. Unlike the rakish and greedy men that had hitherto followed him, these men said they were his equal in both power and wealth, and wanted only to be at his side as brothers stand together in times of peril. The King found joy in their company and was at peace for they asked not for favors. Wisdom and the pain of past betrayals caused the King to walk slowly with his newfound associates and to observe for a time the strength of their filial bond, for the King had known temptation in his own life and understood he must let time pass before he made any of the three men his trusted friend.

The King first met Adnan, a man from Araby whose great stomach rocked with the sounds of his own laughter. The second was a cunning Egyptian named Fayed, and the third was a trader from the Philippine Isles known as Zobel. Between these men there was no love, for they all desired to be the King's favored companion.

As mules carry their wares to the market place, one behind the other, so did these men come before the King in their turn to impress him with their possessions. For the King believed that those who have drunk enough will not return to the wine flask. The young ruler knew not that the drunkard was not able to turn away from the wine.

Adnan declared that he was the richest man in the world after the King. He owned magic carpets on which he flew around the world. Each was so large he was able to fly across the sky with servants and concubines to attend to his needs. He also possessed a great pleasure barge named after his favorite daughter, and such was his wealth that wherever he traveled in the world he might always rest at night in one of his own small palaces of which he had more than could be counted on both hands.

After Adnan came Zobel. Fertile lands where peasants worked under his overseers in a nearby nation had made him rich. He was also a money lender, using his money to gain more, with agents to bring back double the amount of the money loaned.

After Zobel came Fayed. He said he was richer and wiser than Adnan, and possessed inns in many capitals of the west and knew many more powerful leaders in other lands (who gave him large amounts of gold for his work). The blessings of Allah had made him rich, and he would spread the word of Allah even unto the lands of the cold North.

173

The King was at peace with these men, and in trust called upon them to do him service.

'Adnan,' said His Majesty, 'for the sake of friendship and our mutual trust in Allah, go to the bazaars unknown to me and bring back gems of great beauty for my Princess and a magic carpet to give pleasure to us both. We will not speak of money, for you have my confidence.'

Adnan did go forth and return in triumph bearing the jewels and the magic carpet his friend desired. The King's joy was soon ended, it is sad to say, when others in his court told of seeing Adnan carry away more of the King's gold for himself than was just for his deeds. In anger, the King banished the wretch.

Zobel still stood beside the King, and remained a trusted friend. 'Because we both place our hope in Allah,' the King said to Zobel, 'it is my wish that you build a palace for my people where all monarchs of this kingdom shall live in the fullness of time and where I may live and rule in the manner of other kings.'

Soon the tiny nation was dwarfed by the new palace. Its golden domes outshone the sun at noon and its minarets soared above the clouds of the evening. Inside, were banquet halls, state rooms, fountains, prayer rooms, and a throne room lit by millions of candles which hung from the top in beautiful glass sculptures. The corridors were so wide an army could march through them in rank. The walls were covered with gold mosaics and tiles from foreign lands. There was no greater palace in the world.

There came the day of celebration when kings from every part of the world came to gaze upon the new palace. It is not the way of kings to speak ill of other royal friends, so most praised the King for his wisdom and hospitality as they laughed among themselves at the King's lack of worldliness. His Princess read the minds of the royal visitors, and listened to the words they spoke when the King walked away. She had the courage to tell the King that Zobel had made him a fool in the eyes of others and had carried away more gold than Adnan. When the King heard her words, his wrath descended upon Zobel and he, too, was banished.

Only Fayed remained at the King's side. 'Fayed,' said His Majesty, 'You are my only friend. Guard my money and tell me where to buy inns and properties as you have done so I need not worry about greedy men in my court carrying my gold away.'

Now Fayed had witnessed the fate of Adnan and Zobel, and vowed to himself that he would not make the same errors. He took counsel in his heart, thought that which was wise, and was careful in the ways he used the King's money. When Fayed bought for him an inn whose fame was known in every corner of the world, His Majesty believed he had finally found a loyal servant. In this spirit of trust he gave Fayed a royal scroll on which he proclaimed Fayed was empowered to forever act in his name as though the two men and their fortunes were one.

It then came about that a fakir from the land of India was brought to the King's court. The fakir, who had the name of Swamiji, was so fat that two donkeys could not have carried him, and he wore his hair to the middle of his back as the dervish who spins in the wilderness. As he strode through the market place to the palace, the people drew back from this man who blotted out the sun, disturbed by the clattering of his strange prayer beads and his disdain for their stalls of cooked meats.

The King had been told that the fakir was a man of great powers, who had been given a third eye by Allah to see the good or evil in the hearts and minds of those who sat with him. 'Oh gracious Majesty,' said the fakir, 'I am a holy man and have no need of gold. I desire only to be your friend and to find other faithful and loyal men to ease the burdens of your position.' The better to show his powers, the fakir looked inside the King's mind and spoke of things even His Majesty dared not speak out loud. Both the King and Princess Mariam opened their hearts to the fakir and, thereafter, sought his counsel.

Alas, the fakir was no more than a magician who wore the robes of a holy man. His piety was that of the hypocrite who knows not Allah, for his third eye did not exist. What he said was Allah's gift to him was merely the trick of a sorcerer. Unknown to the King, the fakir had been offered gold by Zobel to help him regain a place in His Majesty's court.

The fakir took strength from the King's friendship, and thought how he might lessen the power of Fayed in court as a way of demonstrating that Zobel was a better friend.

Fortune led the fakir and Zobel to a distant center of trade in the empire that once gave protection to the kingdom. It was there that Fayed had bought the famous inn for the young King and made his home.

The King found pleasure in this distant land, in the gaming halls and the women who knew not the difference between the day and the night. He made Fayed his eyes and ears in matters of business, out of trust and a desire that his people not know had learned to relish the ways of a world that did not honor the teachings of Allah.

Basking in the warmth of the King's friendship, and with the power given to him in the royal scroll, Fayed purchased the country's most famous bazaar in his own name, even though the gold he used to take control of the bazaar was the King's. Other strong men doubted Fayed's word that he had put forth his own gold. One man of stature had wanted to buy the bazaar, but the grey-bearded rulers of the Empire denied him this right for empty and selfish reasons.

Fayed had forgotten the fates of Zobel and Adnan. Soon many respected men began to speak ill of him and the young King.

The matter displeased the King.

The fakir was told of Fayed's indiscretion and chose this moment to take advantage of him. In words of praise and understanding, he invited Fayed to share his burdens. Fayed was troubled and came to seek help. Fayed was at rest, and whether through wine or the pride that Allah punishes, began to talk. He knew not that the servants stood in the next room to listen and record his spoken words. He spoke as the fool who wags his tongue on street corners for all to hear, even laughing at his royal patron.

No sooner had the fakir bade farewell than he went to the King taking the servants who bore witness to Fayed's betrayal. Upon hearing of the meeting between the fakir and Fayed, His Majesty wondered: 'If the fakir is my friend, why does he take gold from Zobel to destroy Fayed?' The King troubled by Fayed's words, but more angered at the fakir's questions was soon told that the fakir had been seen with Adnan, and asked the Princess: 'Why is the fakir helping Adnan? He cannot be my friend if he works for those who have betrayed me.'

And so it was that the King called the fakir before him. He sat strong in his anger and demanded the fakir give an explanation for his betrayal. As was his way, the fakir spoke words which the King now knew to be false. This time in both sadness and anger, His Majesty rose and looking beyond the fakir, spoke to his court: 'I resolve this day before heaven that Allah may curse me in the eyes of my people if I see or speak to the fakir again! He may never return to my kingdom.' This vow he made, and this vow he kept.

The tales from the lips of storytellers of old need no moral. But I am not of the old generation, and do not have the tongues of angels or the wisdom of past centuries. Therefore, I must beg you to forgive the need to conclude this humble story with a lesson for those who might read it.

If you are, perchance, the richest man in the world, look not to those who say they have mountains of gold and want no more than to offer you advice and counsel in the spirit of friendship. While they say they seek nothing in return, they will carry away as much of your gold as possible, in the way a drunkard will consume your wine. If these men had been your equal, as they had deigned to say again and again, there would have been no need to make such a proclamation.

Above all, beware of any man who comes in white robes and portrays himself as a messenger from Allah, especially the sweet-tongued fakir who embraces all religions, claims to know what the future will bring, and, with the benefit of a third eye, looks inside your heart and mind. Such men are cunning magicians who feed on the fears and dreams of others, while trading in deceit. For indeed, no fakir can change a man's worth in the eyes of Allah, and no one, from the richest man on earth to your humble scribe, can do other than walk alone before Him.

# – Appendix –

## Transcript of Conversation at 1 Carlos Place, London W1, between Mohamed Fayed, Swamiji and Mamaji, on 6 and 7 June 1985.

*(Part of the conversation is in English, part in Hindi. The translation of the Hindi appears on the right-hand side of the transcript and the English appears on the left-hand side)*

**Swamiji:**
The thing I need is your love, good feeling, mutual confidence – this I require. As I told you these type of things are not required.

**Mamaji:**
Swamiji says I have desired some more valuable good from you. And the invaluable thing that you can give is your love, affection,

178

| | |
|---|---|
| | trust and confidence. |
| Mohamed Fayed: | Yeah, OK, correct. |
| Swamiji: | (*inaudible conversation*) |
| Mamaji: | He says that's most invaluable for me. |
| Mohamed Fayed: | Thank you. |
| Mamaji: | He has always valued your thoughts for him, your love and affection for him. |
| Mohamed Fayed: | Thank you. |
| Swamiji: | As you have brought this with love, I am accepting your love. Otherwise these things are mortal/materialistic. The best is our true love and hearty affection should be maintained heart to heart. And in future, also, these things should be continued, it is most important. |
| Mamaji: | Swamiji thinks one must have, how do you say it? They are materialistic. |
| Mohamed Fayed: | Yeah |
| Mamaji: | No doubt, and, since you have brought it with that love and affection and you have cared to think in these terms, I thank you very much for this. I appreciate it, but, above all, still request and desire that you continue your good wishes, love |

|  |  |  |
|---|---|---|
| | and affection towards him. | |
| **Mohamed Fayed:** | Yeah. That's over? Good. You have good relations with me. | |
| **Swamiji:** | | As you know, I am not restricted to any religious sect. If anybody called me Hindu, perhaps nobody will have more faith in Islam than me, nobody will have more faith in Christianity than me. I am talking about the essence of humanity from these religious sects. And that is the only relation between you and me. |
| **Mamaji:** | I already told you yesterday ... | |
| **Mohamed Fayed:** | Yeah | |
| **Mamaji:** | ... that my philosophy of this, this religion is above the temporal bondage. No doubt I may be born in a Hindu family, | |
| **Mohamed Fayed:** | Yeah | |
| **Mamaji:** | ... but ever since I have adopted these robes ... | |
| **Mohamed Fayed:** | Yeah | |
| **Mamaji:** | ... I have no religion. Communal religion. My religion is humanity, | |
| **Mohamed Fayed:** | Humanity | |
| **Mamaji:** | ... and its vestments are love and affections, | |
| **Mohamed Fayed:** | Affections | |

| | |
|---|---|
| Mamaji: | ... and, with that, |
| Mohamed Fayed: | Of course |
| Mamaji: | ... he says, I respect a Muslim, the Koran, equally as well as I would respect a Hindu and the Veda or a Christian and the Bible. |
| Mohamed Fayed: | Yeah. |
| Mamaji: | He says that has been my principle and, as I told you yesterday ... |
| Mohamed Fayed: | But not, not the Jews, not the Jews (*he laughs*). |
| Mamaji: | ... because, he says, when we are born, |
| Mohamed Fayed: | Yeah |
| Mamaji: | ... when The Almighty gave us birth, |
| Mohamed Fayed: | Yeah |
| Mamaji: | ... he never imprinted on our body anywhere, yeah, that I am Hindu or I am a Muslim. |
| Mohamed Fayed: | Yeah I know, I know. |
| Mamaji: | We are all breathing the same air. |
| Mohamed Fayed: | Yeah. |
| Swamiji: | And the love which I have received from an Islamic person like you, perhaps I have not received that type of love, confidence, co-operation and sacrifices from the people of other religious sects. This is true. |
| Mamaji: | But actually and factually, if you ask the |

181

|  |  |  |
|---|---|---|
|  | love and affection and the following which I have received from persons of – like you, let us – let me be very clear – from Islamic friends of mine, that, in fact, I have not received from any other community, maybe from Indians or anywhere. |  |
| **Mohamed Fayed:** | Yeah |  |
| **Mamaji:** | Not only confining to you, he says, anywhere he help others, indeed, as he showed me yesterday. |  |
| **Mohamed Fayed:** | Yeah |  |
| **Mamaji:** | In so many Middle East and Arabic countries ... |  |
| **Mohamed Fayed:** | Yeah |  |
| **Mamaji:** | ... he has his friends, but all of them have given him good regards and respect ... |  |
| **Mohamed Fayed:** | Yeah |  |
| **Mamaji:** | ... to an extent which others have not given and which he values. |  |
| **Swamiji:** |  | Want to tell you one thing, that today you must clear any doubt from your mind and heart that I have ever said any evil or bad/ wrong words for you anywhere at any time. |
| **Mamaji:** | I only want to tell you today, with |  |

182

|                   |                                                                                                                                                                                                                                                                                              |
|-------------------|----------------------------------------------------------------------------------------------------------------------------------------------------------------------------------------------------------------------------------------------------------------------------------------------|
|                   | confidence ...                                                                                                                                                                                                                                                                                |
| Mohamed Fayed:    | Yeah                                                                                                                                                                                                                                                                                          |
| Mamaji:           | ... that anywhere, at any time, I have never whatever used any single word against you.                                                                                                                                                                                                       |
| Mohamed Fayed:    | Yeah, I'll believe you.                                                                                                                                                                                                                                                                       |
| Mamaji:           | I'll never forget you like that. Like that ...                                                                                                                                                                                                                                                |
| Mohamed Fayed:    | No                                                                                                                                                                                                                                                                                            |
| Mamaji:           | ... I don't say a friend. And if I say that he's a friend and you see that I am carrying your picture in my album and that I can carry of my friend, not of foes. How can I say something wrong against you?                                                                                   |
| Mohamed Fayed:    | No, no, no. What I heard and I explained, it's finished.                                                                                                                                                                                                                                      |
| Mamaji:           | It is finished.                                                                                                                                                                                                                                                                               |
| Mohamed Fayed:    | That's only proper – because Zobel is, you know – he's evil you know. He make so much damage to the Sultan, so much damage. It is beyond decent explanation. Because, basically, Jews exploited through the magazines, the building of the palace. The minute he finished, those terrible people from all over the world, photographers |

183

(*interjection of* 'Yeah')
he prostitute all these
things everywhere in
the magazines.
Anywhere in the
magazines. 'Zobel,
Ayala build the best
palace. Anyone would
like to build a palace
knows where to go, to
Ayala, Enrique Zobel
you know. Whose
pictures of mosques in
the palace, everywhere.
It took me six months
to stop and get pictures
he sold with architects,
with decorators –
American decorators
called, uh, er, Top
Decorator make hotel.
Everywhere, every . . .
everybody make fun,
you know, because you
can't do things like that.
OK, you make a palace,
er, then you don't go
bring people from all
over the world make
fun with one thousand
nights, one thousand
nights like *The King
and I*. You see film *King
and I*?

| | |
|---|---|
| **Mamaji:** | Uh-huh |
| **Mohamed Fayed:** | This is exactly the same story. |
| **Mamaji:** | I see. |
| **Mohamed Fayed:** | And everybody was making fun of him, you know. |

184

| | | |
|---|---|---|
| **Swamiji:** | | *(unclear Hindi sentences but some references to pictures of a woman in the Swami's file)* I want to tell you some of the things, which you will confine to yourself only. |
| **Mamaji:** | Mohamed Fayed, Swamiji says in trust and confidence . . . | |
| **Mohamed Fayed:** | Yeah | |
| **Mamaji:** | . . . and in consideration of the love and regard which I have maintained for you and you have reposed in me, I want to tell you a couple of things and with this confidence, that you will confine this to yourself only. It's for your knowledge and help. | |
| **Swamiji:** | | I had thought of in my own way regarding the confusion you had about me. There is a third person between you and Sultan. |
| **Mamaji:** | The confusion that you got about me in relation to my meeting with His Majesty and your terms, and the person – there's some third person in between you and Sultan who is continually working, who has applied, | |

185

presumably, my name
and I feel and that's
what I see in my
intuition responsible
for (*Swamiji interjects –
inaudible*) if at all
between you and His
Majesty.

Mohamed Fayed: It's not this. It's not this
but – Sultan, you know,
he gets influenced. I
can't go sit with him all
the time, you know. It's
impossible for me, you
know. Because he has
one terrible, evil man,
his aide, Ibnu.

Mamaji: Pardon?

Mohamed Fayed: General Ibnu.

Mamaji: Uh-huh

Mohamed Fayed: Terrible man. This man
takes money from
everybody, everybody.

Swamiji: I think girls also.

Mohamed Fayed: Yeah

Mamaji: Girls?

Swamiji: Girls

Mohamed Fayed: Girls, everything,
everything, everything.
He is the big man, but
the Sultan don't trust
him at all. Bad man.
And this Ibnu and
Zobel are like that.
Build the palace
together. Ibnu gives
permission to all those
people go inside, take
pictures of his bedroom,
everything, anything.
And he's a bad man,

186

|  |  |  |
|---|---|---|
| | you know. But for me, I don't – you know, er I don't need the Sultan. Sultan doesn't need me. But I made so much good for him, you know, with support him with the British Government, you know. | |
| Swamiji: | | According to the enquiry I have made, I am told that you are having huge amount of Sultan's money, which Sultan took back from you – that is what Zobel's son had told me. |
| Mamaji: | Who are the sources of –<br>We have been talking of Zobel ... | |
| Mohamed Fayed: | Yeah | |
| Mamaji: | ... having heard from you, he says I have talked to Zobel myself. | |
| Mohamed Fayed: | Yeah | |
| Swamiji: | Yesterday. | |
| Mohamed Fayed: | Yeah | |
| Swamiji: | In here. | |
| Mohamed Fayed: | Yeah, right. | |
| Mamaji: | And ... | |
| Swamiji: | In Intercontinental Hotel. | |
| Mohamed Fayed: | Yeah, yeah. | |
| Swamiji: | I call from ... | |
| Mohamed Fayed: | Yeah. | |
| Swamiji: | Afghan | |
| Mohamed Fayed: | Yeah. | |
| Swamiji: | He was here. | |

| | |
|---|---|
| Mohamed Fayed: | Right, right. |
| Swamiji: | I start to, to spend two hours with him. |
| Mohamed Fayed: | Yeah. |
| Swamiji: | What he told I tell my language. Mamaji explain to you. |
| Mohamed Fayed: | Right, right. |
| Swamiji: | But please, confident. |
| Mohamed Fayed: | Right. Absolutely. |
| Swamiji: | I trust you. |
| Mohamed Fayed: | Right. Absolutely. Why don't if you tell me something, I don't go tell him. Why I tell him? |
| Mamaji: | It is more so for your knowledge and its security as it's said by me Swamiji thinks whether ... how far they are right or wrong, you know it better ... |
| Mohamed Fayed: | Right |
| Mamaji: | ... whatever he's saying, because they have been told to you. |
| Swamiji: | He told that by putting trust in you Sultan has left huge amount of money – nearly one billion dollars at your disposal. |
| Mamaji: | He told us that His Majesty has left at your disposal a huge sum, amounting about a billion dollars, at your disposal. |
| Mohamed Fayed: | Zobel told you? |
| Mamaji: | Yes. |
| Mohamed Fayed: | All rubbish, all rubbish, |

188

| | | |
|---|---|---|
| | all rubbish. | |
| **Swamiji:** | | On that basis you have purchased Harrods etc.... |
| **Mamaji:** | And his information is that it is on the basis of that or by the support of that, you bought Harrods and made an investment. | |
| **Mohamed Fayed:** | Yeah, but this is rumors, see, is rumors, all rumors. | |
| **Swamiji:** | | He said that Sultan has took back his money from you during last two months, and some balance still left with you and that difference of opinion is going on between you and Sultan. Sultan wants to take back two things from you. He wants his money back, but you are unable to return now, you are passing through money crisis, this is the position between you and Sultan. (*Garbled conversation – inaudible exchange*). |
| **Mohamed Fayed:** | All – he will tell because he ... | |
| **Mamaji:** | He said since last two months – er – His Majesty has been demanding his money back from you and that you have also returned | |

|                    |                                                                                                                                                                                        |
| ------------------ | -------------------------------------------------------------------------------------------------------------------------------------------------------------------------------------- |
|                    | some money back to His Majesty.                                                                                                                                                         |
| Mohamed Fayed:     | Huh?                                                                                                                                                                                    |
| Mamaji:            | Uh-huh                                                                                                                                                                                  |
| Mohamed Fayed:     | No that's not me . . .                                                                                                                                                                  |
| Swamiji:           | What about here, 4 million . . .                                                                                                                                                        |
| Mamaji:            | And there is still some – there's still some balance left . . .                                                                                                                        |
| Swamiji:           | Nearly hundred million.                                                                                                                                                                 |
| Mamaji:            | . . . which His Majesty has to recover.                                                                                                                                                |
| Mohamed Fayed:     | His Majesty never talked to Zobel like that, never tell Zobel this, and, er, personally, at all. There is money – Khashoggi – I take – I sell for him Khashoggi to fund the . . . (*inaudible*) |
| Swamiji:           | Maybe Jander (*phonetic*) told to Zobel.                                                                                                                                                |
| Mohamed Fayed:     | Yeah Zobel. Maybe Jander.                                                                                                                                                               |
| Swamiji:           | Jander told everything about you.                                                                                                                                                       |
| Mamaji:            | Honestly I am telling you how much I appreciate Mr Zobel's fellowship's a lie, yes . . .                                                                                                |
| Mohamed Fayed:     | Right. Yeah.                                                                                                                                                                            |
| Mamaji:            | . . . that this is what has been going on . . .                                                                                                                                        |
| Mohamed Fayed:     | Yeah.                                                                                                                                                                                   |
| Mamaji:            | . . . and that is there.                                                                                                                                                               |
| Swamiji:           | Some balance of money                                                                                                                                                                   |

190

|  |  | still left with you, you are not giving it, since a long time you are not giving it. |
| --- | --- | --- |
| **Mamaji:** | And because you are not giving the balance of the money and because nor you are not returning the Dorchester to His Majesty, that's why His Majesty ... |  |
| **Swamiji:** |  | He wants to sell all that in his own way and you are preventing him to do so. |
| **Mamaji:** | ... he says His Majesty wants to manage his own affairs, |  |
| **Mohamed Fayed:** | Yeah. |  |
| **Mamaji:** | and, er, because Mohamed Sahib doesn't want him to – doesn't allow him to manage his things ... |  |
| **Mohamed Fayed:** | Yeah. |  |
| **Mamaji:** | ... that's why the accounts are not better and I am helping him. |  |
| **Mohamed Fayed:** | Yeah, Zobel helping him? |  |
| **Mamaji:** | Helping him? |  |
| **Mohamed Fayed:** | Yeah. |  |
| **Mamaji:** | To get over yourself? But ... |  |
| **Mohamed Fayed:** | Yeah. |  |
| **Swamiji:** |  | He is saying that on Tuesday His Majesty – out with him. |
| **Mamaji:** | ... and he is also taking HM out ... |  |

191

| | |
|---|---|
| **Mohamed Fayed:** | Yeah. |
| **Mamaji:** | ... with him somewhere. He didn't say where. |
| **Mohamed Fayed:** | Yeah. |
| **Mamaji:** | He is taking him out somewhere for some special work in this area. |
| **Swamiji:** | On Tuesday, morning to evening. |
| **Mohamed Fayed:** | Yeah, Zobel? |
| **Swamiji:** | Yeah. |
| **Mohamed Fayed:** | Is taking His Majesty? |
| **Swamiji:** | Uhm |
| **Mohamed Fayed:** | On Tuesday somewhere? |
| **Mamaji:** | I don't know but that's what he said. |
| **Mohamed Fayed:** | He is leaving, and flying today. You know, for the same trouble, never, I mean he don't trust Zobel. Because he didn't talk Zobel, only two months ago, three months ago. That's all. Before that Zobel was not allowed to come to Brunei because the palace falling down, furniture falling down. 600 million dollars, gone with the wind, all his pictures, every ... |
| **Swamiji:** | But Zobel was every month in Brunei. |
| **Mohamed Fayed:** | Yeah, but now. But before, no. It is only since March. Before no. |
| **Mamaji:** | I think that he himself |

192

|                    |                                                                                                                                                                 |
| ------------------ | --------------------------------------------------------------------------------------------------------------------------------------------------------------- |
|                    | was saying                                                                                                                                                       |
| Mohamed Fayed:     | Yeah.                                                                                                                                                            |
| Mamaji:            | ... that this last three months 'I am helping His Majesty (Mohamed Fayed. Yeah) to um, er recover his money from Mr Al-Fayed.                                    |
| Mohamed Fayed:     | Yeah, you know. I have clearance and somebody, clearance completely.                                                                                             |
| Swamiji:           | (*muddled conversation Mamaji and Swamiji*)                                                                                                                      |
| Mamaji:            | Swamiji told him.                                                                                                                                                |
| Mohamed Fayed:     | I was with him. Every day he talks to me, two-three times. Still take my advice, still talks to me (*lost*) but with me – I saved him 400 million dollars, gone with the wind, from Khashoggi and still 50 million dollar I am still 50 million short. |
| Mamaji:            | Swamiji told him ...                                                                                                                                             |
| Mohamed Fayed:     | And this money gone. Yeah.                                                                                                                                       |
| Mamaji:            | Swamiji called Mr Zobel.                                                                                                                                         |
| Mohamed Fayed:     | Yeah.                                                                                                                                                            |
| Mamaji:            | And he said I have known Mr Al-Fayed for a long time.                                                                                                            |
| Mohamed Fayed:     | Zobel?                                                                                                                                                           |
| Swamiji:           | I told him.                                                                                                                                                      |
| Mohamed Fayed:     | Yeah.                                                                                                                                                            |
| Mamaji:            | Swamiji told him.                                                                                                                                                |
| Mohamed Fayed:     | Yeah.                                                                                                                                                            |
| Swamiji:           | And he got across. He                                                                                                                                            |

193

|  |  |
|---|---|
|  | said, 'Why you did not told me before?' |
| Mamaji: | And so – yeah, he said, how you come to know, but you never told me that you are (*inaudible*) ... say I am more than a year-old teacher. |
| Mohamed Fayed: | Yeah. |
| Mamaji: | When he said that, as I have said, there is nothing with me to hide. |
| Mohamed Fayed: | Right. |
| Mamaji: | My life is open just so anybody can see. |
| Mohamed Fayed: | Right, right, right. |
| Mamaji: | If I know a person, I say it – I'm not scared of anybody – |
| Mohamed Fayed: | Right, right. |
| Mamaji: | ... and, all types of people, good or bad, irrespective of religion, cast and creed they come to me I meet them. |
| Mohamed Fayed: | Right. |
| Mamaji: | So, knowing them is not a sin ... |
| Mohamed Fayed: | Yeah. |
| Mamaji: | ... and as far as he said, I know Mr Al-Fayed, |
| Mohamed Fayed: | Yeah. |
| Mamaji: | he said he is a person of five, six billion dollars minimum. |
| Swamiji: | Assets. |
| Mamaji: | Assets, cash, according to Swamiji's |

|                    |                                                                                                                                                                                                                                                                                                                                                                                                                                                         |
| ------------------ | ------------------------------------------------------------------------------------------------------------------------------------------------------------------------------------------------------------------------------------------------------------------------------------------------------------------------------------------------------------------------------------------------------------------------------------------------------ |
|                    | estimation.                                                                                                                                                                                                                                                                                                                                                                                                                                              |
| **Mohamed Fayed:** | Right.                                                                                                                                                                                                                                                                                                                                                                                                                                                   |
| **Mamaji:**        | He said how a paltry sum of . . .                                                                                                                                                                                                                                                                                                                                                                                                                        |
| **Mohamed Fayed:** | Yeah.                                                                                                                                                                                                                                                                                                                                                                                                                                                    |
| **Mamaji:**        | . . . of hundred million dollars . . .                                                                                                                                                                                                                                                                                                                                                                                                                   |
| **Mohamed Fayed:** | Uh-huh.                                                                                                                                                                                                                                                                                                                                                                                                                                                  |
| **Mamaji:**        | . . . would hold him back for his relations between His Majesty and, er, yourself?                                                                                                                                                                                                                                                                                                                                                                        |
| **Mohamed Fayed:** | He is with me and, you know, I help him politically a lot at these times with the British Government. Myself and the Prime Minister are like that, always. He knows that I took him there. I made the Prime Minister go there, to Brunei. It was not in her program when she goes there, you know in March – end of March beginning of April. She put and went there. I arranged it all. Zobel can't do things like that – I, you know, with this property I have, that is, gold, banks, I mean 500 million, 600 million, I don't need him that much. It's my reputation, my businesses. |
| **Mamaji:**        | That's what Swamiji told him. He said that fellow that . . .                                                                                                                                                                                                                                                                                                                                                                                             |

| | |
|---|---|
| **Mohamed Fayed:** | They imagine, because, you know, he sees me, he comes to me, he goes, you know and all those people jealous, you know. He's just putting things to talk to reporter in the press, you know, but for me, the Government knows you know, British Government. |
| **Swamiji:** | I will tell you one thing, that was asked by him in our today's and yesterday's meeting. He asked that he has got four-five people – 'whom should I trust more? You tell me this according to your thinking'. |
| **Mamaji:** | One thing, of course, I will tell you. Yesterday and this morning, and also this morning at lunch ... |
| **Swamiji:** | In my meeting ... |
| **Mamaji:** | ... in my meeting and conversation with him, His Majesty, he inquired from me that I have got four or five persons and how he needs 'and which, according to your spiritual thinking and meditation, you would consider whom should I trust upon more in the matter of money and |

|                   |                                                                                      |                                                        |
|-------------------|--------------------------------------------------------------------------------------|--------------------------------------------------------|
|                   | advice?'                                                                              |                                                        |
| **Swamiji:**      |                                                                                      | First name he took was of Zobel.                       |
| **Mamaji:**       | The first name is this that of Mr Zobel.                                              |                                                        |
| **Swamiji:**      |                                                                                      | Second was yours.                                      |
| **Mamaji:**       | Second was – was you.                                                                 |                                                        |
| **Swamiji:**      |                                                                                      | Third was of Manoukian.                                |
| **Mamaji:**       | The third was Sadiqui Manoukian.                                                      |                                                        |
| **Swamiji:**      | Hu, Hu, Dato bin Hu ... (*some garbled conversation*)                                 |                                                        |
| **Mohamed Fayed:**| Yeah, Dato bin Hu those Chinese, the one who bought from him that place ... the Holiday Inn. |                                                |
| **Swamiji:**      |                                                                                      | He told me that give me two days time I will tell you. |
| **Mamaji:**       | And wish for reasons which you think, to what degree, to what extent I should take their support, because whatever it is they plot with this ... (*lost*) Swamiji has met him on several matters he has tested, tried and felt satisfied that whatever spiritually and psychologically Swamiji has told him have come out perfectly well, according to him. So that – these are the things which he reports back as I say. | |

197

| | |
|---|---|
| **Swamiji:** | His Majesty told me this morning. |
| **Mohamed Fayed:** | Yeah, yeah. |
| **Mamaji:** | These are the things which also impressed you when you first met Swamiji ... |
| **Mohamed Fayed:** | Yeah. |
| **Mamaji:** | ... because he believes in things like that. And he could say and probably he did say something about you, about your life and things like that. |
| **Mohamed Fayed:** | Yeah. |
| **Mamaji:** | These are such personal, private matters and after PM's office never a politician, he will try. |
| **Swamiji:** | You have called me at home and asked about Karim, I told you that he has long life – you believed it or not. |
| **Mamaji:** | You will agree when they first went there you were worried about myself – Abdu Karim's life. You and your wife, both were worried. Within my own power, whatever I could do spiritually and I told you that he will have a long life. Of course, at times a bit hard so will be like that OK? And even then to say – to maintain what I have |

198

|                    |                                                                                                                                                                                    |                                                                                                                                                               |
| ------------------ | ---------------------------------------------------------------------------------------------------------------------------------------------------------------------------------- | ------------------------------------------------------------------------------------------------------------------------------------------------------------- |
|                    | said, believe it or not, I have been praying to the Almighty to pass over this period, not as attention for you or for your wife, but for your little boy who was suffering and I have been asking to the Almighty to give this suffering to me not to this boy. |                                                                                                                                                               |
| Mohamed Fayed:     | So and I feel that he is a poor man after he's going there ... and always going to have something in life.                                                                          |                                                                                                                                                               |
| Swamiji:           |                                                                                                                                                                                    | When he asked me about those four people I told him that I will let you know within two days.                                                                  |
| Mamaji:            | Swamiji has inquired about you. Swamiji says will you do this thing.                                                                                                               |                                                                                                                                                               |
| Mohamed Fayed:     | Yeah.                                                                                                                                                                             |                                                                                                                                                               |
| Mamaji:            | Can you please meditate whatever you like. Whatever comes to your mind please do mention.                                                                                          |                                                                                                                                                               |
| Swamiji:           |                                                                                                                                                                                    | I would like to know something from you, in your confidence, about that Manoukian, that Jew, that Zobel – if you can tell me as a true friend.                |
| Mamaji:            | Just for my own using and knowledge apart                                                                                                                                         |                                                                                                                                                               |

199

|  |  |
|---|---|
| | from what – |
| **Swamiji:** | In confidence |
| **Mohamed Fayed:** | Yeah. |
| **Mamaji:** | This is valuable advice. I would like to pretend give me something one can like about these people – Mr Zobel, Sadiqui Manoukian and Hirschmann the Jew, |
| **Mohamed Fayed:** | Yeah. |
| **Mamaji:** | do you think you, you know something about them? |
| **Mohamed Fayed:** | All these, er, people, General Ibnu, all these people, all crooks. Zobel is out of it, out of it, his business is hardly nothing at all it's going out because Ibnu is no good Ayala, Ayala, his business is going out, Mr Zobel Ayala, Ayala is a liar. Took the money and made a hotel and he used all the money he made from the Sultan for that. But three months ago he was completely down nearly bankrupt. And he used Ibnu all the time to come back again because Ibnu was worried because I don't talk to nobody. (*Swamiji and Mamaji – joint mixed inaudible Hindi conversation*). |

200

Swamiji:

He has also asked about Ibnu whether he is trustworthy or not – about Isa too. (*Inaudible conversation*).

Mohamed Fayed: Ya, yeah.

Mamaji: Asking me, he is saying will Zobel be loyal to me . . .

Mohamed Fayed: Yeah.

Mamaji: Uh – Pehin Isa – What you . . . He wants to get honest opinion and certainly travel, the children also so he will get a correct opinion at least one from me – you will agree that with all the goodness His Majesty has got, it is our duty in the name of the Almighty – that he is such a gentle fellow we should work trying to carry on the work together do you agree?

Mohamed Fayed: Yes, absolutely. You know there is a hard core that surrounds him like Lee Kuan Yew, Lee Kuan Yew Prime Minister and I teach him the word of Mohamed . . . I say go. I have great respect for this great man who took Singapore back, rose from nothing – great man – no oil nothing. If you believe in God and

this is it everything goes
fine. He told me, 'what
are you doing in
Brunei?' I said the
Sultan my friend and he
ask my help from time
to time and the Sultan
likes to do the Trade
Centre I have in Dubai
one which ... one
billion dollars. If for
Government I do, I
manage dollar one
billion. And the Sultan
likes to do one. And this
is why, I you know. I
met him but when they
know like that,
everybody – because ...
I just deal directly with
him and if anybody in
the middle I don't want
you know but this is all
much talk because of it
but I find him good man
to be able to move
things given the
guidance that you have
to give him ... ability.
In one year time I have
50 million dollars for
... in England. In
Europe I am building
mosque, church for two
million pounds. I
participate in France, in
United States, in Egypt,
in Thailand – in
Thailand I spend two
millions dollars. I have
three colonels in the

202

army retired. They go
and dig in. They don't
give to people they do
the thing themselves.
From the Crown Prince
in Dubai, Crown Prince
Abu Dhabi I have
another twenty,
hundred million ... All
Arabs, of course,
because this is ...
basically I don't need
his money because I am
sophisticated you
know. What I am going
to do? I have Harrods.
Now I don't sleep
because people talk
unbelievable topic you
know. I was at peace
before, at peace before,
you know quiet man,
the minute I do this I
hate the minute I done
it because everyone
wanted to took, take
Harrods from me.

| | | |
|---|---|---|
| Swamiji: | | This power of attorney ... power of attorney (*slightly inaudible conversation*) |
| Mohamed Fayed: | No, you can't do it any longer. | |
| Mamaji: | Zobel also says that His Majesty has given him the power of attorney. | |
| Swamiji: | | The power of attorney, the power of attorney. |
| Swamiji: | The power of attorney, the power of attorney. | |
| Mohamed Fayed: | Yeah, I have a power of | |

|  | attorney. You ask His Majesty. I have power of attorney, I can do anything, anything ... |
| **Mamaji:** | Zobel said |
| **Mohamed Fayed:** | ... on earth right I can go to the bank. I can have 10 billion dollars I want. You can ask him. I say I don't want, ten people start talking. I say I don't want half that. You know because, Isa, Pehin Isa I say I don't want given all this power of attorney. Everything. We are good friends. Don't want anything because people say, everything I do they say Sultan. Everything I have is his I have one he bought in New York at 75 Rockefeller Plaza, only one building, one single building 500 million dollars, you ask – 75 Rockefeller Plaza in New York. You go there in New York in front of 21 Club (yes) only one building, 500 million dollars. The Ritz Hotel, you know the Ritz Hotel. One big company not only hotel, only name you know, Ritz Crackers, Ritz – you know – licences only the Ritz |

|  |  |
|---|---|
|  | establishments are worth 700–800 million. The Ritz companies, the (*inaudible*), the Trade Center in Dubai this is Zobel was talking about. It's stupid you know. It's stupid, they don't understand. |
| Swamiji: | (*Hindi rather inaudible*) – just what is the information you have been passing to the Sultan |
| Mohamed Fayed: | British Government |
| Mamaji: | ... Sultan frightened – you know yeah because security is Zobel, owns security Sultan is tied, is tied to Zobel ... Zobel, he can do all these things, when you and me are outside ... |
| Swamiji: | Sultan |
| Mamaji: | (*inaudible*) Who will help me? Al-Fayed, you phone the Al-Fayed ...! |
| Mohamed Fayed: | He have Michael, Michael (?) the OSS man, you know, the paratrooper ... and he can't sleep at night without my people around, on top, because if he trusts my people. My own butler, butler you know, the butler who feeds me, doing for me dark tall he was the |
| Swamiji: | Yah Yah ... |

| | |
|---|---|
| **Mohamed Fayed:** | Duke of Windsor, he is the Duke of Windsor's butler (*inaudible conversation*) |
| **Mohamed Fayed:** | He is with the Sultan all the time. If the Sultan don't trust me he say Mohamed this is (...) He is the man inside. He make breakfast for the Sultan. He look after him. He is my man. I stay without and I give him. Because this man I live with, you know, you know, many year I worked with ... with me for many years ... but I have Ali's assistant with me now. But when he comes, says Mohamed I want. What he want I will give him how can Zobel say – er – Sultan doesn't trust me? |
| **Mamaji:** | What about your opinion about Hanbury? |
| **Mohamed Fayed:** | Hanbury, good man – Christopher Hanbury. |
| **Mamaji:** | Yeah. |
| **Mohamed Fayed:** | Is Estate Manager here, one man you can trust with everything, top man. |
| **Swamiji:** | Good man. |
| **Mohamed Fayed:** | Good man. Right. Top of the class ... Lee Kuan Yew say 'Mohamed how can |

206

Sultan all corruption
there? Sink in
corruption ... Always
around Sultan there is
these people are bad.'

*(Swamiji and Mamaji – inaudible Hindi conversation. Mohamed Fayed joins in, Lee Kuan Yew mentioned)*

**Mohamed Fayed:** And I told Lee Kuan
Yew ... you can't, but
there are limits, you
know. I say 'I don't
want to be anything to
do with it, no trade
centre'. He needs my
help and what I want
from you to give to the
gods, give to the poor.

**Swamiji:** Second wife.

**Mamaji:** The second wife?

**Mohamed Fayed:** Second wife.

**Swamiji:** However, what is your
explanation?

**Mohamed Fayed:** The second wife's
relations – yeah the
brother and relations
you know in the family.

**Mamaji:** He has a lot of money?

**Mohamed Fayed:** Yeah, everybody,
everybody, it's just, it's
just unbelievable how
the poor don't have
anything. I took this
one paper, you know. I
say all mandates, I give
all power of attorney
and I have nothing. And
we sign, he sign, I sign
and give one copy to
Bin Isa. Bin Isa, I sign
give the copy to Zobel,
to Ibnu and I find in

*Observer* newspaper.
And this was Isa, only
one person I see I can
trust. I give him all
paper and documents
... you know all these
people like that. Now
Zobel likes to make one
Jumbo 747. I cancel.
One ... he would like to
make a crown room
and, er, unbelievable. I
say 'look King Faisal,
King Fahd of Saudi
Arabia 300 million
dollars one aeroplane' I
say, 'You don't need it.'
Because Zobel likes to
make and you like
palace on top of that
and I cancel. I say its no
good ... not even
thinking about, just to
put him down ...

**Swamiji:** ... regarding that ...
**Mamaji:** How about er
Manoukian ...
**Mohamed Fayed:** Terrible, terrible man
(*Hindi conversation
Manoukian
mentioned*) he works.
Nobody knows. He
shirtmaker, he makes
shirts in Jermyn Street,
yeah in Jermyn Street.
He's one shop, shirts,
and he bring girls to er
Jeffri – his brother –
younger brother.
**Mamaji:** How he come – how he
came close of His

208

|                 | Majesty? |
|-----------------|----------|
| Mohamed Fayed:  | He's close to brother Jeffri. He works for Jeffri. They buy houses, they buy castles (*inaudible*) and they buy furniture, buy paintings but now they caught him in in the customs two weeks ago – Manoukian – er smuggling, er, art work silver and he gives one false information and he is now under investigation – against Inland Revenue and they go in his house – took everything from there. |
| Mamaji:         | Sultan knows it? |
| Mohamed Fayed:  | Sultan knows. |
| Mamaji:         | Between you and Swamiji, this interview. (*Swamiji and Mamaji inaudible conversation*) |
| Mohamed Fayed:  | Sultan? No no. Terrible hah hah. He got to be worse. He lied to you. But, you know, two people, Ibnu, Zobel, Ibnu perhaps. |
| Mamaji:         | Bin Isa? |
| Mohamed Fayed:  | Bin Isa? No, Bin Isa is nice man, but you can buy him you know and see I give ... I trust the man. And he wants ever, he took. Sultan, you know is good, he is |

such a nice man. He is
a wonderful man you
know but Hu Hu is
terrible. He is crook
you know. He sold him
the hotel ...
unbelievable – the hotel
was worth, when he
sold him the hotel, 30
million dollars. He took
125 million dollars –
125 million dollars!

| | |
|---|---|
| Mamaji: | How could he do it? |
| Mohamed Fayed: | He told me he look for the Holiday Inn, I put my people there from the Ritz. |
| Mamaji: | Oh? |
| Mohamed Fayed: | Yeah. |
| Swamiji: | So then you do not have any amount of money belongs to Sultan? |
| Mamaji: | So all these rumours be put out strictly out of jealousy? |
| Mohamed Fayed: | Yeah. |
| Mamaji: | You are not really keeping half of billion? |
| Mohamed Fayed: | All the money I have for him he have it back and this not my money. It's the money which he lost. I tell you I took it from Khashoggi, from Lavia, from Hirschmann people like that from Zobel. This is why Zobel ... |
| Mamaji: | Hirschmann, Zobel |
| Mohamed Fayed: | Because Zobel, Hirschmann poured |

|               |                                                                                         |
| ------------- | --------------------------------------------------------------------------------------- |
|               | money over airplane and when I go he come ... (*Only short sentences can be heard until the end of the tape*) |
| Mamaji:       | What you ... what you are doing, Swamiji says you are doing all the accounts? ... Zobel |
| Mamaji:       | Swamiji says I don't want money today                                                   |
| Swamiji:      | They are all evil men, all evil ... Manoukian                                           |
| Mohamed Fayed: | You know, I don't want ... because I like Margaret Thatcher, you know ...              |
| Mamaji:       | I have been advised they will believe my relationship is like that ...                  |
| Swamiji:      | I do not want Sultan to take any advice from ...                                        |
| Mohamed Fayed: | The only good man is Hanbury ... very personal, I do not like ... Bin Isa ...          |
| Mohamed Fayed: | Father? nice man, good man ... my father ... (*Total speech loss*) (*Two thuds*) (*Total speech loss*) |
| Mohamed Fayed: | For my part, he is very rare, and suddenly here I am, I can find one billion – I have one tenth ... buy ... |
| Mamaji:       | How you are making                                                                      |

211

|                    | yesterday?                         |
|--------------------|------------------------------------|
| **Mohamed Fayed:** | Oh very good – just                |
|                    | talking and trying to,             |
|                    | you know, really to                |
|                    | work out things                    |
|                    | because he want the                |
|                    | Dorchester, but I don't            |
|                    | want to give him the               |
|                    | Dorchester to give to              |
|                    | Zobel, or you know or              |
|                    | to give it to                      |
|                    | Manoukian, I say,                  |
|                    | because this Dorchester            |
|                    | I bought for myself,               |
|                    | because it's next to my            |
|                    | building, 60 Park Lane.            |
|                    | Straight away. And                 |
|                    | then 55 is all connected           |
|                    | together. Right.                   |
| **Mamaji:**        | That they know.                    |
| **Mohamed Fayed:** | And I bought the Hotel             |
|                    | for me ...                         |
| **Mamaji:**        | Right                              |
| **Mohamed Fayed:** | ... and I told him if you          |
|                    | want the Hotel, then               |
|                    | the Ritz Hotel has to              |
|                    | manage because it's the            |
|                    | best hotel in the world            |
|                    | I own and this, the                |
|                    | Dorchester, I bought               |
|                    | for myself. But he                 |
|                    | dream the Dorchester.              |
|                    | He want to own the                 |
|                    | Dorchester OK ...                  |
|                    | because his father, I              |
|                    | think, had his – his               |
|                    | father and mother they             |
|                    | have their, er,                    |
|                    | honeymoon there and                |
|                    | his mother was                     |
|                    | pregnant in England in             |

|  | the hotel, in the Dorchester. He have sentimental value, otherwise I never give the hotel for anything because this hotel make profit – 20–30 million pounds a year possibly – if I manage you know because this ... |
|---|---|
| Mamaji: | But in that case I think you lose? |
| Mohamed Fayed: | No, no, no, I will still in November – no, but those people will go out, because bad company, Regent, terrible company ... |
| Mamaji: | They will go out? |
| Mohamed Fayed: | ... they want – from Washington, they've been thrown out. Last month in Washington they have a hotel there. |
| Mamaji: | According to the papers ... |
| Mohamed Fayed: | Yeah but – there is arbitration in November, because the employees don't want them. |
| Mamaji: | Yes. |
| Mohamed Fayed: | I finish, I say I finish Regent – I sit with you because I have management contract. I say what you want I do to make you happy, no problem, between me and you there is no |

money but just let me
finish Regent first, take
Regent out and I bring
you a good general
manager. He work for
you and I'm out – but
on the condition you
don't give it to Zobel or
give it to Manoukian or
Cockstop you know,
because they're dying
for, you know, to have
Dorchester you know. I
say is mine. You take
your money back,
here's one check, take
your money. I'll take
hotel now on this
condition you know.

**Mamaji:** Zobel is a rich man?
**Mohamed Fayed:** Pardon?
**Mamaji:** Zobel is a rich man?
**Mohamed Fayed:** A Jew?
**Mamaji:** Zobel has he furnished
wealth?

**Mohamed Fayed:** No, no. Only the
Sultan's money he took
lately from him. He
took some money from
him to make bank and
things like that, you
know. But he have so
many liabilities, you
know, so many
liabilities. He was
relying, but I think he
has done two/three bad
deals for the Sultan and
he lost ...

**Swamiji:** You have purchased
this Harrods for you,

214

not purchased for
Sultan?

| | |
|---|---|
| Mamaji: | And this, er, excuse me . . . |
| Mohamed Fayed: | Yes. |
| Mamaji: | . . . may I ask you a personal question if you don't mind? |
| Mohamed Fayed: | Yeah. |
| Mamaji: | Swamiji says that, er . . . |
| Mohamed Fayed: | Yeah. |
| Mamaji: | . . . that this Harrods is bought for yourself, not for His Majesty. |
| Mohamed Fayed: | Hum, on my children's life it's mine. All mine. Me and two brothers . . . nobody. And the British Government, they don't give permission . . . they give me permission in ten days because they know who is Mohammed Fayed for twenty-five years. I give this country business, over six billion sterling worth of business, in the last ten years. They know who is Mohammed Fayed. This is why they give me permission and before they give that, they have to know that this is my money . . . right? . . . Not anybody money, because the man who has, who owns this Lonrho, Tiny |

|  | Rowland, who's always writing ... bad man. |
| Mamaji: | This much I read in the papers. |
| Mohamed Fayed: | Bad man. |
| Mamaji: | This much I've seen. The ... paper also carried the story. |
| Mohamed Fayed: | Yeah |
| Mamaji: | About that, er ... |
| Mohamed Fayed: | That I have no money and this is Sultan's money? |
| Mamaji: | Yes. |
| Mohamed Fayed: | Everybody says it. But, er, the British Government they have ambassadors there, High Commissioners. They go out to Sultan, 'have you any interest in', 'No' he say and he have nothing for them. And I've never ... you know the Sultan also likes to be my friend. It's my business and he have nothing to do with this business. But people just ... er ... but I am adept you know all those people bark, you know and God is blessing me and saving me because I do no harm. I only do good, that's all. And always here are the results, people bark, they talk it doesn't shake, you know, because we are |

216

|  |  |
|---|---|
| | stronger than all that. |
| Swamiji: | I feel it is necessary that ... God bless him. Brother. I have received much understanding on the subject. I will talk on this basis. And our contact will be perfectly maintained. And time will tell you that how I have maintained friendship. You will by yourself realize in next few days because our contact will be maintained as it was before. So that we can do something. I expect proper cooperation from you. |
| Mamaji: | I am grateful for many information which I have received from you. |
| Mohamed Fayed: | But this confidential. |
| Mamaji: | I am the ... |
| Mohamed Fayed: | But he trusts me – I trust him. |
| Mamaji: | No, no word what we have said is going to be repeated to anyone. |
| Mohamed Fayed: | Because I'm going to the Sultan tomorrow to say thank you. He knows I am always his friend. No problem. No problem. For me I need nobody, only my God, you know, what I have between me and him, just spiritual things. |
| Mamaji: | Yes that is what he said. |

| | |
|---|---|
| **Mohamed Fayed:** | I have a message in my bottle, that wealth you know, I have, half of it will go, to God. |
| **Mamaji:** | And ... |
| **Mohamed Fayed:** | You know ... |
| **Mamaji:** | Swamiji says only future, Swamiji will tell you what I regard for you. My thoughts are with you and what my prays go for you. |
| **Swamiji:** | I will try to make his relation more closer. |
| **Mamaji:** | I have agreed I would certainly like to get you out of this trouble, this misunderstanding and the nuisance which others are creating like clouds round you. |
| **Mohamed Fayed:** | Yeah, but ... Your conscience is clear. You sleep, worry about nothing. You see your children. You see your brothers. You keep healthy and everybody is happy. |
| **Swamiji:** | That time will tell. |
| **Mamaji:** | I will do my role and only the (peak) time will tell you that I have been and I have proved to you as a good real true friend today. |
| **Mohamed Fayed:** | But you tell him I have a difficult time, you know, the last few months you know, really difficult time you |

|  |  |  |
|---|---|---|
|  | know. By the wife was also, you know having the baby, traveling, was not feeling well. I have pressure from I make mistakes you know. I made a mistake to have this house and this company, you know. Was a mistake but you make mistakes what can you do? Ha Ha |  |
| Mamaji: | Sometimes. |  |
| Mohamed Fayed: | Because, you know, you make everybody look at you, before nobody knows Mohamed Al-Fayed. Who is Mohamed Fayed? Quite calm you know that nobody knows, no. |  |
| Mamaji: | Sometimes blessings in disguise come like this. |  |
| Mohamed Fayed: | Yeah but, that's alright you said yourself you have to go through for it you have not to retreat you know. You go all for it. |  |
| Mamaji: | That's the cycle of the world. |  |
| Mohamed Fayed: | Er, tomorrow alright? What you decided your program or not yet. |  |
| Mamaji: | Yes. |  |
| Swamiji: |  | No, Sultan wants to talk tomorrow so I will stay tomorrow and will go day after tomorrow. |
| Mamaji: | Because His Majesty |  |

219

| | | |
|---|---|---|
| | wanted to have some talks tomorrow. So the Swamiji is traveling tomorrow he is going day after. | |
| **Mohamed Fayed:** | Yeah, is that so? | |
| **Swamiji:** | | Their development minister of that country must have reached there from America. |
| **Mamaji:** | Because what time he says go there, I'll be going to America. | |
| **Swamiji:** | | In future how contact can be maintained with you? ... anything else? |
| **Mamaji:** | There are our debts and other subjects as in the past. How can we maintain our level of contact ... | |
| **Mohamed Fayed:** | Right. | |
| **Mamaji:** | ... so that this mission is standing by this, mushroom growths. | |
| **Mohamed Fayed:** | But not through Vini Kapoor you pick the phone, you call Mamaji say you are there and leave a telephone number and all will be taken care of. | |
| **Swamiji:** | No that actually is when I may tell you. I will leave my number for you. | |
| **Mohamed Fayed:** | I like to help, you know. I like to go there and help because I know it's poor country, you know and people, with | |

220

my relation with
Sultan. I say Sultan
please, because now I
am ask Sultan to help
Egypt, to help, er, in
Jordan also people, a
lot of people there, in
Afghanistan you know.
A lot of people ...
orphan people have no
heart.
You know, all this. I
want him to help them,
the Sultan. It was my
plan, you know, to
have loans for him to
help Sultan make some
develop, you know, its
good, you know. Yeah.

**Swamiji:**                                                    I will be there in the
weekend and from
there I will give you
important instruction.

**Mamaji:** Next weekend,
wherever I am I'll again
pass on some really
important useful
information to you
(*inaudible Hindi*) it may
not be so possible so ...
But, er, will it be
possible for you that,
should he remember
you or it may be
necessary to avoiding
the telephonic talks.

**Mohamed Fayed:** Yeah.

**Mamaji:** If you can spare it days
or two's times and meet
in America or
somewhere?

221

| | | |
|---|---|---|
| **Mohamed Fayed:** | Yeah ... <br> Travel really kills me <br> and I am an old man <br> you know. | |
| **Swamiji:** | | Hope can that happen <br> ... you ... I ... years <br> ... years (*laughter –* <br> *unclear*) |
| **Mamaji:** | Oh no, Swamiji is <br> saying that I can give <br> you guarantee and <br> assurance for another <br> thirty years of lively life. | |
| **Mohamed Fayed:** | That's good, that's <br> good, fine, that's very <br> good – hope so <br> (*laughter*). | |
| **Swamiji:** | | Physically healthy, also <br> immensely and you will <br> be also successful in <br> (worldly) enjoyment <br> you do. |
| **Mamaji:** | He says, I guarantee <br> you will be healthy by <br> physically that right by <br> your heart and even for <br> the worldly <br> enjoyment – good. | |
| **Mohamed Fayed:** | Without that we cannot <br> live, you know. Ha ha! <br> No life for me ha ha! I <br> go from the window, <br> finito Mohamed Fayed! <br> (*laughter*) ... but pray <br> for me ... for that <br> (*laughter*). | |
| **Mamaji:** | He says yes that, ha ha! <br> I'll endorse your view <br> after all coming to that <br> date that's the only <br> official left available. | |

| | | |
|---|---|---|
| **Mohamed Fayed:** | OK. If you want to talk to me tomorrow, I will be in the evening I will bring some, some dollar, you know for a trip and some also sterling for London visit. OK? And you let me know if you need anything, yeah, good. | |
| **Swamiji:** | | Alright (we will) meet between eleven to one there in the evening at what time you will be able to meet? |
| **Mamaji:** | From eleven to one Swamiji will be with His Majesty. | |
| **Mohamed Fayed:** | The evening for me is better. | |
| **Mamaji:** | What time? | |
| **Mohamed Fayed:** | Tomorrow I'm so busy all day. | |
| **Mamaji:** | What time will you be coming in? | |
| **Mohamed Fayed:** | Around 7 o'clock, 8 o'clock. 8 o'clock is better. Yeah, 8 o'clock is better. Yeah just 4 or 5 in ten minutes I will tell you goodbye. And if there is anything you need, let me know. As I told you it's confidential, you know what we talked and it's very important but I like you to put him in peace with himself, you know, because what the only important thing | |

for him is the British
Government because
they have been there for
a hundred years
protecting him and he
has his soldiers there.
All black boys, two
thousand Gurkhas,
people there like and
with me, I am his
friend. I just want to
support him, with that
because when the
British Government
upset and we see that he
can't – he has so many
crooks around him and
so many publicity and
so many bad things,
then it's bad for him,
you know, and I am
holding the line for him
which is very
important. The
support of the British
Government, against
the brother and against
his father, and it's very,
very important,
because I believe he is a
man can do a lot of
good to his country,
but he's still not and
also to all the other poor
countries around,
which is very, very
important.

**Swamiji:**                                    Leaving tomorrow.
                                               These two people are of
                                               not much importance
                                               to him, but for their

government if they can be kept at a distance then it would be good for him. He should be alert because they are going to live here for about hundred years – although they are good people it is advisable to be alert because who know that what they mean by their heart. And I will tell him that their contacts are here and in foreign countries also. Oh God, you save I hope you will come to the temple with me.

Mamaji: Makes a wish come true. Allah is great. The Guru has faith ... if you guard him, guide him, politically financially and I'll be especially with him. We have to help for a good cause.

Mohamed Fayed: Right!

Mamaji: And let us join hands.

Mohamed Fayed: That's right.

Mamaji: To help our common ...

Mohamed Fayed: OK, absolutely.

Mamaji: ... friend ..

Mohamed Fayed: Yes.

Mamaji: ... for his better achievement and success in life.

Mohamed Fayed: That's all what we are for this life because ... is too short and if he doesn't make good, you know, it stay with you. You surrounded with angels, helping you guiding you so on and so forth. Whatever we do there is nothing can keep us safe except the goodness we make, for others and for ourselves and not only for ourselves only, but for others and this is a big thing. I mean fifty thousand people I look after OK? Their homes, look after them and this is a pleasure you know and as much as I can make I'm always here (*inaudible*) I like to take from people can afford to give. I like to do things for India, like Mother Teresa, like you know, which very important I like you to see where can we do to also offer, to do things for people, which is very important.

| | | |
|---|---|---|
| **Swamiji:** | | Time will tell him that he needs . . . we will talk tomorrow . . . contact will be maintained. |
| **Mamaji:** | You know but somehow we have come. | |
| **Mohamed Fayed:** | Have you met. | |
| **Mamaji:** | And met again you might. | |
| **Mohamed Fayed:** | Is God always with us? | |

|  | Beside us again, you know, but sometimes it comes and I am down, you know, spiritually, you know, but not mentally, you know, (*laughter*). |
|---|---|
| **Swamiji:** | And ... |
| **Mamaji:** | (*Inaudible conversation*) |
| **Mohamed Fayed:** | Because when you have work all the time, work will put you down, you know, you just, you just, come to a time you don't want to see anybody, you know you don't want to talk, you know, because you find people are so vicious and so jealous, you know, just want to put you down, you know. You better just relax and keep away from this world for a little until you get yourself again. Swami, I'll be seeing you again and I'll see you tomorrow. |

|  |  |
|---|---|
| **Swamiji:** | Salahm ah Leikum. |
| **Mohamed Fayed:** | Salahm ah Leikum. |
| **Swamiji:** | Say ... we met today and had a very lengthy discussion. Essence of that is when you will meet him next, you will by yourself realize that what effect has been |

|  |  | created by our discussion and it will take some more time, and, by grace of God, future will be stonemarked for him. |
| --- | --- | --- |
| Mamaji: | I met His Majesty this morning and, er, had some valuable discussions about you, too, in particular, and what should I say more? Indeed, I can tell you that when you happen to meet His Majesty next and the resulting state will be seen by you and whatever confusions or misgivings have been in the mind you will find those are clear not only you but also to him. |  |
| Swamiji: |  | And on Thursday let me know over the phone how your conversation went with him. |
| Mamaji: | And after talking to him on Thursday, please let me know how your conversations with him have gone through. |  |
| Swamiji: |  | I will be contacting you from America. |
| Mamaji: | I will be contacting you on Thursday from America. I have given him my impressions, complete impressions, on the lines that were |  |

|  |  |  |
|---|---|---|
| | suggested by you. | |
| Swamiji: | | And based on the opinion that you expressed that those people I have expressed same to him. |
| Mamaji: | And, er, speaking about the persons ... that I, he was anxious to enquire about ...? | |
| Mohamed Fayed: | Yeah | |
| Mamaji: | And the opinion as you expressed about them, Swamiji says he has more or less found the same in his meditation and he has given the same opinion to His Majesty. | |
| Mohamed Fayed: | Yeah. I appreciate that, both thanks. And, er, but there is still those people, you know, Ibnu, Isa, Zobel, you know all the time but, you know ... | |
| Swamiji: | | If I get your love, then they can be removed from the way but I need your heartiest cooperation. |
| Mamaji: | If I get your cooperation, heartiest cooperation, sincere don't mind it. | |
| Mohamed Fayed: | Yeah | |
| Mamaji: | Then you will find that I will have them all removed from the way. | |
| Mohamed Fayed: | You know, that they are bad. But the most | |

229

important thing, you
know he can't spare
those people because
those people they are
like, you know, spiders,
you know, they sit
there. For him, he is not
a strong person, you
know. He is a kind
person and it's difficult,
you know, with those
people because they are
bad people.

**Swamiji:** Yesterday you
mentioned something
that the Prime Minister
of Singapore expressed.
Some opinion, what is
that?

**Mamaji:** Yes, I appreciate that.
How about yesterday?
You mentioned
something that the
Prime Minister of
Singapore expressed.
Some opinion.

**Mohamed Fayed:** Yeah

**Mamaji:** What was it?

**Mohamed Fayed:** Er, that he is sinking in
corruption. People all
around him are bad
people. In Brunei, forget
about it. Don't waste
your time, because bad
people, he can't just
live, he lives but in a –
how do you call?

**Swamiji:** Lee Kuan Yew told
you?

**Mohamed Fayed:** Yeah, and I told him
that was these people.

230

Because he say 'Lee
Kuan Yew is like my
father' I say 'Lee Kuan
Yew is not like your
father. He is worried
about you. He say that
you sink in corruption.
Because Lee Kuan Yew
give one of his favourite
man, one friend like
brother, to the Sultan
three years ago. This
one ... this person he
made Singapore
straight, no corruption,
no drugs, no crime. And
he send to the Sultan.
He told him 'if you
want Brunei to be like
Singapore I give you this
man for six months to
clean up for you
everything and then he
started and then one
minister took him,
invite him to the seaside
for lunch and they sink
the man alive in the
water.

**Swamiji:**                                     Sink the man alive in
                                                 the water.

**Mohamed Fayed:**     And he died and
                       nobody say that he
                       drowned. He was
                       swimming and
                       drowned. He have
                       heart attack but they
                       can't discover how.
                       And since this time Lee
                       Kuan Yew is finished
                       from Brunei. He did no

|  |  |  |
|---|---|---|
|  | good he lost, you know, but because … |  |
| Swamiji: |  | Are you sure that Swamiji was telling, in my opinion Zobel has taken the contract for making it? |
| Mamaji: | Are you confident, Swamiji says, I think probably Zobel has taken the contract for making the … |  |
| Swamiji: | New Palace |  |
| Mamaji: | … New Palace |  |
| Swamiji: | Second wife who is making? |  |
| Mohamed Fayed: | The brother of the second wife. Second wife's brother-in-law you know. |  |
| Swamiji: | Brother-in-law. |  |
| Mohamed Fayed: | Brother-in-law. |  |
| Swamiji: | What's his name? |  |
| Mohamed Fayed: | Not Jaffa. I don't know. I don't remember the name. He is doing it because he is the husband of the sister. |  |
| Mamaji: | Tooma? |  |
| Mohamed Fayed: | Yeah Tooma, sure. |  |
| Swamiji: | Tooma is making money? |  |
| Mohamed Fayed: | Yeah, yeah. Tooma. I don't need, you know, inside business. I have nothing to do with those people. This has nothing to do with Zobel because Zobel was out only three months Ibnu brought |  |

|  | back. |
|---|---|
| Mamaji: | Oh no. |
| Mohamed Fayed: | Ibnu brought back. |
| Swamiji: | (*inaudible Hindi*) |
| Mohamed Fayed: | Because he is with Ibnu. Ibnu – Zobel build the palace with Ibnu together. Everything partner, you know. |
| Swamiji: | (*inaudible Hindi conversation*) |
| Mohamed Fayed: | And Hirschmann, the Jew, the one with the airplane, also partner with Hirschmann. This was big things for Hirsch – for Zobel. |
| Mamaji: | But one boy, one old man which one bad? |
| Mohamed Fayed: | Both of them bad, one worse than the other. Terrible people. |
| Mamaji: | Jewish? |
| Mohamed Fayed: | From Israel. They are from Israel. |
| Swamiji: | (*inaudible Hindi conversation*) |
| Mohamed Fayed: | Terrible people, terrible people when the (*sounded like* 'suscart') talk the voice, the mouth, horrible! It's like, evil, you know. Terrible people! and I salvage because I went, he show me the paper I say, 'this boy, young boy, tell him to stay in the hotel and if you are not going to take your |

|                  |                                                                                                                                                                                                                                                                                                                                                                                                                                                                                                                                                                          |
|------------------|--------------------------------------------------------------------------------------------------------------------------------------------------------------------------------------------------------------------------------------------------------------------------------------------------------------------------------------------------------------------------------------------------------------------------------------------------------------------------------------------------------------------------------------------------------------------|
|                  | money back I ... 125 million dollars. And he listened to me 'tell the boy if the money don't come tomorrow it shall transfer to my bank you can't leave' and without that I also brought Khashoggi; I brought the money 220 million dollars gone! All money gone with the wind, you know. The biggest crook, you know and this all the money I have in my account that he can have it back. He asked me where the money is? 'Where is your money?' But I don't need the money. |
| Mamaji:          | Yeah.                                                                                                                                                                                                                                                                                                                                                                                                                                                                                                                                                                     |
| Mohamed Fayed:   | Because my friendship with him is more important than anything.                                                                                                                                                                                                                                                                                                                                                                                                                                                                                                           |
| Mamaji:          | Friendship.                                                                                                                                                                                                                                                                                                                                                                                                                                                                                                                                                               |
| Mohamed Fayed:   | I don't need, because today one minister going from the Government, British Government ... again because this man, Tiny Rowland, writing you know, and he told him he have anything in Harrods, House of Fraser? He say no. Isa was sitting, you know, and Isa told the                                                                                                                                                                                                                                                                                                      |

|   |   |
|---|---|
| | minister, 'If Sultan like to buy Harrods, House of Fraser, he buy it. Don't need Mohamed Fayed to behind – to hide behind you know. |
| **Mamaji:** | Today? |
| **Mohamed Fayed:** | Yes, today and he is going to the Government straight away because too much talk – you know, those people, Tiny Rowland talk and the Prime Minister would like to put this person in prison, you know, because he also talk, you know, in the newspaper – 'Prime Minister have something to do with the Sultan. This is why they give to Mohamed Fayed' the man crazy, you know. |
| **Mamaji:** | This Rowland? |
| **Mohamed Fayed:** | Yeah. Yeah, you know, you know, is for me, is God always with me, you know, calling me. He has to be happy because the British Government think Mohamed Fayed is up there, you know. If Mohamed Fayed up there inside Prime Minister, British Government, they will never give clearance for |

me to have one big
institution, because this
is one of the biggest
institutions in the
world, you know. To
give to one foreigner,
they must know who is
Mohamed Fayed. But
those people see that
because they know my
ability, you know, and
I can know you know?

**Swamiji:** Mr Fayed is a self-made
man. He has become
hero from zero. Knows
your personality and
you with a great deal of
trust ...

**Mamaji:** I have drawn a picture
about you – that Mr
Fayed is a person who
is a self-made man.
From zero he has risen –
he has risen – to such a
high position just
because of his qualities
of head and heart,
ability to manage. It's
not that he has just
pocketed things here
and there and got it. He
has his own personality
and that fact is very well
known and he is one of
the shining up-coming
investors and that's
why he is the center
point of jealousy of
many people. So.try to
understand him.

**Mohamed Fayed:** No in his trance, you

236

| | |
|---|---|
| Mamaji: | know that ... That's what His Majesty told him. Just to try to understand him. Don't go by what people say. Try to analyze the subject with your own eyes and then only learn by it. He said 'I have no bias and I hold brief for nobody'. |
| Mohamed Fayed: | Right. |
| Mamaji: | What correct thing is, what correct attitude should be, that's what I am telling. The rest is up to you what decision you take. |
| Swamiji: | Jeffri is close to him, yeah, Mohamed is close to him? Jeffri? |
| Mohamed Fayed: | Jeffri, |
| Swamiji: | Very close to ... |
| Mohamed Fayed: | Jaffa, Jaffa |
| Mamaji: | Jaffa. |
| Mohamed Fayed: | Jaffa. |
| Swamiji: | No, no, no. Brother, brother Jeffri. |
| Mohamed Fayed: | Jeffri, very close, but he is no good. He's good, he likes him because he is younger brother, but he makes also – he brings bad people to him, you know this Manoukian, for example, you know, also not good people. He's Armenian. Armenian people worse than the Jews. |

237

|  |  |
|---|---|
| | (*laughter*) |
| Mohamed Fayed: | Worse than the Jews. And he is Lebanese. Lebanese/Armenian, you know. |
| Mamaji: | Lebanese Armenian. |
| Mohamed Fayed: | Yeah, but those people (*inaudible*) |
| Swamiji: | Prince Mohamed, Sadiqui, which country he belongs? |
| Mohamed Fayed: | Sadiqui is Malaysian. Singapore. Sadiqui lives in Singapore. |
| Swamiji: | Oh, resident, but original from where? |
| Mohamed Fayed: | Malaysia. |
| Swamiji: | I heard he was from Pakistan. |
| Mohamed Fayed: | Sadiqui? |
| Swamiji: | Ah ha. |
| Mohamed Fayed: | No, no. Singapore, but may be from originally – Pakistan originally, yeah yeah yeah. |
| Swamiji: | What type his person? |
| Mohamed Fayed: | He was before with Sabah, Prime Minister Harris. |
| Swamiji: | Where he met you? |
| Mohamed Fayed: | Sadiqui? Yes, I met him also. |
| Swamiji: | Where? |
| Mohamed Fayed: | He came here to London. |
| Swamiji: | He came to London? |
| Mohamed Fayed: | Yeah, yeah, just to say, you know, he like me to support and you know. And then he |

|                |                                                                                                                                                                                                                                                                                                                                                                                                                                  |
| -------------- | ------------------------------------------------------------------------------------------------------------------------------------------------------------------------------------------------------------------------------------------------------------------------------------------------------------------------------------------------------------------------------------------------------------------------------- |
|                | called me in Singapore. We talked. I say, you know, he's a Mohamed to be. He's younger brother to Sultan. Together they work. They are three brothers one person. If those four brothers not one person, no hope for Brunei, no hope, because they have to work together, but everyone fight each other. You go and tell him I don't need him. I don't need business because I have enough business and I think he knows. |
| Swamiji:       | And, I think he has money?                                                                                                                                                                                                                                                                                                                                                                                                        |
| Mohamed Fayed: | Yes a lot (*whistle*).                                                                                                                                                                                                                                                                                                                                                                                                            |
| Mamaji:        | Oh?                                                                                                                                                                                                                                                                                                                                                                                                                               |
| Mohamed Fayed: | He is second after Shell.                                                                                                                                                                                                                                                                                                                                                                                                         |
| Mamaji:        | Second after?                                                                                                                                                                                                                                                                                                                                                                                                                     |
| Mohamed Fayed: | After Shell Oil Company in Brunei. Very big, insurance, everything, big business and Sadiqui manage for him.                                                                                                                                                                                                                                                                                                                     |
| Mamaji:        | Is he having something to do with the Shell also in Brunei?                                                                                                                                                                                                                                                                                                                                                                        |
| Mohamed Fayed: | Yes, yes. Also Jeffri has some things oil ... some things like that.                                                                                                                                                                                                                                                                                                                                                              |
| Mamaji:        | I see. That too with the knowledge of the, His Majesty or ...                                                                                                                                                                                                                                                                                                                                                                     |

Mohamed Fayed: Of course, every
brother, they work
together, you know.
They don't work
together. Each one has
his own business, you
know, and each one
don't want to, you
know, mix with the
other you know.
There's difficulty there.

Swamiji: Everybody has his own
business one's own way
this second wife not
from good royal family
(?) not from a rich
family?

Mamaji: The second wife she
does not hail from ...
Swamiji: Royal Family
Mamaji: The Royal Family?
Mohamed Fayed: No, no, no common;
common.
Mamaji: What are her
antecedents?
Mohamed Fayed: Middle – medium-class
family, medium-class.
Swamiji: Making money?
Mohamed Fayed: Yeah, she was air
hostess. Yeah, she was
air hostess.
Swamiji: Huh?
Mohamed Fayed: She was air hostess in
Brunei air lines.
Swamiji: Ahm.
Mohamed Fayed: Met the Sultan, loves,
but she wonderful lady,
wonderful, wonderful
lady, very very nice,
and, you know, because
she is human, you

|  | know, and from common background. She is natural, you know ... also the Sultan, he is 20. He is natural. He is not big-headed, you know, very, very, very human person. You leaving tomorrow? |
| --- | --- |
| Swamiji: | Yeah, tomorrow I am leaving. |
| Mohamed Fayed: | Sultan going to Germany tomorrow? |
| Swamiji: | Germany? |
| Mohamed Fayed: | Yeah, Germany. |
| Swamiji: | With (Joseph) Zobel? |
| Mohamed Fayed: | For one day, yeah, to see airplane. This also disaster for him, I say, because they ask him, you know, do things which can be destruction. |
| Swamiji: | He is going to see plane. |
| Mohamed Fayed: | Yeah, because this 747 – |
| Swamiji: | Are you not? |
| Mohamed Fayed: | Yeah, I am. |
| Swamiji: | For purchasing it? |
| Mohamed Fayed: | No, no, because we have lawyers in Washington going and saying Zobel is going there – take the Sultan. They talk to my lawyer, you know, to see the plane, you know, and then again give again to the Jew, to Hirschmann again, another time his partner to make ... to |

|  |  |  |
|---|---|---|
|  | fail to make one exact partner. I finish this because ... |  |
| Swamiji: | (*inaudible*) |  |
| Mamaji: | Huh? |  |
| Swamiji: |  | Zobel has convinced him that whatever he should take from you and he should give it to him. |
| Mamaji: | Zobel has convinced him, or trying to convince him that, he should get the Dorchester to manage ... |  |
| Mohamed Fayed: | Yeah |  |
| Mamaji: | ... and that Sultan should take it out of your hands and give it to him. |  |
| Mohamed Fayed: | Yeah |  |
| Mamaji: | This is Zobel's idea which he has pumped into His Majesty's mind. |  |
| Mohamed Fayed: | Yeah but ... |  |
| Mamaji: | Huh? |  |
| Mohamed Fayed: | No, no. I say, Dorchester if he gives to Zobel he'll never see Dorchester. He take his money back. Because he bought ... Dorchester is my hotel. Right? I give only on condition that my hotel Ritz be involved, because that's dear to me and this place freehold, in Park Lane. You know Park |  |

242

Lane, you know Park Lane, all Mayfair, no freehold, only this place. And for me is diamond, you know, jewel. I give to him because he die own Dorchester. I say 'fine'. Because like brothers, you see, that's fine. Is one brother take one piece, for me no problem. But he take over to give to Zobel, he never see hotel, because he own the hotel but I manage the company. The holding company is in my hands.

**Mamaji:** Holding company is Ritz?

**Mohamed Fayed:** Yeah. On this condition that I have one contract with him twenty years. I manage the hotel for twenty years. Ritz manage the hotel for twenty years. And I told him, 'What's fair is fair, you know. You sign papers, your contract, I give you the hotel. You stick to paper you sign.' He can just go and come back. We can't just be up and down in this way. It's not musical chairs, you know, now Mohamed Fayed, Zobel go,

|  | Mohamed no – no more, it's like that, you know all the time. (*Mohamed Fayed clapped his hands for emphasis while speaking in the above speech*) (*Laughter*) |
| Swamiji: | (*inaudible*) |
| Mohamed Fayed: | I say I don't need … Zobel needs that but you know, now he understands the situation because he knows, you know, Zobel is not a good person, you know. He is CIA, works for the CIA it's all … |
| Mamaji: | Huh? |
| Mohamed Fayed: | Of course. Yeah. This document paper, I send you newspaper. |
| Mamaji: | Who? |
| Mohamed Fayed: | Zobel, CIA agent. |
| Mamaji: | Which country? |
| Mohamed Fayed: | He worked with Marcoses. |
| Mamaji: | I see. |
| Mohamed Fayed: | And, er, everybody around Sultan, servants, cooks, nannies, all by Zobel around him. I mean it's bad news. All those Philippine agents. |
| Mamaji: | In Brunei? |
| Mohamed Fayed: | In Brunei, yeah. Bad news. Because when he build the palace he |

|  |  |  |
|---|---|---|
| | brought people, you know, and managed them, the servants in the kitchen and all that. It was very bad. In *Washington Post*, very important article. | |
| Swamiji: | | Our contact will be maintained. |
| Mohamed Fayed: | At what time you leaving tomorrow? | |
| Mamaji: | *Washington Post* very important article it's coming or it's ... | |
| Mohamed Fayed: | It's already in the newspaper. Already. One very important article. | |
| Mamaji: | In *Washington Post*? | |
| Mohamed Fayed: | Yeah | |
| Mamaji: | When? | |
| Mohamed Fayed: | This was, er, three months ago, four months ago. About one big Hawaiian – it was in Hawaii polo club and one big company, CIA company, and they worked with Zobel, and this man shot himself because he took money from CIA and he spent it, you know, making polo clubs and Zobel was partner. It was big scandal in America. | |
| Swamiji: | | What is your program for the next week? Because I am going tomorrow and I will |

245

|  |  |
|---|---|
|  | maintain contact with you. And I am also going to reach there within two or three weeks hence it is necessary that ... |
| **Mamaji:** | How are you placed next week because we are going tomorrow ... |
| **Mohamed Fayed:** | Yeah |
| **Mamaji:** | ... And next week 2/3 weeks we maintain contact. And as requested to you yesterday that it should it be necessary if – I may need to call and discuss some things ... |
| **Swamiji:** | Zobel is going to have him some papers, perhaps I may also get a chance to see it within two to four days – |
| **Mamaji:** | ... some papers which Zobel wants to give to His Majesty? |
| **Mohamed Fayed:** | Yeah |
| **Mamaji:** | Maybe I may get those papers and may be of interest to you. |
| **Mohamed Fayed:** | Yeah |
| **Mamaji:** | So certainly those are the things which instead of – either talking on the phone or sending will not do. |
| **Mohamed Fayed:** | Yeah |
| **Mamaji:** | We can face to face discuss it, and talk about that and as you know, I have got, |

|  |  |
|---|---|
|  | myself, peace for you so I would like that. If an eventuality like that arises, I would like you to ... |
| **Mohamed Fayed:** | Absolutely |
| **Mamaji:** | ... inform you so that you can come over there. |
| **Mohamed Fayed:** | Yeah, no problem. |
| **Mamaji:** | No problem. How are you placed during the next week? |
| **Mohamed Fayed:** | How God works ... I live day by day because I ... |
| **Mamaji:** | But you can adjust your program? |
| **Mohamed Fayed:** | Yeah, if a thing is important, you know I will. |
| **Mamaji:** | Because we are about three weeks in the States. |
| **Mohamed Fayed:** | Yeah |
| **Mamaji:** | And then after – you tell me after three weeks that on his route, via Japan, His Holiness will be reaching Singapore and Brunei, and will be meeting His Majesty then. |
| **Mohamed Fayed:** | Right |
| **Mamaji:** | What are your directions, or just indications, what you would advise His Holiness to speak to His Majesty on the lines or the terms? |

**Mohamed Fayed:** His Majesty got quite good advice, because he knows that the British Government don't like Zobel and, only destruction for him by have contact with Zobel, because Zobel take business from British companies and gives to American companies. And they don't like that. And advice. All the money was British, with the Crown Agent. Zobel advise give Union Banque Suisse, Citibank Corporation and the agent take money, 7 per cent from fees and everything else. And all contracts go to Bechtel, American company, palace. He don't give anything to British companies. Plus, they know that he is evil person, you know, and he corrupt everybody around the Sultan and it's no good for me, I need to corrupt nobody. I talk to nobody. Ibnu always for me, I don't see, I don't need, because I go to Sultan, straight to the door, to his bedroom, no servant, nothing, you know, and it is very

|                    |                                                                                                                                                                                                                                                                                                                                                                                                                                 |
|--------------------|--------------------------------------------------------------------------------------------------------------------------------------------------------------------------------------------------------------------------------------------------------------------------------------------------------------------------------------------------------------------------------------------------------------------------------|
|                    | important, you know and they gape (phew!) how this Fayed do the things like that? But this is the way, you know, for me, because I don't need to have people like that, because I don't need to pay Ibnu to have things from the Sultan. If Sultan like to have my advice, my help, I am here for him, you know. |
| Mamaji:            | Right                                                                                                                                                                                                                                                                                                                                                                                                                            |
| Mohamed Fayed:     | And this is very important. And they don't like this because before they have to buy Ibnu. Ibnu hates you because you don't go to him. *(Laughter)* For me he can go to hell. |
| Mamaji:            | It's good psychology.                                                                                                                                                                                                                                                                                                                                                                                                            |
| Mohamed Fayed:     | Yeah, yeah, that's right. Because no cuts, you know, because all the time he take, you know, and it's bad, you know. Bad for him because if you can buy the person, it's dangerous for him to have around, you know, because he can do anything for money. |
| Mamaji:            | Right                                                                                                                                                                                                                                                                                                                                                                                                                            |
| Mohamed Fayed:     | For security it's no good. It's bad. Head of State, you know, he's |

the Head of State and a
young man. I see he has
a good fortune you
know. In area there's
only Lee Kuan Yew
that's all, nobody else.
Suharto is OK, you
know. Far away, but so
many problems in
Indonesia, so many
poverty, so many
people, you know. Big
problems. But for him
and the country have
future have career, he
has to prepare and have
good reputation
before, because Brunei
has corruption
everywhere, like Africa,
you know worse than
Africa.

**Mamaji:** Worse than Africa?

**Mohamed Fayed:** Worse, yeah, worse.
When he tries to talk,
you know, he's OK. He
comes and you can't go
sit with him all the time.
It's difficult you know.
OK, my friend, I leave
you with these – some
other presents.
(*Handing over of
something*)
OK and . . .
. . . My cook is sick and
this why I don't want –
he have cold. He can't
make the rice pudding.
You tell him – he have
cold. I want him to do

|  | rice pudding and then |
|---|---|
|  | he have the cold. |
|  | And makes fat. |
| Mamaji: | His Holiness is saying |
|  | that your love and |
|  | affection and your |
|  | regards are more |
|  | valuable to me than any |
|  | materialistic thing. |
| Swamiji: | I will call you. |
| Mohamed Fayed: | Yeah, OK. All the best. |
|  | Have a good trip and I |
|  | will be in touch, huh? |
| Swamiji: | Yeah |
| Mohamed Fayed: | And you call me about |
|  | it, thank you very |
|  | much. |
| Swamiji: | That same number? |
| Mohamed Fayed: | Yes, same number, all |
|  | the best, bye. |